HUGH MacDIARMID: MAN AND POET

for Dan, who shares my love of Scotland

HUGH MacDIARMID

NATIONAL
POETRY
FOUNDATION, INC.
UNIVERSITY OF MAINE

EDINBURGH UNIVERSITY PRESS
EDINBURGH, SCOTLAND

MAN AND POET

Edited
with an introduction by
Nancy Gish

Co-Published by

The National Poetry Foundation
University of Maine
Orono, Maine 04469-5752
United States

and

Edinburgh University Press
22 George Square
Edinburgh, Scotland

Printed by Cushing-Malloy, Ann Arbor, Michigan, U.S.A.

Library of Congress Number: 92-81089
NPF ISBN: 0-943373-20-4 (cloth)
NPF ISBN: 0-943373-21-2 (paper)

Edinburgh ISBN: 07486-04057

ACKNOWLEDGEMENTS

I wish to thank the National Poetry Foundation for making this book possible, especially Professor Carroll F. Terrell who first suggested it; Professor Burton Hatlen, who has supported the work throughout; and Marie Alpert, who has provided consistent help and advice as well as produced the text.

I am deeply indebted to Lorrayne Carroll for sustained help in copy editing and to Wendy Lamb for typing many sections of the manuscript. I also wish to thank Michael Grieve for his support in providing permissions and photographs, Joy Hendry and Raymond Ross for their interest in the book, and F. C. McGrath for invaluable commentary and criticism on my own contribution. I am grateful as well to the University of Southern Maine for consistent support for travel and manuscript preparation.

The author and publishers wish to thank the following for permission to quote copyright material: Carcanet Press for the extracts from Hugh MacDiarmid's poetry and prose.

Carcanet Press will be issuing a 12-volume *Collected Works* of Hugh MacDiarmid by the year 2000.

TABLE OF CONTENTS

NANCY GISH

INTRODUCTION

Centennial years are appropriate times for reassessment: new information, new insights, and new theories combine to shift the center of critical concern and value. And in the case of culturally validated writers, writers who have been labelled "great" and who have profoundly affected others of their generation, the lapse of time allows for fresher, more independent and critical readings.

It is ironic, then, that for studies of Hugh MacDiarmid assessment and reassessment inevitably coexist at the one hundred year mark. For like his critically acknowledged contemporaries--Pound, Eliot, Yeats, Williams--and more recently re-examined women of the early modern period such as H.D. and Marianne Moore, MacDiarmid helped define an era. Indeed, for Scotland, he did so almost alone. Yet unlike his contemporaries he remains little known and less studied outside of his own country, and the complexities of his work--of language, sources, and cultural context--have been treated as barriers to authentic interpretation rather than challenging hurdles on a compelling path to understanding. Scholars of his work are continually placed in the difficult position of introducing him anew for non-Scots, in every article and every book, thus perpetually going over the same ground, or pushing the boundaries of knowledge and theory at the risk of losing those who have not yet achieved ease with a Scottish lexicon and a separate, marginalized history and culture.

To approach MacDiarmid's work is thus to enter at once, and unavoidably, into the literary politics which both frame his own persistent assertion of a Scottish voice and sustain his location in the margin. On the one hand, a traditional perception of Scotland as provincial and secondary--what T.S. Eliot defined as a "satellite" culture--remains in much English commentary; on the other hand, any choice genuinely to attend to the *difference* and significance of MacDiarmid's art requires of Scots and non-Scots alike a complex linguistic task. Even to

Scots, much of MacDiarmid's lexicon is unfamiliar--archaic or regionally specific to any one of Scotland's own dialects. Perhaps more significant still is the fact that Scottish history, culture, and literature are simply not taught in English and American schools and seldom in Scottish schools. Thus Eliot's assumption of a "tradition" on which he could draw for allusion, quotation, and mythic background could rest on a significant if not extensive core of readers who *would* recognize scenes from Dante, lines from Spenser, or voices from Ovid. The same cannot be said of Dunbar, Alasdair MacMhaighstir Alasdair, or the ceremony of the Common Riding. Yet the sources are there to be found and used, and the question remains why the specific forms of MacDiarmid's complexity are resisted.

The question, in one sense, presents a Catch 22: seriously to address MacDiarmid's work involves familiarity with Scottish language, literature, and culture; until one achieves some level of familiarity, however, it remains difficult to enter into the poetry in the first place. Yet it is precisely MacDiarmid's difference from and challenge to the familiar, comfortable, and canonized that makes his work both startling and important. He forces us to reframe our understanding of both modernism and post-modernism.

MacDiarmid's early lyrics in *Sangschaw* and *Penny Wheep* as well as *A Drunk Man Looks at the Thistle* are or seem (depending on one's perspective) both recognizably modernist and amenable to formalist analysis. Moreover, the Scots Vernacular, in MacDiarmid's words, "is a vast store house of just the very peculiar and subtle effects which modern European literature in general is assiduously seeking. . . ." It is the language, he claimed, which represents a specifically Scottish contribution to European Modernist aesthetics. But it can be argued that even in the early work MacDiarmid cannot be understood through theories of organic unity or balanced tensions, and his linguistic mode projects a radical indeterminacy. His purpose, moreover, is always expressly political and cultural. Reading the late, long, very loosely assembled "poems of fact," it becomes far more clear that a new theoretical method is necessary.

Harvey Oxenhorn, in fact, who champions the early poems as brilliant lyrics in a universally compelling style, explicitly chose in his book, *Elemental Things: The Poetry of Hugh MacDiarmid*, to focus only on the early work, since "any satisfactory consideration of MacDiarmid's "poetry of wisdom" [would] depend on critical approaches and assumptions significantly different from those that have governed this study" --that is, New Critical assumptions focused on Modernist style. It now seems increasingly clear that MacDiarmid wrote post-modern works in the early 1930s, works that seemed simply unpoetic or aesthetically unsuccessful by accepted critical standards of their time. They are only now coming to be appreciated in light of changed critical approaches.

This collection includes not only essays on the multiple facets of MacDiarmid's work, but a wide range of theoretical perspectives. It thus helps to place MacDiarmid in twentieth century critical views and to define his position on the crux of modernism and post-modernism.

I. Grieve and MacDiarmid: Portrait(s) of a Poet

"Hugh MacDiarmid," poet, polemicist, Marxist, Nationalist, is the nom de plume (or de guerre as one friend would have it) of Christopher Murray Grieve, an often distinctly different character, who did not necessarily, by his own account, always agree with MacDiarmid. If it was Christopher who broke with and yet deeply internalized the values of his family, it was Hugh who took up a combative alternative stance. If it was Hugh who fought for a Scottish Renaissance on all fronts, it was Christopher who attended, with courtesy, concern, and irascibility, to friends, relatives, and fellow artists. Deirdre Chapman, his daughter-in-law, and Morag Enticknap, his niece, recall the private man at very different stages of his life in vivid detail and in ways that reveal both the split and the continuity between the personae of Christopher and Hugh. For Naomi Mitchison, fellow writer and activist in the heady days of the Scottish Renaissance, it was MacDiarmid whose personality and style provided both a focus and a critical challenge for what she calls a "gale of change."

II. In Memoriam Hugh MacDiarmid

Although MacDiarmid has been comparatively neglected in England and America, the Scots and the Irish have always recognized him as a poet of great stature and, in varying degrees, a major voice of an alternative tradition. For Norman

MacCaig, MacDiarmid's closest friend, he was "a bonnie fechter," an uncompromising writer who needed--even created-- opposition as a way of sustaining his work. More important, perhaps, his personal complexity helped direct his poetry.

For John Montague and Seamus Heaney, MacDiarmid represented a tradition and poetic resource outside the London center and, in differing ways and degrees, an influence. All three interviews in this section include evaluations of MacDiarmid's place in twentieth century poetry and commentary on the man, his impact, and details of his poetic styles. Donald Davie's poetic tribute is itself an evaluation from another position.

III. "The Company I've Kept": Contexts and Intertexts

MacDiarmid began his career as a journalist; he was a voracious reader, an inveterate browser, and a general pack rat for information and ideas which he appropriated (some say "plagiarized") for his own poetry and prose. Throughout his life he drew on a wide array of writers, friends, and literary sources, which he put to poetic use with a persistent refusal to force consistency or singleness of vision. His "autobiography," *Lucky Poet*, is primarily a compendium of quotation, paraphrase, and commentary on others' ideas as they inform his intellectual life and vision. Because he read so widely and eclectically, his materials are seldom drawn from canonized texts of the kind taught in British and American universities: he read Russian philosophers, little known Scottish poets, and writers of small countries, with a relish equal to the usual interest in Shakespeare or Kant.

Alan Bold, Raymond Ross, and Peter McCarey trace three of these connections, focusing on MacDiarmid's specific intellectual links with the poet/minister T.S. Cairncross who influenced him as a young boy, the philosophy of empirio-criticism, and the metaphysics of Shestov. Alan Riach traces parallels in the life, work, and poetics of MacDiarmid and Charles Olson. He argues that MacDiarmid's later work is akin to Olson's, and he places both in a post-modernist context.

IV. "Whaur Extremes Meet": The Work

Although Christopher Grieve had written rather derivative lyrics in English, Hugh MacDiarmid's poetry began in 1922 with "The Watergaw," a striking departure from Grieve's work and a startlingly new use of Scots Vernacular for modern poetic purposes. His first two books, *Sangschaw* and *Penny Wheep*, consist of short lyrics in "Synthetic Scots"--a literary language constructed of Scottish words from any region or time. Both because of their originality and force and because of their linguistic demands, the early lyrics created a controversy, still unresolved, over the status of Scots as a literary language as well as MacDiarmid's specific use--for poetic purposes--of words found in dictionaries.

Kenneth Buthlay and Harvey Oxenhorn address both issues from contrasting points of view. While Oxenhorn, an American, focuses on the lyric and poetic values of the early work, and sees the use of the Vernacular simply as a method, Buthlay, a Scot, examines MacDiarmid's lexical sources, challenging a history that taught Scots to eschew their native speech. For Oxenhorn, MacDiarmid's poems are most poetically significant when evaluated against aesthetic criteria not specific to Scots or Scotland. For Buthlay, MacDiarmid's practice of appropriating words, lines, and phrases from Jamieson's *Etymological Dictionary of the Scottish Language* went beyond idiom or colloquial speech to mine that "quarry of subtle and significant sound," taking images, metaphors, sounds and patterns of rhythm for their whole cultural value.

In *A Drunk Man Looks at the Thistle* MacDiarmid moved beyond the individual short lyric to a long, complex, and philosophical poem in Scots. His own comments and advance blurb, as well as the poem's explicit themes, represent the poem as a political act of resistance to what he elsewhere called "linguistic imperialism." Rena Grant--addressing the poem as nationalist text--argues that it embodies a contradiction: that is, it assumes the position of a national epic for a country "which has not been a nation-state since before the time when the nation-state arose" and hence can "only very problematically "retrieve" the essentially Scots," a project MacDiarmid unquestionably intends. Assuming that project as, nonetheless, his political goal, my own article focuses on MacDiarmid's strategies for such a retrieval and his overt tactics for subverting the hegemony represented by T.S. Eliot's *The Waste Land. A*

Drunk Man and *The Waste Land*, I argue, play out the politics of literary margin and center in Britain, a politics contextually defined by the two poets' critical prose on politics, language, and culture.

MacDiarmid's shift, in his later poetry, to English, has been as controversial as his early work in Scots. If the latter has been seen as brilliant but linguistically difficult of access, the former has been called understandable but not poetic. It is, in fact, equally complex in different ways and, as Carl Freedman argues, equally subversive of English hegemony.

Perhaps the most widely admired of MacDiarmid's late long poems in English is "On a Raised Beach," a philosophically dense meditation on "being and non-being" which opens with an astonishing passage of synthetic English as obscure and impenetrable as any poem of dictionary Scots.

Roderick Watson opens his study of the poem's atheist stance and confrontation with physical matter by another contrast with T.S. Eliot. "On a Raised Beach," he suggests, serves--like *Four Quartets*--as a career and conceptual turning point. Drawing on post-structuralist theories of language as an open-ended process of signification, Watson argues that in "On a Raised Beach" MacDiarmid sought "an irreducible stability" in the world of stone before turning toward a fresh conception of the "world of language, and then of the world *as* language."

"In Memoriam James Joyce" is taken from a projected longer work entitled "A Vision of World Language." If Roderick Watson finds in "On a Raised Beach" MacDiarmid's turning point, Carl Freedman defines "In Memoriam James Joyce" as his culminating contribution to a new form of language that goes beyond attempts to retrieve the essentially Scots--though that would be redefined, not absent. While the poem continues to privilege marginalized Scotland and Celtic nations as a whole, it adds a "more general praise of process and fluidity, and a concomitant opposition to identitarian notions of fixity and stable meaning." Examining *Finnegans Wake* and *In Memoriam James Joyce* as parallel and related texts, Freedman posits a mode of social organization in which these "unreadable" texts might become "readable" because our waking lives would be less alienated from unconscious discourse.

Lucky Poet, MacDiarmid's self-proclaimed "autobiography" tells very little about his "life." Rather, it consists of a sweeping survey of his ideas, convictions, political views, and hyperbolic self-representations. It has been easy to dismiss and easier to ignore. Stephen Smith, however, redefines its unfamiliar tactics through the Scottish tradition of flyting. This "oratorical autobiography," he maintains, serves more important functions of the genre than the provision of "facts" about a life; it functions as a "symbol or parable of 'consciousness in quest of its own truth.'" It offers as subject not the history of an individual life but the "persona of the exiled bard."

MacDiarmid's poetry and persona are inseparable because he persistently fused them. Assuming the stance of Bard, voice of a nation, he launched a poetic revolution in Scotland that is still--in new forms--under way. In the year of his centennial, Scotland is again seeing a rise in nationalist politics, and small nations--as he claimed--are demanding a voice. His life and poetry are a cultural resource we have only begun to tap.

GRIEVE AND MacDIARMID: PORTRAIT(S) OF A POET

Allen Ginsberg and Hugh MacDiarmid.
Photo by Photo Meier/Groep 45.

DEIRDRE CHAPMAN

A MEMOIR

When I married his son and got to know Christopher, I knew none of his work. Since Christopher *was* his work, talking to him in the early days was like trying to engage the Queen, whom one had failed to recognize, in conversation about rates or house prices. His position on almost everything was known to the people he spent his time with so that it was seldom necessary for him to discuss basics, and like the Queen his day-to-day experience was of concentrated isolation, keeping up with current affairs, reading, and writing letters. Other people (Valda) made appointments and arrangements and dealt with money. He turned up.

Looking back, I think my ignorance may have eased the relationship. Since I could be neither a groupie nor a student, analyst, and potential over-simplifier of his point of view, he had no need of either his dancing shoes or his flak jacket. In the company of all but family and a handful of well-tried friends there was always the gleam of one or the baffle of the other.

I was lucky, then, to see him straight. And at home there was no-one straighter. He sat suit-jacketed and upright in his perpendicular fireside armchair between the tower of newspapers he meant to cut and the radio he would turn on ahead of the next news bulletin, keeping his pocket watch slightly fast for this purpose. He was sixty-four, acclaimed but not yet feted, and already quite deaf. I was twenty-one, tentative, and eager to make a start on understanding this plainly nice but reputedly disturbing man. I would ask a question or make a remark and he would fail to catch it. He was known not to care for tentative people and he was anxious not to be known for being deaf, but he was a kind man. "What is she saying?" he would appeal to Valda, cupping his hand behind his ear. Valda would repeat the remark and he would define the problem. "She has a very soft voice."

The loss of hearing underlined his self-containment and his tendency to speak in statements, prompting others to do the same. Whether it contributed to these I couldn't say, but certainly at this time he seemed cut off from any possibility of a wry, speculative, off-the-cuff exchange. His close friends were people who expressed themselves concisely. Norman MacCaig, his closest friend at the time, whose own conversational style was reflective and questioning, had the schoolteacher's knack of turning up the volume and coming to essentials. And with strangers of his own intellectual calibre he would concentrate hugely, leaning forward and cupping his ear, which itself flattered and clarified thoughts. His social infill at the time seemed to consist largely of groupies who would make statements of their common views for the satisfaction of having them endorsed. What was lacking were dissident voices, flashes of humour, background colour, overheard remarks, clues to the way unremarkable people were thinking. His line at the time was that ninety-nine per cent of people (or perhaps it was ninety-nine point nine--he was precise about that sort of thing) had nothing to say that he wanted to hear. But years later when he had come to terms with a hearing aid, there was no domestic exchange so trivial that he could let it pass, insisting on having everything beyond his hearing range repeated to him in full. The whole truth about Christopher was always better than whichever aspect of it he promoted for purposes of his own.

But Christopher sitting in his fireside chair, looking at his watch and waiting for the news to come on, had eccentricities that were undisguised and very endearing. He would turn on the radio at full volume three minutes early and, when fiddling with the tuning knob failed to halt the weather forecast, he would fiddle with his watch instead, shaking it and holding it to his ear. After several years of observing this, I gave him a watch one Christmas in the belief that his distrust of gadgets might yield to one that had not had time to break. I was mistaken. It was in the blood. Other people who keep their watches fast know they are doing it. Christopher surprised himself every time.

When the news came on at last, all the Grieves would start to shout at the radio, heckling and jeering so that it was hard to hear any of it. When television came to Brownsbank, they shouted just as vigorously at the television news though it went on much longer. By the end they were extremely stimulated. Valda would make coffee. Christopher would give half his biscuit to the dog and be ticked off. Then he would clear away the cups and wash up. This was his regular job and he did it after every meal as if programmed, with a predictability and a docility that would have astonished people who only knew his public style. A distinguished visitor, ambassador from another cultural movement or seat of learning, who had travelled across land and sea to meet him and been invited to stay for the convivial Brownsbank lunch in front of the fire with food and conversation flowing freely, would suddenly have his pudding plate whipped away as Christopher recalled himself and headed for the kitchen until persuaded he was off duty.

There were two other domestic triggers he responded to. One was the sound of a vacuum cleaner. It made him hold his legs straight out in front of him and keep them there till the noise stopped. On the occasions when he came to stay with us for long enough to be hoovered round, I would hoover along the landing and into the sitting room to find him already sitting like this with his pipe in his mouth and his eyes on his book. I would scurry round the chair and tell him to relax, but he wouldn't, not till I'd switched the machine off. The other trigger was knitting. If I took out needles and wool he would lay down his book and hold his hands up in front of him as he had in Whalsay when Valda did Fair Isle knitting to supplement their income and needed to wind the wool.

Christopher at home was courteous, formal, kind, irascible about small things, astonishingly patient with grand-children, and above all consistent. Occasionally a fireside debate would touch on one of his public positions--his contempt for the preoccupations of the common man or his decision to rejoin the Communist Party over Hungary. Then he would fly into one of his rare rages. It was a point of view that could not be articulated in fireside style. He had to clothe himself in pomposity to carry it through. Yet it was a point of view that had to be maintained despite the softening influences of the grandchildren, the dog, and the dishes. Possibly he felt it was unfair of us to bring it up at such a time. He was in his slippers being nice and we were pushing him on wanting to machine-gun people with low IQs.

His literary friends tended to tolerate his politics as an occasional posture, and socially his two fields had a fence running a long way down the middle. He would castigate a literary gathering held in his honour for neither understanding nor giving sufficient weight to his politics, and a political one for being incapable of responding to his poetry. When, at home, we, uncategorised, hovered too obviously hoping for him to go on being calm and rational and shed light on one of the areas of apparent irrationality, he became austere and dismissive or resorted to polemic. We were on the line between the place where he could take people and the place they had to reach on their own or not at all. We stepped aside.

Christopher was extraordinarily generous with his time and, lacking any sense of status, would agree to attend or address just about any gathering he was invited to. He often came to stay with us in Glasgow on these occasions and would be ready to leave far ahead of time, standing in the hall with his raincoat over his arm for ten or fifteen minutes waiting till it was time to go. When he came home his conviviality kept us up till two or three in the morning, and in his last years he developed a knack of sleeping off late-night excess throughout the following day and night, turning up shaved at the breakfast table two mornings after the night before.

In later years when Valda took to holidaying in the sun and Christopher spent longer periods with us, devouring detective stories by day and erupting into reminiscence and anecdote in the evening when the glasses were brought out, he developed a patriarchal shade to his personality and would inquire after the state of my marriage and advise me against the dangers of emotional over-investment in children. "They grow up you know." His delight in company coupled with the obligation he felt to be decorous towards me led to some amazingly verbose and euphemistic anecdotes. One night he told me how a bomb had fallen on the red light district of Salonika while he was stationed there during World War I. "All the ladies of easy virtue," he said, "were incinerated in a night."

While he was staying with us, I was co-opted to the family task of trying to save Christopher from himself. Valda and Mike were very good at this, cajoling, bullying and circumventing sorties to pubs in uncontrolled circumstances with extraordinary imagination and energy. I found it harder. "Papa's escaping!" one of my children would cry, and we would gather nervously at the door watching him scurrying down the path on his small feet, his coat over his arm, the most orderly of escapees.

Because I was not a nanny but the agent of nannies, he would outwit me with more consideration than, as a man of his age and nationality, he felt obliged to show to those who had his interests closest to their hearts. He would come back soon so that I wouldn't be blamed. He behaved with the same consideration towards friends who picked him up and brought him back from meetings, readings, or receptions, but under the surface he was always slightly touchy about his competence. When a friend showed an inclination to help him up our front steps, he would stand back on the threshold and wave him through the door ahead of him with a display of magnanimity, redressing the balance.

The contrast between his public stances and his personality gave Christopher an amazing facility for making people happy. Arriving in an Edinburgh or Glasgow pub off the lonely bus from Biggar, he responded physically to the presence of friends and acquaintances. In this mood he listened, encouraged, endorsed views, promised (and remembered later) to give support, and suffered fools, if not gladly, patiently. Acquaintances and strangers who knew of his elitism felt special and chosen. Pippa passes.

MORAG ENTICKNAP

A MEMOIR

I was, I suppose, about eight years old when I first became sharply aware of my uncle Chris. I entered for a verse-speaking competition at school, and my father suggested that I choose one of my uncle's poems, as this would make a change from the likely choice of the other entrants. I knew of course that my father's only brother wrote poetry. From time to time I overheard my parents discussing the latest volume to appear. My father bought all of these, and was fiercely critical of his writing, yet proud in a dour Scots way of his achievement, and a great admirer of the early lyrical works. The poem he suggested for me was "A Herd of Does" from "Penny Wheep." I did not win any prize, nor did I receive any of the reflected glory I rather unworthily hoped might rub off on me as a relation of the poet. So I was brought face to face with the puzzling contradiction that I had a famous uncle--he must after all be famous if his poetry was printed in books--yet my teachers, who in my eyes were omniscient, had apparently heard neither of him nor of his work.

We were living in Edinburgh at this time, and were well placed to visit my grandmother, my father's mother, who by now married to her second husband had settled in East Lothian, a few miles south of Edinburgh. My brother and I loved our visits there. We enjoyed the freedom of the countryside after the city streets, and although my grandmother lived in very humble circumstances, to us there was a richness of life that we were always to remember. We "helped" our grandparents about the house and estate--my step-grandfather was a lodge keeper there. Here there was much more talk about uncle Chris. My grandmother always called him by the contracted version of his name --Christie--and usually referred to him in conversation as "puir Christie." To her it was beyond understanding that any man could choose writing as a profession, and so she assumed that he was unable to get a job. Being a journalist and writing for a newspaper was just about comprehensible, as it did bring in a wage, but writing verse was a total bewilderment to her. He was her son, and she loved him, and it was not right that he could not get good honest work--hence "puir Christie"!

In the early nineteen-thirties my uncle was going through a very difficult time. His first marriage was breaking up, he had suffered a street accident, and together with his chronic money worries his health was being affected. How much of this his mother knew I cannot tell. She was always hoping to hear from him, or for him to come to see her, and she especially longed to see her grand-daughter Christine, of whom she was very fond indeed. I never met my cousins Walter and Christine, nor did I meet their mother, my aunt Peggy. To my brother and me this did not seem strange. We were not a close-knit family, and we seldom saw the aunts, uncles, and cousins on my mother's side either, although most of them lived in the same town as we did. When my uncle's first marriage broke up, my aunt Peggy took the children. This was a tremendous blow to my uncle, who loved his children, and suffered a sense of enormous injustice that they should be taken from him. He was unable to explain this to his mother either, and indeed I do not believe that she ever knew of his divorce. To her it would have been unthinkable anyhow, such things were a terrible disgrace and in her view did not happen to decent people. It seems to me that to spare her, he never explained what had happened. It must have been very hard for them both. Granny would always be asking for the children to come and visit her, and my uncle would run out of excuses for why this could not be. In the end I think he just stayed away. I do know that my aunt Valda and my cousin Michael, the son of the second marriage, never met my grand-mother, and I think that she probably never knew of their exis-tence.

After the death of her second husband, my grand-mother moved back to Waterbeck in Dumfriesshire to live with her sister. Her health had been failing for some time, and it was eventually disclosed that she was suffering from inoperable can-cer. During her final illness, my father visited her as often as possible. As always, she was concerned for Christie, and kept asking when he would come to see her. He of course was far away in the Shetlands and unable to be at her bedside, but my father's anxiety and worry led him to outbursts of impatience and resentment at his brother's absence and seeming lack of concern. Looking back down the years, I can see just why this resentment arose, but at the time all I knew was that my uncle was considered to have behaved badly. I had not yet met the man himself; all I knew came from the words and opinions of other people. This, however, was soon to change.

Our first meeting came in 1936, and was preceded by a typically bizarre introduction. Coming home one evening after a family outing, we found a note, written in pencil on a sheet of toilet paper, propped up on the living room table. Uncle Chris had called round, found nobody at home, climbed in through the unlocked bathroom window and, seizing on the only visible writing material, had left his message and gone. The note said that he was in Edinburgh on some literary business, and had brought Valda and Michael with him. Based as they were then in the Shetlands, this visit was an opportunity for aunt Valda to do some shopping and the like. For Michael it must have been like going to the moon. He had probably never seen a street, let alone a city like Edinburgh.

I remember this visit principally for my uncle's colourful clothes. All the men of our acquaintance at that time wore sober suits, plain shirts with hard collars, restrained neckties, overcoats and always hats and gloves out of doors. Admittedly my brother and some of his school friends wore kilts on Sundays or holidays, but my brother's kilt was of the dark green Graham tartan, and if the other boys might wear a brighter variety, yet their shirts and jackets were plain. My uncle was like some exotic bird. He wore a kilt of predominantly red tartan, a bright red soft woollen shirt, yellow tie, tweed jacket, kilt stockings and a balmoral cap. In this glorious apparel he strode the streets of grey Edinburgh, accompanied by my sober-suited father. "Folk turned and stared at us," my father complained. Being stared at was disgraceful of course, but I cannot feel surprised that folk did! On this first meeting, apart from the clothes, I remember a friendly and cheerful man who laughed a lot, talked a lot, and who played games with Michael on the floor--something amazing to my brother and me, who were not at all used to such behaviour from grown-ups. They stayed only three days or so, and then vanished as quickly as they had come.

At the end of 1936 my family moved away from Scotland. My father's work took him to London, and for the next four years the family home was in Surrey. In 1940, wartime conditions meant that my father's work moved away again from London and was based in Glasgow, and we went there in the early winter of that year. My mother had died suddenly in February, and we had a short letter from uncle Chris at that time, but otherwise there had been no communication, although my father continued to get his books, and friends in Scotland would send him newspaper cuttings from the Scottish papers, which kept him abreast of public events in his brother's life at least. He was not reported in the English press at all, as he had quarrelled with, and upset, too many of the editors and reporters!

Early in 1942 uncle Chris left the Shetlands to come to Glasgow, where he took up war work in an engineering firm. It was arranged that he should come and stay with us. I have no knowledge of how this came about, and it seemed then, and seems even more so at a distance of time, to have been a very strange decision. The relationship between my father and his brother was a difficult one, and although they managed well enough at a distance, living under the same roof for any period of time was likely to strain matters considerably. On looking back, I think that probably it was meant to be a very brief stay, as it was understood that my aunt Valda and Michael would soon be coming to join him when he had found suitable lodgings. Also, my father's work took him from home for periods of a week or so at a time, so no doubt he thought that his brother's brief stay would not cause too much friction. So uncle Chris arrived, more soberly attired this time, with piles of books and papers, and very little else but the clothes he was wearing.

He was on shift work from the start, so sometimes at home during the day and sometimes during the evening, leaving at around ten at night and coming back early next morning, or rising early to go to work and finishing late at night. On these shifts he rarely returned straight home. He had friends in Glasgow, mostly of political views sympathetic to his own, and would meet and talk with them, attend and take part in public meetings and so on. Some of these friends occasionally telephoned him at the house, or came to call, and this became a bone of contention with my father. He had never liked my uncle's political activities, had no sympathy for his political views, and thoroughly disapproved of his house being in any way connected with such goings on.

My uncle was during this time at work on *Lucky Poet*, although I do not remember his having very much time to devote to this. He would make copious notes on bits of paper, which were bundled together in untidy heaps. How he ever got a book together I cannot imagine. He was of course possessed of enormous mental energy, and even when dozing in his chair by the fire after coming off shift, he would awaken with a great start, leaping out of the chair, so active was his mind. Until one got used to this it could be most alarming, and I remember that my brother, who had to share a bed with him on occasion, was startled almost out of his wits by these upheavals, which occurred at night as well. Of the household, I was the one who saw him most as I was at home all the time, having taken over the housekeeping after my mother's death. He was the first adult of my parent's generation who talked to me on equal terms, and this I found very much to my liking. He was prepared to talk and to discuss any subject in which I was interested, to treat my opinions with courtesy and without any taint of patronizing, and to put forward his own opinions for us both to consider and debate. Many evenings were spent in talking on so many different subjects, for at this time my mind was avid for new knowledge and experience. He never made me feel that my opinion was beneath consideration, nor that I should defer to him because he was older, and also my father's brother. I later met many people with whom it was possible to talk widely and objectively, but he was the first, and I have never forgotten that.

I can see him now, sitting forward in the armchair, emphasizing his words with stabbing gestures of his long, slender fingers, half-smoked pipe in his hand. At my request, he was trying to explain Dialectical Materialism, among other things. This after a hard day's work, for no matter how tired he might be, the prospect of some kind of argument or discussion would renew his vitality. Of course he must have lived on his nerves. He was no longer a young man, and was engaged in hard unfamiliar work. He might go on from his shift to address some meeting or other which could last late into the night, and then have to make his way home through the blacked-out streets to snatch some sleep before starting work again. When he was engaged on any task or undertaking he gave it his whole attention, absolutely to the exclusion of anything else, or indeed anybody else; and this undoubtedly gave rise to the appearance of insensitivity at times. He would use other people to further his own ends without compunction, not cynically, nor because he thought they did not matter, but because when his thoughts were concentrated, anything extraneous just did not exist for him. I know that my father felt that he had been used in this way on several occasions, and found it hard to accept.

When he had an afternoon free, he would sometimes suggest that we go out, and I remember going to see *Citizen*

Kane with him. This was a strange and very different film from any I had seen before, and led to much discussion later--discussion that taught me to think of film making as more than just entertainment. We also set out one day for Glasgow University, where T.S. Eliot was to give a lecture. Uncle Chris knew him, and promised to introduce me, which was a most exciting thing to look forward to. Unfortunately for me, when we got to the venue, the hall was packed to the doors, and my uncle decided to abandon the visit. I was very disappointed, and have to admit once again that this partly arose from missing the chance of shaking hands with the famous.

His stay with us, however, was not to last long. When there was no progress in finding lodgings for Valda and Michael, my father I think decided that uncle Chris was making no effort and that he would stay indefinitely. Relations, already inflamed by the political activities mentioned, became more strained, and finally came to a head one evening when my uncle arrived back a little the worse for drink. Here was a good excuse to put an end to what had never been a welcome visit between the brothers. An argument developed into a quarrel, harsh words were exchanged, and my uncle left the house there and then. I missed him very much but, schooled never to question my father's actions, could not talk about this, nor mention his name. A few weeks later, my uncle came back to collect his belongings. His manner to me was unchanged. I saw him go down the road with a sense of loss. I was never to see him again.

More than twenty-five years were to pass before we had any contact again. I had married, moved to London, and my three sons had grown up. When my youngest son was at university, he wanted to make a study of my uncle's work and, unable to get the necessary books from my father, I decided to write to uncle Chris asking if he would be willing to help. I did not know where he lived, but got his address from "Who's Who" and wrote to explain my request. I had the most delightful letter in reply, and although we had heard and seen nothing of each other in all the years between, it was as if we had parted only the day before. He told me about his travels, and about all his children--for he had by now made contact again with the children of his first marriage, and had grandchildren in all of whom he was deeply interested and in all of whom he clearly delighted. He was immediately ready to help Alasdair by lending whatever books he wanted, and excused my father's rather odd refusal to lend his own copies, writing:

> Perhaps your father in refusing to lend Alasdair my books wasn't altogether acting in a dog-in-the-manger way, but feared that my work--or some of it--is too subversive and might have a bad influence on your son.

This seemed to me then, and does so even more now, to show that my uncle had not forgotten the episode of being asked to leave our Glasgow home because he might be a bad influence on my younger brother. In this letter too, he referred back to another incident from the Glasgow days. My fiance was staying with us for a holiday, and one morning came down to breakfast to find his shoes missing. He knew where they had been left the previous night, but a search failed to find them. They were the only pair he had brought, so for that day he was confined to the house. The mystery was solved in the evening when uncle Chris came home wearing the shoes, which were much too big for him and must have been very uncomfortable. On being queried he replied, "Well, it was wet, and mine were letting water." Twenty-five years later he wrote, referring to my husband:

> He is the only man into whose shoes I ever stepped--briefly and unsuccessfully--an escapade for which I hope he may have long ago forgiven me.

In 1972 my father died, after a long and painful illness. I thought it right that his brother should be told by one of the family, and so I wrote again with the news. Again I had a prompt reply. There was no hypocrisy in the letter; he merely said he was sorry to hear of the death, but that it was

> one of the effects of Scottish individualism that members of the same family so often have little or nothing in common and can't get on with each other. It was hereditary in my family. My father and one of his brothers lived in the same small town and never visited or even spoke to each other.

At this same time my own marriage had ended and that, together with my father's long illness and death, of whom in spite of many difficulties I had been very fond, had left me in a vulnerable state. Remembering my uncle's kindness when he had stayed with us, I wrote to him, unburdening myself at some length. I had no reply, and so resigned myself to losing touch again. I did not follow up the letter, thinking that perhaps the long gap in our lives had broken the tie. I was reluctant, too, to press any claims on my uncle in view both of the relationship between him and my father, and of the fact that he was now a well-known and eminent man. The passage of time had long erased my desire for reflected glory. I could not now presume upon our family connection. Over the next four years there was no direct contact between us, although I did from time to time hear of my uncle's activities--for example I saw him on television once or twice. Then in 1976, my eldest son drove up to Scotland on holiday, and on the way called in on my uncle. He told me later how he had to pass Aunt Valda's scrutiny before being allowed in. My aunt was rightly very protective of her husband, who was now the focus of much attention from all over the world, and who, although we did not know it then, had been quite seriously ill. My son was received with the greatest pleasure and friendliness, although my uncle had never before met him. He was interested in Nicholas's own work and activities although apparently was not able to find out all he would have wished. In a long and affectionate letter that closely followed this visit he wrote:

> Nicholas, as you must know has a very soft voice, and I am very deaf even with a hearing aid, so I couldn't glean much information from him. Not that I could have asked him many questions anyhow. He might well have resented that.

It was from this letter too that I learnt why I had not heard for so long. He wrote:

> Not receiving my letter you must have thought I just didn't care. That would be very far from the truth. I have thought of you ever since and wondered how you were fixed, and also how your sons all were. I had thought I'd never get in touch with you again. When I got your long letter I wrote you at once. Unfortunately you had given no address, so I addressed my reply to your married home in London and some time later had it returned via the Dead Letter Office marked "not known here," so I had no means of getting in touch with you, but I have always wanted to. . . .

After this, I sent cards at Christmas and for his birthday. In the summer of 1978, my youngest son called in at Brownsbank on his way to a holiday in the western isles. Alasdair sent me a postcard to tell me of this visit, and to let me know that my uncle was suffering from terminal cancer. I had just sent off a card for his 86th birthday on August 4th, and on the heels of Alasdair's card came a letter to thank me, saying also:

> I would have written long ago if I had not, characteristically alas!, lost your address and had no way of getting in touch with you.

He told me of his illness, but wrote cheerfully also about his visit to Dublin to have his D. Litt. conferred, and he ended his letter:

I am sorry I can't write at greater length, but even this short note takes more out of me than I have to give--but I send you my love and best wishes and hope to hear from you when you feel like it.

These were his last words to me. The news of his death came in a brief item on the radio just over a month later. He had faced life always with great courage, and he was indomitable to the end.

May he rest in peace.

NAOMI MITCHISON

MacDIARMID AND THE SCOTTISH RENAISSANCE

I never knew Hugh MacDiarmid at all well. We moved in rather different circles. We were fellow parents at Kilquahanity school, but probably our children knew one another better than we adults did. I remember him, at a large and chaotic Edinburgh meeting, defending me from a fairly vicious attack by some young Scots writers--it must have been in the fifties. He was always gentle, even over-polite. But I have nothing of interest to recall.

What I think is important is his political effect: nothing to do with his "political" verse which I find unreadable, but with his putting Scotland onto the map after so many years of sliding down. I don't think he was wise to stand as a Communist Party candidate in Perthshire (I contributed to his election fund partly to annoy my own relatives up there) and the party didn't exactly welcome him. But he did get what at the beginning was called the Scottish Renaissance really seething. For instance, the Glasgow Saltire Society, where he could sometimes be found, was a real centre for artists of all kinds, in music, in paint, and in words. And it probably would never have got going without a feeling that we had produced a great poet. These were the days of his earlier Scots lyrics. Many others followed him, some of whom will probably survive and be read, the best any of us can hope for.

This stirring was more easily felt in Glasgow than in Edinburgh. Others were joining in the stream. There was the Citizens Theatre with Bridie always at hand--I remember so well how, when my fisherman co-author and I were producing *Spindrift*, he would suggest alterations, but in such a way that his idea went straight through to the part of one which was constructing and came out, not at all in his words but following the way he wisely wanted the shape of the scene. It was a marvellous experience. For me too there was always Neil Gunn. Equally there was John MacCormick and the Scottish Convention.[1] But probably much of the general ferment that was going on was started off by the fact that here was undoubtedly good poetry being written in Lallans[2] and getting around to people who were not the normal poetry audience. I am sure that this stirring was due on one level at least to Hugh MacDiarmid. On other levels it was due to Tom Johnson, whose works are directly in stone and concrete and indirectly in such things as my own term of work on the Argyll County Council, where I would probably not have been but for a meeting he held in Carradale.

I was much less directly associated with the national poet because I just can't do with drunk men looking at thistles. I want to see it unaided by any drug, however reputable and connected with--presumably--the difficulty that so many of my countrymen find in loosing themselves from social constraints and what they feel is the dominance of women. It is all very odd and goes back many generations. H. M. had to depend on a certain intake of alcohol in order to reach the heights he was bound for. He led a good many young poets and others the same way. Certainly that was bad for some of them. I was never tempted to join the Rose Street[3] gang, nor would it conceivably have helped my writing if I had. But why worry? They wouldn't have wanted a woman-body there anyway. Perhaps I missed hearing the first pouring out of a poem, who knows? It all became part of a legend.

Various magazines were started in the period of Scottish excitement, including several short-lived and often badly printed Glasgow ones. There was never any lack of eager contributors! Painting sprang to life with such people as Joan Eardley, Ann Redpath, Morrison, Henderson Blyth--I take the names almost at random; there were a dozen more, all strongly motivated by the Scottish scene. And of course there was J. D. Ferguson and Margaret Morris, both powerful personalities, but probably they too were hit by the same gale of change, sweeping away the old stalks in the Scottish kailyard.

How much was Hugh MacDiarmid responsible for all this? I doubt if one person can ever be responsible for the Zeitgeist of a country or community. It is only that words have a habit of spreading. Other words get loose, are used. For good or

---

1. The Scottish Convention was a nationalist organization which split off from the Scottish National Party in 1942 and worked to promote Scottish Home Rule.
2. Scots, the language of the Lowlands of Scotland.
3. A street in Edinburgh lined with pubs.

evil there is a shift. Scotland is very different now from what it was even half a century back. Hugh MacDiarmid was responsible for some of it. But the same wind that was blowing him blew on others and has not stopped blowing.

IN MEMORIAM HUGH MacDIARMID

Ezra Pound and Hugh MacDiarmid, Venice, 1971.
Photo used courtesy of Michael Grieve.

NANCY GISH

INTERVIEW WITH NORMAN MacCAIG
NOVEMBER 12, 1979

NG: Could you tell me when and where you met MacDiarmid and how long you knew him?

NM: I suppose I was his closest friend outside of his own family, but I didn't meet him till 1946. He was very well known, of course, even before that, but I didn't know any of the writers in Scotland until that annus mirabilis when I met them.

NG: And did you then spend a lot of time with him?

NM: Yes. It was a most extraordinary thing, because in many respects, we're quite unlike each other, but we took to each other just immediately.

NG: Did he ever talk about his early life in Langholm and Montrose? I find that letters are sort of cut off there, and if you look at *Lucky Poet*, the whole early part is lost.

NM: He didn't often talk about his early life. There are references, of course, in his poems; many many images come from Langholm. There's a path in Langholm, for instance, known as the Curly Snake, which is the original of Cencrastus, the Curly Snake, and there are numerous references to the topography of the place, but when he brushed the dust of Langholm off his feet, he made a thorough job out of it.

NG: That's really why I wanted to ask about it because he says in *Lucky Poet* that his political and metaphysical vision very much develops out of his early life in Langholm, yet in *Lucky Poet* he doesn't really talk much about his life at all. So I wondered if there was any place where he had gone into any more detail about that.

NM: No, I don't think so. He very, very seldom mentioned it. In fact, I don't think he would ever mention it unless he was actually asked.

NG: Is that true for Montrose and London as well? He didn't talk about it?

NM: Yes. I knew him for many, many, many years, and I kept on discovering that he'd lived somewhere--Longniddry, near Edinburgh, for instance. Now I knew him for twenty years before I knew he had spent some time there. He was an egomaniac but not an egotist, and, of course, one accepts the egomania because he had the most extraordinary ego. If I had one like that, I'd have a mania too.

NG: Could you elaborate on that? In what sense was his ego so extraordinary?

NM: I suppose like many great artists in the past, in any of the arts, he was finally really only interested in what would stimulate him to write poetry, and this had some very odd facets to it. He was an omnivorous reader in his young days, read everything, but from the time I knew him, he read a tremendous lot, but they were all detective stories.

NG: By 1946 that's what he read?

NM: Oh yes. His wife had a terrible job keeping him in detective stories, and he was really . . . he was not into so many other poets. The only ones that he was interested in were those who rather shared his interests and who excited his mind to writing more poetry. He was very apt to brush the whole lot off as being mindless oafs that knew nothing whatever about poetry, you know, because he always expressed him- self with extreme violence. "I am whaur extremes meet." You know, the famous phrase. And he had a marvelous gift for denunciation. Some of my friends tell me I have it too. Perhaps [that was] one of the things that made us close friends because we were fully aware of the fact that vitu- peration is an art form, and he and I used to quarrel and, oh, say terrible things to each other so that eavesdroppers thought we hated each other. Actually we were enjoying ourselves fine. He never had a lukewarm idea. If you men-

tion, say, Ted Hughes, Philip Larkin, he just totally abol-
ished them in one or two sweeping sentences. That's what I
mean by egomania. But it was necessary for him, just as it
was necessary for Cezanne or plenty others. He was seeking, unconsciously, something that would enable him to
write more poetry.

NG: Do you feel then--when you say that the things he was
doing, the things that he was reading, thinking, were stimuli
for poetry--do you feel that his whole political and Scottish
cultural mass of interests was secondary to poetry? Was
poetry the center?

NM: Oh yes, poetry was the center all the time.

NG: Do you think that if he had not gone through that terrible
time in the '30s, if he hadn't been on the defensive, he
might have moved in a different direction in his poetry, or
did he create that situation?

NM: Oh, he very much created it himself, but it was a hostile
environment, no doubt about that. This is a Philistine country, and he was up against the Philistines, of course, all his
life long. I don't know what he would have done if he was
heaped with blushing honors. No, he was a "bonnie
fechter." And without opposition I think he wouldn't have
done what he did do. As a poet the extraordinary thing that
happened in the '30s was, of course, his desertion of Scots
and his return to English in his poems. He was once here,
just the two of us, and he said--we had been talking, talking, then a pause--and he said, "You know, Norman, why
I've been writing all that rubbish these last forty years
(meaning the long English poems), and I said, "No, what
do you think?" "I lost my sense of rhythm." Well, I had
noticed that; anybody could if you read the poems written
in the '30s, you know "Scots Unbound," the "Raised
Beach." He simply and totally lost his sense of metrics. I
don't know anything like it. He couldn't write an iambic
pentameter if you gave him five pounds. Suddenly over a
couple of years or so it totally deserted him.

NG: At what point?

NM: About 1933 or 4. 4 perhaps. And he started writing these enormous poems in English and in free verse--because he couldn't write in metrics anymore--and switched over from the lyrical to the intellectual: poetry of ideas, scientization of poetry, etc., etc.

NG: How do you evaluate those later poems?

NM: They have extraordinary passages in them, but they're nothing compared with the poems before then. He knew that himself. "My best poems are in Scots." Oh, he knew it.

NG: Do you think that his sense of rhythm, when he had it, demanded a Scots medium?

NM: Well, it was very closely linked with the Scots language, and when the meter went the language went. There are beautiful passages, as in *The Cantos* of Pound, beautiful passages, but the whole thing, the whole poem is so full of added pedantry, like quotations from scores of languages.

NG: You say that he knew they weren't as good, or anything like, the early things, and yet he was absolutely committed to them at some level, wasn't he?

NM: Oh very much so, and you get very defensive about your own procedures. He would say things like, "they tell me I once wrote some good lyrics. Rubbish, sentimental balderdash. It's my later poems, you know."

NG: But you think he didn't really believe that?

NM: I really don't know.

NG: T. S. Eliot said the important thing about long poems is the structure of the whole and that inevitably what matters is how one can handle the more prosaic interstices that hold together magnificent sections. Can that concept be used to justify the structure of MacDiarmid's later poems?

NM: I don't think so. I don't think he was very good at the structure of long poems when he was writing in English. It's a most extraordinary psychological thing. In the poems in

Scots, the lyrics and *A Drunk Man*, of course, the masterpiece, he never puts a foot wrong in terms of structure.
Never. Or in metrics--absolutely impeccable. . . .

NG: What do you think about something like "On a Raised
Beach"?

NM: I think that's a masterpiece, of course, terrific. . . . I think
that's one of the great poems of this century, absolutely
remarkable. The lyric thing hadn't yet been clubbed to
death by the intellectual, political, philosophical, techno-
logical interests.

NG: Do you feel that if you want to evaluate MacDiarmid as a
poet in the twentieth century, you have to throw the late
English poems out, or simply select bits, or do you think
that they do have some power as a whole?

NM: Well I don't think that they can be discarded. . . If you want
to understand the man and the work, you have to read
them, oh yes. The best defense of these long, later poems
that I've read was by Edwin Morgan. *In Memoriam James
Joyce* was reviewed by W.H. Auden, and he said that he
was baffled and bamboozled, but it was such a remarkable
poem and put you in touch with such a remarkable mind
that he'd prefer not to make a judgment on them for
another ten or twenty years. I used to say exactly the same
thing. I was unwilling to admit to myself, you see, they were
less than the work he had done before. But over the years
I've come to face up to it. . . .

NG: Do you think that he did have a vision of a kind of poetry
that he wanted to write, and that his problem was finding a
way to write a long poem for the twentieth century?

NM: Yes. That's a common ambition with poets, isn't it, to write
a long poem. . . . I really only remember Chris expressing
anything like real admiration for another poem when he
was talking about Ezra Pound and David Jones. Long
poems crammed with learning--that's what attracted him.

NG: You said one thing earlier about *A Drunk Man* that I'm not
sure about. You said the metric is impeccable. I do find

places, even in *A Drunk Man*, where he seems to find it necessary to end on a preposition or an insignificant word-- to lose power by putting a tag to get the meter.

NM: I don't think that happens accidentally very often in *A Drunk Man*; I don't think so. But one or two, yes, I'm now remembering; in one or two places there was even bad grammar.

NG: I don't think that would have worried him.

NM: It doesn't worry him at all. He was not worried about such things whatever. . . . He wasn't a man to revise, you see. He just poured the stuff out.

NG: He never did revise?

NM: Couldn't be bothered revising.

NG: Do you know his work method? Did he produce a certain amount of material in a day or did he just work by inspiration?

NM: Well in Whalsay, Valda tells me, when he was writing these long, long poems, he used to write all night--just page after page--and never revised it. I don't know his methods when he was writing the lyrics of *A Drunk Man*. I just don't know.

NG: They look more intricately controlled.

NM: Oh they are; they're absolutely extraordinary, quite extraordinary. The "Bonnie Broukit Bairn," for example. It's so perfect that you're quite unaware of the art, you know. *Ars est celare artem*. I think I knew it for a number of years before I realized that the first line rhymes with the last one and the second one, the second last one, and there are two couplets in the middle. More than that, the first line and the last line rhyme very weakly: "Mars is braw in crammasy," then "The haill clanjamfrie!": single syllable, weak rhyme. The second and the second last are a single syllable, strong rhyme: "Venus in a green silk goun,"-- "Greet and in your tears ye'll droun," and in the middle are two double rhymes, in couplets; the poem is shaped like a half moon.

NG: I never saw it either. I have wondered how conscious his technique was in those intricate lyrics.

NM: Well, when a great poet is on his game, he does these things quite unconsciously, absolutely, and it amuses me to read critics talking about consonants and vowels and internal rhymes, as if the man had consciously planted them. He did it because he was working at the whole bent of his powers.

NG: But isn't it important that they're there? As an observation about the poem, its valid.

NM: Absolutely important that they're there but the implication that the boy sweated over it and said "I better have an image here"--nonsense.

NG: One of the things he does that fascinates me is the sudden overturning of pompous expectation. One of my favorite lines is "--Thae trashy bleezin' French-like folk." That's a description of the angels in heaven.

NM: There's a poem about going back to Langholm. The second last verse is beautifully written, conversational, perfect rhythmically. The second last stanza is about chaps in the river fishing for salmon in February or thereabouts. It's early in the year because they're cold, up to here with chest waders. And the last verse is "Their queer stane faces and hoo green they got! / Juist like Rebecca in her shawl o' sly. / I'd never faur to gang to see doon there / A wreathed Triton blaw his horn or try."

NG: Yes, that's wonderful.

NM: "My name is Norval. On the Grampian Hills / It is forgotten, and deserves to be." " 'Let there be Licht,' said God, and there was / A little."

NG: It's wonderful.

NM: The "reductive idiom" the scholars call it.

NG: I'm fascinated by the degree to which my students immediately take to it. Even though they look at Scots and don't think they can read it, in a very short time they love it; they'll do the work to get it.

NM: Revert to that verse I quoted: first two lines, "Their queer stane faces and hoo green they got! / Juist like Rebecca in her shawl o' sly." I loved that poem for years before I met him, and after I got to know the man, I used to amuse myself by asking him the meaning of esoteric Scots words because of this rubbish they talk of him dredging in a dictionary, you know. But he did. He did. He said so: "I wanted to enrich my Scots. How do you do it? Where do you get words? A dictionary." Etc. That's when he was writing in English, in his early days in Montrose. So he bought Jamieson's dictionary. The way I put it is, "C. M. Grieve dived in at one end and Hugh MacDiarmid splashed ashore at the other." Oh, I never once caught him out. His vocabulary in Scots, never mind English, was enormous. And "Juist like Rebecca...."--I didn't know who Rebecca was. I looked up the Bible Rebecca because he's got an awful lot of Biblical references. No mention of shawls, "in her shawl o' sly," and I didn't know the meaning of the Scots word "sly," so one night I said, "You know the meaning of the Scots word 'sly,' Chris?" and he ejaculated a wee phrase in Latin, a language he doesn't know, and I said, "Come on, come on, come on--in your hamely mither tongue, what's the meaning of 'sly'?" And he said "It's the green scum that forms on a pool," and he had given me the scientific name for it. So I gave in. I said I only saw that word in this line: "Juist like Rebecca in her shawl o' sly." I said "Who is Rebecca?" You know what the old devil said? "I don't know; she just fitted the meter." So I thought of American scholars truffle-hounding through the libraries of Europe trying to find out who the hell Rebecca is. He had a mischievous sense of humour which many people didn't realise.

　　　　He was, in fact, an extremely complex man, a bundle of opposites, which meant, amongst other things, that he often contradicted himself. When accused of this, he liked to quote the famous lines of Walt Whitman:

Do I contradict myself?
Very well then, I contradict myself
I am large. I contain multitudes.

And he did.

NANCY GISH

INTERVIEW WITH JOHN MONTAGUE, 1980

NG: How did you meet MacDiarmid?

JM: I have the impression of knowing Christopher for a very long time. I think this may be because he was always accepted in Ireland, in Dublin, where I was a student, as a major poet, and I was aware that the *Drunk Man* was a major poem. Now hunting around the libraries of Dublin, I came across *Stony Limits*. Then I became aware there was very little of MacDiarmid actually available. But he was very definitely a name to us and a very real name, and I came across a copy of *Stony Limits* and of *Lucky Poet* in the Kevin Street library. I was so fascinated by these two books that I was tempted to steal them, but I came to the conclusion that it would be better to leave them in case they would have the same volcanic effect [upon others] that they had upon me, and periodically I was mildly puzzled that he didn't seem to be mentioned inside the English reviews that we read: the *Observer*, the *Sunday Times*. But on the other hand we were quite aware that the Scots had their own scene: Pearse Hutchinson had been born in Glasgow, and we were familiar with the publications of MacLellan and various of the Edinburgh publishing houses and also-- being in Dublin--with the idea that one could have a fame inside one's own country and one's own capital and this need not necessarily hold across the water in England. It was almost normal to us because after all, Austin Clarke and Patrick Kavanagh, our two leading poets, were not known in England either. Now, when he actually physically entered my universe, I'm not quite sure. I think it began when there was correspondence in the *Guardian*. I was living in Paris at the time and roundabout his seventieth year there was a page on MacDiarmid, an article on him, and a statement by MacDiarmid. This led to a correspon-dence, and this correspondence included an extremely nasty little letter from John Wain whose main objection seemed to be that MacDiarmid had rejoined the communist party at the time of the invasion of Hungary in 1956, and I wrote to say that while I could agree with some aspects of John Wain's objections, he and I were in the position that we didn't have the evidence, and that as with Pound and the Pisan Cantos, it was the poetry that we had to judge. So we would have to wait until we had the *Collected Poems* before we could pronounce on MacDiarmid, and Wain's kind of attitude was not a very serious one.

Now when I actually met him, I'm not sure. As I say I was as familiar with his work as one could be considering that most of his books were out of print. When I met him I was struck by the way he had solved one of the central psychological problems of a controversial poetry writer. He was a creative schizoid; that is to say any one who was angry at Hugh MacDiarmid would be confronted with Christopher Murray Grieve, who was one of the most gentle and agreeable persons that one could possibly meet, and provided that you didn't keep continually bringing up subjects that he was bound to disagree with, you could have a most serious conversation with him. All of my conversations with him were always very amicable indeed. I found that this was also true of any older poet of real quality, and there was a receptive gentleness in him towards any idea and certainly a great courtesy towards the visitor, and the visitors often would be Englishmen of course. He might be an Anglophobe, but if it were Tom, Dick, or Harry, he was a bit like Swift: he would take the Englishman on his own merits.

NG: Can you explain what you mean by a "creative schizoid" and the separation between Hugh MacDiarmid and Christopher Murray Grieve?

JM: I don't know when or how Christopher took to the habit of having a pen name. I don't know his reason for it. He said he was against being called Christ and that he preferred the name Hugh, and he had a whole argument for it, which was that he was against the Christian myth but he was for the divine wisdom which was Sophia and that Hugh represented to him the divine wisdom and that Christopher represented Christ and that he wanted to show his allegiance in terms of his personal behavior; Hugh MacDiarmid could say or do anything but Christopher Murray Grieve was a Christian gentleman.

NG: Did he say this to you about Christ as Christopher?

JM: Yes. This was inside a long mystical conversation about Christianity and about views of the world and about communism. Something was mentioned also about stones and the material universe and the fact that no matter how you looked at it, whether you looked at it from the point of view of Christ--especially after Teilhard de Chardin--Christ seen as the evolving Logos and Word that the earth is trying to utter, that this could be acceptable to a communist and that there is no reason why the two things couldn't be acceptable as in the case of certain Russian mystics like Solovyov. I was saying that the reason for the Russian Orthodox Church being alienated from the Church of Rome was also why Austin Clarke objected to the Church of Rome. The Church of Rome destroyed the Holy Spirit, Santa Sophia, because the Holy Ghost originally was a woman, was feminine. But when you change from Greek to Latin you get the Paraclete, which was masculine, so it was a change of languages and a change of order, and once Roman order came into the church, then out went the feminine element and the whole Roman world was geared against the feminine principle.

NG: Did MacDiarmid comment on this?

JM: He was agreeing with me the whole time.

NG: I'm fascinated by what you said about Christopher representing Christ and Hugh being another, being aligned with Sophia, because in his early poetry he identified himself with Christ, even in *Drunk Man*. The *Drunk Man* himself is frequently identified with Christ.

JM: But Christ gets rejected in the middle and late work.

NG: Yes, right.

JM: I mean that's connected with the change inside the man.

NG: Can you tell me about MacDiarmid's readings in Ireland?

JM: He was a public performer; he didn't have the elan or the kind of verbal music of somebody like Dylan Thomas, but they were very good public readings. They were very sound, and they usually attracted a full house, and when you had him over for something like that, whether at the Peacock or at the Lantern Theater, which was burned down at the same time as the British Embassy, after Bloody Sunday, most of the poets in town would come along and would be there. He was always very pleasant to them. People like Tom Kinsella came, people like Douglas Sealy, of course, whom he had known for a long time. Douglas Sealy was with a nephew of Douglas Hyde, and as you know from your work, he used a lot of Douglas Hyde's translations from the Irish. He had encountered a lot also of the young Richard Ryan, Eavan Boland. There would be a kind of mustering of the poets to meet him. One person he dearly wanted to meet, another old codger like himself of socialist background, was Peadar O'Donnell. And Paddy was also over 80. Peadar had cancer, but they met; we got them together in the Shelbourne Bar. This was the kind of marvelous thing about Christopher, that despite his socialist views and the proletarian sympathies, he didn't mind meeting in the best places, and Paddy had a long chat about Larkin, John Maclean, Frank Ryan, the kind of Socialist links between the two countries because, after all, the 1913 strike had been in Dublin, and there had been a point when it had seemed that that first real socialist revolution would be in Ireland, not in Russia, and there was a kinship for a period between Glasgow and Ireland which would now be out of the question. The kinship now would be between Glasgow and Belfast and on a much more narrow basis, but these two old men chatted a lot about their socialist past and about their hopes for the future, and they had a high old time. He also met Austin Clarke on both occasions. He declared from the platform, I think of the Lantern, that Austin Clarke was doing more for Irish poetry than W. B. Yeats had done.

NG: Does MacDiarmid's work have links with Irish Poetry?

JM: Now it seems to me I always placed MacDiarmid among
poets who are not accepted in the kind of London center,
the English center, although they belong to these islands,
and in the case of all four or five of them their interests in
a mythology, even the case of David Jones's interest in
British mythology, was something which was not acceptable
to the central English tradition of a well made poem. And
so you found that people like MacDiarmid were isolated,
but so was Austin Clarke, who only achieved recognition in
England, only got a Poetry Book Society Choice, when he
was about 70 years of age. I think Graves kept going . . .
they won through mainly longevity. They wore down the
English by just living longer than them and by producing
more. Graves, of course, only came back into public recognition long after his novels. I remember a headline in the
New York Times after his great poems came out, mid-way
through the 1950s I think it was. Graves would have been
round about 65. It says, "Famous Author Has Turned to
Verse." This was the collected poems of Robert Graves
being reviewed as if he was a new poet! Graves with his
books like *The White Goddess*, the mythomania of the
White Goddess, the extraordinary leaps of the imagination
which Graves takes dealing with horse goddesses, triple
goddesses, hags, guardians of the well, moon goddesses, all
this kind of mythomania which you also find in David
Jones, the mania that you find in MacDiarmid and Austin's
addiction to early Irish, which he couldn't read very well
but which he was very much influenced by. All of these
men--I used to class them in my mind as four masters, and
the four masters were four Irish writers, at a particular
period in Irish history--they were actual monks I think--
who decided to assemble the existing body of knowledge
before it was dispersed, and in some way these people and
all of these authors made glorious antheaps out of material
which might possibly be threatened or might disappear.

NG: Who are these authors?

JM: Well, there is Christopher with his wide-ranging sympathies. You would never know what he might bring in: his
whole kind of theory of the east-west synthesis, his belief in
the Gaelic thing, which he related to the Coel Mor, which
he related to the ragas of India. In the case of David Jones,

his belief in the Sleeping Lord, King Arthur, who is buried under the hills of Britain, his belief in the Island of Priden, which is the old name from which Britain comes, his continual quotation of the fragment from the old British historian who was called Nennius, who said, "I have made a heap of all that I could find." And David Jones's two long poems, *In Parenthesis* and one about the First World War and probably his masterpiece, *The Anathemata*, which is a remembering of everything beginning from a priest who was saying mass and the altar stone becomes a stone of all the ages, becomes Troy, and slowly every one thing is mentioned and all the others are accreted to it. Now of course David in his haphazard way was a much more systematic scholar than Christopher, and also the Roman influence was inside David because after all the mainland of Priden, say south of Hadrian's wall, had been subjected to the Roman order and the Roman roads, whereas that is what is absent from MacDiarmid's mind, which keeps reaching from the lowlands to the highlands. And Christopher, of course, is a literal inheritor of the Lowland Scots tradition which gave him access into the Border Ballads and to Robert Burns. He was much better, I often think, than Robert Burns, who was rather good in the longish poems.

NG: Do you mean like "The Cotter's Saturday Night"?

JM: Yes, and "Tam O'Shanter," which is a marvelously readable poem.

NG: Does MacDiarmid's interest in the Gaelic tradition link him to the other poets you mention?

JM: All these men had a smattering of the Gaelic. It's extraordinary how much they were able to absorb through their pores, without in any of their cases, even Austin Clarke, being able to read the original. They could get close to it, and Robert, as you can see obviously from *The White Goddess*, is chock full of all the English have rejected, all the magic of the English countryside, the fairies, and all the deposits of Britain. I find this a very Irish book just like *A Vision*. It's an extraordinary kind of gathering together of many layers, often wrong, but even when it's wrong, it's creative. There's the same kind of mind working behind it as works behind the later long poems of MacDiarmid, where these extraordinary leaps are taken, leaps often in the dark, between one subject and another, and the same assumption that any one man can know everything. So Robert Graves ends up his life as a Sufi, declares that his view of poetry, especially love poetry, is based upon Sufi poetry because early Irish love poetry was very close to the Sufi. This is the same kind of argument that MacDiarmid uses to prove, not to prove but to claim that the Coel Mor, the Pibroch, is close to Indian music. He's taken long leaps of the imagination which nobody could prove but which are lovely to dwell upon. This is the kind of thing that you remark in all of them. Austin Clarke was more modest, more shy, had been profoundly hurt by the new Irish state, his inability to get a divorce. He was a much more constrained person than MacDiarmid, but MacDiarmid clearly recognized in the collected Clarke, in the later Clarke, the same kind of wide ranging imagination. In the book, *Flight to Africa*, Austin is dealing with Irish clerics throughout Africa; he's dealing with a flight to a PEN Congress in Yugoslavia; he's dealing with lust, love, the Roman Church, the Celtic Church. He traces all the ills of Ireland to the fact that we had our independent church here, the early Celtic church, and it was destroyed by Rome. And it was true that St. Patrick, when he came, he came to organize the early Irish Church, and when the Normans came, they came with a Papal Bull of Hadrian IV to reform the early Irish Church. Now all of these men were very conscious in their different ways of belonging to a tradition which was wider than that of the English, which included the British deposit as David Jones called it, and David would argue that if the British were to accept their own tradition and the meaning of their own name, the Island of Priden or Britain, and to accept the many deposits because, after all, the landscape of Britain contains the same stones and the same linguistic deposits as our own island, then there would be no intellectual quarrel between us. It's the censoring of British history after the defeat of the Jacobites, the censoring consequent upon the Hanoverian view of things: this is what they would have all contended against in their imaginative way.

NG: Is your poetry influenced by MacDiarmid?

JM: I think for me he was very much a father figure. This may come in my case from the absence of a father as a presence in my own life that I was so fond of these older men, but he touched me in a completely different area from Graves and Clarke; it does seem to me that I might not have done the *Rough Field*, which he enjoyed even in progress, if I hadn't read *A Drunk Man Looks at the Thistle*; I'm not making any comparison between the two works because they have very different principles of organization, but there is the kind of shift of mood, which is often misunderstood and what I loved in the *Drunk Man* and sometimes missed in the later work, the move from one kind of mood to another, from the sublime to the ridiculous in one quick shift, and of course absorbing the pain of history and also giving a kind of harsh laugh at the end of it. So I found the *Drunk Man* a marvelous example, and I found his pertinacity, the way he kept going also in the face of extreme odds and through long periods of exhaustion and isolation, I found this base sympathetic. I also probably would be sympathetic to his vision of the kind of Union of Celtic Socialist Republics that is so marvelous a utopia that we are not likely to see it in our days. All these men were examples to me as you can see, examples of people who lived as poets, people who were proud of being poets and proud of being to some extent the voice of the better aspects of their people, of the genuine aspirations of their people often when those aspirations were nearly extinct.

NG: You've said that you don't feel that other Irish writers were influenced in the way you were, but of course many of them met him when he came over here to read. How did they respond to him? What would you say is his reputation in Ireland now?

JM: His reputation in Ireland was always high, as I said, from the beginning, from the first time I began to read poetry, but it's as if it was the reputation of a poet writing in some other language. His reputation was like the respect one had for Neruda or maybe also for Pound, somebody who was apart from the *Observer* and from the *Sunday Times* culture box. Somebody who was doing something large and lonely and who summed up a whole culture. So he always had this audience in Ireland.

NANCY GISH

INTERVIEW WITH SEAMUS HEANEY 1980

NG: Did you know MacDiarmid well?

SH: I couldn't claim to be an intimate of MacDiarmid, and I didn't meet him until 1969. There was a big poetry reading in Dublin on United Nations Day, sometime in early December, and Hugh MacDiarmid came over. Austin Clarke, the doyen of the Irish Poets, was there, and a number of younger people including myself. It was held under the auspices of the trade union movement in Liberty Hall in Dublin, a very big hall. It was a very big audience too, and a great success. But I had a sense of MacDiarmid before that. Obviously he had a resonance; and I had read some of his early lyrics and assented to them, but I didn't really inhabit them. The impression I remember that night, meeting him--the first thing about him was that he didn't come on as monumental or institutional. There was a tremendous sense of modesty and eagerness and no barriers at all. If you compared him with a famous poet like Robert Lowell, whom we also knew and liked a lot, Lowell negotiated through the persona in some way, you know. You were aware that you were meeting a poet; but MacDiarmid, well, he was low-key, although he certainly talked out of an obsession with poetry and out of a tremendous sense of his own reputation and his own greatness.

NG: Could you be specific?

SH: He would tell you what he had written and what he had said. Yet at times there would be modesty and a self forgetfulness; he would just be that small man smoking a pipe like a million anonymous ancestors by the fire in Biggar, like a thousand countrymen that I knew--his legs crossed, smoking a pipe, saying "Aye, aye, aye." There was an ordinariness about him and his manners. On the other hand a lot of his personal authority derived from his being the poet that he was, *and* he knew he wasn't just an anonymous poet. The house was surrounded by pictures by modern masters. And that was all assimilated into the domesticity. There was a sense of it being the poet's house, yet the objects weren't displayed self-consciously--the portraits of him, I mean.

NG: But his house was filled with portraits of himself.

SH: He certainly was very egocentric, but that's okay.

NG: And he had plenty of reasons to be, really. Could you describe that first meeting a bit more?

SH: Well, I don't have many clear recollections of it. One thing I recall about it is that we were being kept away from the drink as far as possible because MacDiarmid of course had a reputation for taking a few drinks, and the man who was running this reading was quite peremptory about the way he treated MacDiarmid. "You mustn't have any of that until after the reading," and so on; but somehow or other a bottle was smuggled into the dressing room, and we all had a few drinks, so although I was very junior, the young poet making up the tail end of the program, I was still brought into the circle. We went afterwards to this man's house, and I remember MacDiarmid saying to me, "I like your poems, but they are too short. I only write long poems." So I felt some kind of confirmation just because he had actually deigned to look at the things. But I remember more a presence, more this vitality and this grace, you know, and a feeling of not being daunted, partly because of the intimacy of the Scottish voice and the democratic style.

NG: Did he influence you in any way?

SH: He didn't influence me technically, insofar as the procedures of writing verse are concerned. Maybe he influenced me in a different kind of way, helped me to think about the relation between poetry and cultural foundation, what it meant to diverge from the English tradition. When I did a review of *The MacDiarmid Anthology*, I had just resigned from a job at Queens University, and was free-lancing, trying to work full-time as a poet, and thinking about that commitment, about what it meant. I'm certain that *his* commitment and the ferocity of it came through to me as exemplary. And also his ability to keep a life-line open always to the childhood self and to Langholm and to the dialect. I liked that fidelity in him.

NG: It would seem to me that technically you have more affinity with someone like Norman MacCaig, but that in content and approach you may be nearer to MacDiarmid. Would you say that's accurate?

SH: That's right. I think the timbre of MacDiarmid's feeling is closer to me. And I have MacDiarmid's gift for falling flat on my face in a poem, which MacCaig could never do.

NG: But MacDiarmid can soar.

SH: MacDiarmid can lift. MacDiarmid was a rare challenge and a rare rebuke to the kind of neat new critical notions of poetry which I grew up with in the university: your objective correlatives and your impersonality and all that. Suddenly, here comes this man saying "I," "moi," all the time, you know, and blethering, shouting in poems. Letting fly without any primness or constriction.

NG: Very Whitmanesque.

SH: I would say at times as much Ginsberg as Whitman.

NG: MacDiarmid used to send his material to F. G. Scott every week, and every week Scott would send him back a very intense and close analysis, which MacDiarmid never paid any attention to because he went on doing his own thing, but Scott railed at him several times about being confessional in his poetry. MacDiarmid himself, of course, claims that he wants poetry that is classical and detached. Do you think he ever achieves detachment?

SH: I don't think he's "confessional." I would never use that classification. I never, in a MacDiarmid poem, get any hothouse intimacy. Except in the most distant and classical of poems. I think the intimacy is in them, in *Sangschaw* and

Penny Wheep and those poems. Yet there, the intimacy is grounded upon cadence and on the natural closeness of certain sounds. I feel with MacDiarmid a rhetoric and a stance, the elaboration of a hearth language rather than a confession.

NG: Well this letter was written in the late 20s or early 30s. He didn't mean "confessional" as in Sylvia Plath.

SH: Okay, that's different. It wasn't a technical term. Fair enough.

NG: I think he quite literally meant revealing self.

SH: I think that MacDiarmid reveals himself the best when he has the image, when he stares a long time at the single thing. I mean "A Glass of Pure Water," or "Island Funeral." Those two come to my mind.

NG: Or "On a Raised Beach" where he sits and looks over those stones?

SH: That's right. But actually I can't take that poem because of the language. I find the language actually McGonaglesque in places. . . . Joyce is mad about language, and MacDiarmid addresses Joyce very often, but I think what Joyce possessed was what MacDiarmid, alas, didn't: a sense of the ridiculous. If Joyce had used words like that, he would have given them to the citizenry, or put them into the "Oxen of the Sun" or something. By context he would have "placed" them, you know. Diction has to be carried and redeemed and made live with a tone or a cadence. I think that in "On A Raised Beach" the rhetoric is an external rhetoric, a deliberate cranked up rhetoric almost. But I think that in "Island Funeral" or "A Glass of Pure Water" there's nothing cranked up; the tone of the voice comes in just right. They possess the quality which Robert Frost called "the sound of sense."

NG: How would you say MacDiarmid is viewed in Ireland today? Are Irish poets in general strongly aware of him?

SH: I think his generation and the generation ahead of me--
John Montague--is very strongly aware of him. It depends
on the sense of your platform within Ireland, I suppose. If
you come from the North, and think of yourself in a
minority and in a culturally resisting position, where you
are saying "our culture is not British," then MacDiarmid
has something to say to you. Even though he was kind of
histrionic in his anglophobia, there was genuine vision of a
possible culture other than the metropolitan English for-
mula, and there was also a vision of integrating the archaic
which was in Scotland (and which is in Ireland) with the
modern. I know John Montague is strongly aware of that
position. John knew him better and was probably more
consciously attached to his poetic. In Belfast, among the
young poets I grew up with, the same age as myself--
Michael Longley really liked the lyrics, and Longley's dis-
position towards England would be completely different
from MacDiarmid's. But MacDiarmid was part of what you
attended to. He was a big, thick *Collected Poems*.

NG: Was this awareness and interest from a sheer admiration
of the poetry or was it also from the sense of dealing with
poetry that turns away from an English tradition and
returns to its own ancient traditions?

SH: Well, language in Ireland is something that obsesses the
writers because of this myth of loss that we too have, of the
lost Irish language. Very conscious efforts were made a
couple of generations ago by a writer like Austin Clarke
and by literary theorists like Daniel Corkery, say, or even
Thomas McDonagh to define the proper Irish mode and
the proper Irish note in the English language. Naturally
MacDiarmid's linguistic inventiveness and his conduct of a
campaign on linguistic lines was something that you were
immediately and naturally interested in. So you assented to
that without necessarily attending to the poems individu-
ally or critically. Your awareness of Lallans as a strategy
for refusing certain values and reestablishing others was--it
linked in, I think, to some emerging awareness in the North
of Ireland and in Ireland generally, of our post-colonial situation. Not that Northern Ireland perceives itself politically to be post-colonial, but I think culturally it is. It has to
find its own language. I think that even the writers spring-

ing from the Protestant Unionist establishment culture like John Hewitt, for example, and younger writers with a similar heritage are all strongly aware of having to find myths and images from their own ground. Hewitt was aware of the Lallans regionalist venture. So MacDiarmid in some way was an example. I'm thinking of what Eliot might call the social function of poetry, you know, how the artist percolates and vibrates certain attitudes and values.

NG: In America and certainly in England people are not aware of MacDiarmid as one of the classics, and I'm interested that in Ireland he was and is. Were you introduced to him at school?

SH: No, no, no.

NG: How did he enter into the consciousness of younger Irish poets?

SH: I never have heard a lecture on MacDiarmid at the university; I never saw a poem of his at school. He entered in by being a thick book on the bookshelves and by conversation about him, just an awareness that he was there.

NG: How long do you think that that's been true?

SH: I would date it in my own case from about 1964 or 1965.

NG: Do you think that poets writing in the 50s would have been likely to be aware of him?

SH: Probably knew him as a name. Oh yes. I think that, for example, if you place him along with David Jones in England, you could almost make up an alternative tradition half-outside the usual, received modernist one. David Jones is affected by modernism and uses the resources of modernism, but he refuses the modern world. MacDiarmid, while he stridently shouts himself towards the modern world, has something in him that belongs to the organic archaic community. And that is the difficulty that metropolitan and official, down-the-middle, English critics have had with him. It is this matter of intonation again; his language isn't their language; his culture isn't their culture.

There may be a kind of vindictiveness against the communism, but I don't think so. The British establishment is so fey and trivial about politics, that wouldn't stop them. Maybe what stopped them taking MacDiarmid seriously was the Scottish language; outlandish as far as they're concerned. A kind of English cultural chauvinism keeps him out. He's taken more seriously in America, I suppose.

NG: When he's known, he's taken more seriously, but he isn't as well known as one would think.

SH: There's a bit of difficulty. There's a genuine aesthetic difficulty in placing an artist who literally establishes his own language, actually makes it up out of dictionaries and dialects.

NG: Well, so did Eliot and Pound. It's just that they made it up out of Latin and Greek.

SH: I think he has a lot in common with Pound. There's the same imperfection and zaniness; the same originality in the early melodies. Also, he has a lot in common with Wordsworth.

NG: Why Wordsworth?

SH: Both connect language with cultural vitality and both discover early on, in a series of lyrics, an idiom which will be restorative for the culture. And I think *A Drunk Man Looks at the Thistle* is like the *Prelude* almost. It's a big project early on that turns the lyric flexings into a definitive action. And then the late, long English language stuff--those poems are to the MacDiarmid career what the Ecclesiastical Sonnets were to Wordsworth's; they are doctrine.

NG: Just from your own point of view, how would you place MacDiarmid's poetry in the twentieth century?

SH: I don't know how to evaluate it because I have a feeling that MacDiarmid's poetry is kind of like Irish history: it is moving towards its fulfillment. It will be perceived as ancestral when, say, Caribbean literature and Nigerian literature and Irish literature come into their strength in the twenty-first century. One half of me says MacDiarmid is a flawed poet, deeply gifted, deeply visionary, with maybe twelve or fourteen lyric poems and a couple of longish poems, that the rest of it is a kind of evangelistic wreckage artistically. And the other half of me says "How bloody thin lipped can you get? Such energy, such generosity, such full bloodedness, all that overwhelms the aesthetic claim." But it doesn't, alas, in the end.

NG: In what you're saying about becoming the voice later on, do you accept MacDiarmid's own vision of the emergence of small cultures?

SH: I wish I could do it. I think all that's defeated actually: pious hopes rather than actual achievement. But the lost is what MacDiarmid lived by. And it's maybe what the imagination always lives by. And it is the function of the artist to give--one of the functions--to give valency to those values that seem to be lost, to make them realities of the imagination and therefore alive. And certainly in the post-imperialist world of cultures that have had to deal with English and have to discover through their own particular dialect of English a way of re-saying themselves, MacDiarmid is bound to appear as a resource and an example. And if you take Eliot's notion of a major poet--that poet in whom you can't read one thing without sensing the whole thing--then MacDiarmid is a major poet, and he's also major in terms of the genius that he had and the effort he made.

DONALD DAVIE

IN A YEAR OF THE OLYMPICS

to the late Harvey Oxenhorn,
on his "Poetry of Hugh MacDiarmid."

Closing your patient book,
I mind the scunnersome braid
Scots I have heard in a London
'bus or railway-station,
manfully drunk. So stiff
the clay MacDiarmid tried
to entertain his hopes of.

Those ruffians wore the favors
of some athletic club.
Another of our old
Stanford circle writes of
the frightening image of "mob,"
when he took his adopted son
to a ball-game in Chicago.

Going as you did to
Greenland in a tall
ship was more athletic;
or else his crouching unfed,
unsociable and honest,
MacDiarmid the socialist,
alone on a rock off Whalsay.

An exercise in survival
communally or solo
is a sporting event. Great sport
is to be had in writing
when such as you recount
surviving a difficult voyage
among the books of another.

Tall talk won't do it. How
tall walk the ships? Ships' companies
were a find of the *bourgeois*,
a mercantile invention, as
reading the records of any
18th-century navy
attests, by sorry contrast.

Time that the burgess be
exonerated. Culture as
you, I, and our friends know it is
a tight ship's company, *bourgeois*.
What, short of the lash, could sail us
so near to the glacier's outflow?
What else have we trusted?

Ah Caledonia! That
deluded imperial service
pipe-majors piped them to
is seen for what it was
perhaps, as the hermit of Whalsay
skirls on the mainland pibrochs
for wars not of clans but class.

"THE COMPANY I'VE KEPT": CONTEXTS AND INTERTEXTS

Norman MacCaig, Sydney Goodsir Smith, Hugh MacDiarmid,
Sorley MacLean, Alistar Fowler.
Photo used courtesy of *The Glasgow Herald*.

ALAN BOLD

MacDIARMID AND THE CAIRNCROSS CONNEXION

New readers of Hugh MacDiarmid who approach his work with preconceptions about a militantly Marxist poetry are "frequently astonished"[1] by the pervasive presence of Christian imagery. Though he was "very young,"[2] perhaps fifteen or sixteen, when he abandoned "the kirk o' my faithers" (307), he made profound use, in his poetry, of the figure of Christ and the connotations of Christianity. "The Following Day," from *Annals of the Five Senses* (1923), begins:

'My house is crowned with horns
--Transpiercing horns of deer!
As were His brows with thorns.
Between two thieves He hung
Upon His Cross,
As here 'twixt earth and sky
Hang I. . . .'

(CP 8-9)

The poem, its author acknowledged, "came into my head just as it stands on paper,"[3] so in 1920 the twenty-eight-year-old poet instinctively cast his thoughts in a Christian context.

     Sangschaw (1925) includes "I Heard Christ Sing," "O Jesu Parvule," and "The Innumerable Christ" with its cosmic vision of the crucifixion:

I' mony an unco warl' the nicht	strange
The lift gaes black as pitch at noon,	sky
An' sideways on their chests the heids	heads
O' endless Christs roll doon.	

(CP 32)

1. Hugh MacDiarmid, *The Complete Poems of Hugh MacDiarmid*, ed. Michael Grieve and W. R. Aitken, 2 vols. (Harmondsworth: Penguin, 1985) 197. All subsequent references to the poems are from this edition.
2. Hugh MacDiarmid, *Lucky Poet* (1943; London: Jonathan Cape, 1972) 40.
3. Alan Bold, ed., *The Letters of Hugh MacDiarmid* (London: Hamish Hamilton, 1984) 47.

"Bombinations of a Chimaera," from *Penny Wheep* (1926), seeks (with facetious asides) spiritual release through the experience of resurrection:

> The wecht o' my body,   weight
> The wecht o' my soul,
> Like the stane frae the mooth   stone from the mouth
> O' the sepulchre roll.
>
> (CP 64)

In MacDiarmid's Scots masterpiece, *A Drunk Man Looks at the Thistle* (1926), a spirit-sodden Scotsman is transformed into a truly spiritual individual and held up as an inspirational example to others. First, though, the Drunk Man must carry his burden to a hillside where he--from "Montrose or Nazareth" (CP 88)--is symbolically crucified on the thistle. Early in the poem MacDiarmid introduces the deliberately blasphemous notion that the inebriated Scotsman is capable of becoming a second saviour:

> A greater Christ, a greater Burns, may come.
> The maist they'll dae is to gi'e bigger pegs
> To folly and conceit to hank their rubbish on.
> They'll cheenge folks' talk but no' their natures, fegs!
>
> (CP 86)

That note of caution is subsequently contradicted by the thematic thrust of the poem, which sets out to prove that human nature can, indeed, be changed. Always conscious of "The thocht o' Christ and Calvary" (CP 122), the Drunk Man eventually understands that the revival of Scotland depends on a creative Christ-like resurrection:

> *'A Scottish poet maun assume*   must
> *The burden o' his people's doom,*
> *And dee to brak' their livin' tomb.*   die
>
> *Mony ha'e tried, but a' ha'e failed.*
> *Their sacrifice has nocht availed.*
> *Upon the thistle they're impaled.*
>
> (CP 165)

In his final flourish, though, the Drunk Man turns to

> ... Him, whom nocht in man or Deity,
> Or Daith or Dreid or Laneliness can touch,   death; dread
> *Wha's deed owre often and has seen owre much.*   died
>
> (CP 167)

If the image contains calculated elements of ambiguity, it is because the Drunk Man is ultimately indistinguishable from Christ.

Throughout the 1920s MacDiarmid treated the Scottish Literary Renaissance as a platform from which he could preach his poetic ideal of a resurrection of the self. Inside every individual, he implied, was a potential Christ. The identification with Christ continued in *To Circumjack Cencrastus* (1930) though that sequence is defeatist where *A Drunk Man* is triumphant. Now MacDiarmid sees himself being sacrificed to an unworthy cause, the domestic struggle for survival:

Thrang o' ideas that like fairy gowd   throng; gold
'll leave me the 'Review' reporter still
Waukenin' to my clung-kite faimly on a hill   with bellies shrunken from
O' useless croftin' whaur naething's growed   [hunger
But Daith, sin Christ for an idea died
On a gey similar but less heich hillside.   very; high
Ech, weel for Christ: for he was never wed
And had nae weans clamourin' to be fed!   children
(CP 237)

MacDiarmid's concept of liberty, as expressed in *Cencrastus*, is determined by the Christian precedent:

For freedom means that a lad or lass
    In Cupar or elsewhaur yet
  May alter the haill o' human thocht   whole
    Mair than Christ's altered it.
(CP 257)

Though contemptuous of the institutional Christianity of the Scottish Kirk, MacDiarmid insists:

I'm no' a Christian but I canna say
That Christianity's failed--it's no' been tried,
(CP 260)

The idea of surpassing Christ and achieving the new social order he failed to establish is central to "First Hymn to Lenin" (1931) which acclaims its hero in Christological terms:

Christ's cited no' by chance or juist because
You mark the greatest turnin'-point since him
But that your main redress has lain where he's
Least use--fulfillin' his sayin' lang kept dim
That whasae followed him things o' like natur'
      'Ud dae--and greater!   would do
(CP 297)

"Third Hymn to Lenin" (1957) condemns the capitalist world for pretending to be "Christian--in flat defiance of all Christ taught" (CP 897).

In 1933, the year he came in financial and psychological distress to the Shetland island of Whalsay, MacDiarmid composed "On a Raised Beach," generally regarded as his greatest poem in English. During the course of the poem MacDiarmid searches for "the Christophanic rock that moved" (CP 423) as he meditates on the meaning of physical death and creative life. When he rises majestically to his conclusion, MacDiarmid accepts the death of all men philosophically by noting one exception:

> --Each of these stones on this raised beach,
>   Every stone in the world,
> Covers infinite death, beyond the reach
> Of the dead it hides; and cannot be hurled
> Aside yet to let any of them come forth, as love
>   Once made a stone move
>   (Though I do not depend on that
>   My case to prove).
>   (CP 433)

"Lament for the Great Music," which comes (like "On a Raised Beach") from *Stony Limits* (1934), specifically declares, "I believe . . . in the ineluctable certainty of the resurrection" (CP 480).

With a writer as prolific as MacDiarmid, it is possible to make any number of critical cases by the selective use of illustrative quotations. Nonetheless, the poetic evidence demonstrates that MacDiarmid's verse, and some of his greatest verse at that, is saturated in Christian symbolism. I do not wish to suggest that MacDiarmid was a closet Christian or that he was at all insincere in his many assertions of atheism.[4] Still, he was (to cite his favourite Whitman quotation) a man who contained multitudes, and with his enjoyment of extremes he could be simultaneously materialist and mystic, a self-proclaimed Communist whose ideal of the sacrificial saviour was founded on the Christianity of his childhood. For artistic and biographical reasons, then, I regard it as enormously important that at a crucial period

---

4. "I see [reality] as a spiritual thing, insofar as reality is conceivable by the human mind. It's possible, of course, to think or to imagine that only a very small portion of reality is accessible to the human mind: which is why I am a materialist and an atheist." So MacDiarmid says in *The Thistle Rises*, ed. Alan Bold (London: Hamish Hamilton, 1984) 251. This passage can be contrasted with MacDiarmid's poetic conviction "That the whole astronomical universe, however illimitable,/ Is only one part and parcel of the mystery of Life" (CP 822).

of his life--from the age of nine until the age of fifteen--MacDi-armid came heavily under the influence of a man who was a Christian by profession and a poet by aspiration.

Before he assumed the pseudonym "Hugh MacDi-armid" in 1922, Christopher Murray Grieve (as the poet was christened in Langholm in 1892) was in the process of making a reputation as an enterprising and ambitious personality in Scottish literature. Grieve's first book was *Northern Numbers* (1920), an anthology of living Scottish poets and, as MacDiarmid acknowledged in his intellectual autobiography *Lucky Poet* (1943), its purpose was to promote the aims of the editor:

> The well-known poets represented alongside *les jeunes* in the earlier issues ... were speedily, and no doubt a trifle unceremoniously, 'dropped', and the field was left to the rising school. I have been accused of ill-faith in securing the association in this way of men who were relatively distinguished--and then dropping them. I cannot see that any ill-faith was involved at all. I simply took the position as it then was at its best--determined to proceed thence to a different position altogether. ... And as to these men of established reputation ... [I felt] the necessary development of Scottish poetry necessitated their drastic demotion in critical esteem and popular appraisal. ... [5]

Planned as an annual anthology along the lines of Edward Marsh's *Georgian Poetry* (1912-22), *Northern Numbers* amounted to three volumes, the last being published as well as edited by C. M. Grieve (dated 1922, actually issued January 1923).

It is the first volume of *Northern Numbers* that reveals most about the strategy of Grieve. Of the eleven contributors to the book, John Buchan, Violet Jacob, and Neil Munro (to whom the volume is dedicated "with affection and pride") clearly represent the Scottish poetic establishment while C. M. Grieve, A.G. Grieve (the editor's brother) and Roderick Watson Kerr (like Grieve, a former student at Broughton Junior Student Centre in Edinburgh) are the new names. Standing apart from the categories of the established and the up-and-coming is T. S. Cairncross with eight poems including "Langholm," a tribute to the town in which C. M. Grieve was born on 11 August 1892:

> It lies by the heather slopes,
> Where God spilt the wine of the moorland
> Brimming the beaker of hills. Lone it lies
> A rude outpost: challenging stars and dawn,

---

5. MacDiarmid, *Lucky Poet* 179.

And down from remoteness
And the Balladland of the Forest
The Pictish Esk trails Glory,
Rippling the quiet eaves
With the gold of the sun.

Here casts the angler,
Half-hid in shadow: his eyes
Veiled with rapt contemplation,
Where raider and reiver darted and harried.
Those mild terrible eyes
Came down from Flodden.

He hints and bends over the crystal waters
In large content,
The Roman Road all empty
By death's stern sure outlawing,
With here in great spaces of the wind and sunshine
Life at the full!

O border shadow!
A silhouette of silence and old years
Ever abide: now the clang of the long day over,
The little town shall fold itself to rest
With through its dreams the chequered river gleaming
In luminous peace!

Though MacDiarmid claimed, "Basically, I don't
think I've been influenced by anybody at all,"[6] there are echoes
of Cairncross's "Langholm" in the early poems, particularly "A
Moment in Eternity." Compare Cairncross's "Brimming the
beaker of hills" with Grieve's similarly alliterative "Burgeoning
in buds of brightness" (CP 3), Cairncross's reference to "crystal
waters" with Grieve's "crystal sources in dim hills" (CP 5),
Cairncross's "luminous peace" with Grieve's "luminous boughs"
(CP 5), Cairncross's "great spaces of the wind and sunshine"
with Grieve's "wind . . . Multitudinous and light" (CP 5). The
stately movement of Cairncross's verse, the contemplative presentation of his theme, the exclamations: these are features
Grieve fashioned in his English poems. Quoting "Langholm" in
Lucky Poet, MacDiarmid comments:

> I thought that was great stuff when I was a boy of twelve to four-
> teen, not recognizing then that what really attracted me to Cairn-
> cross's work was his technical experimentation, with Henley's
> rhymeless rhythms, and that I was very soon to recognize in myself

---

6. Bold, ed. *The Thistle Rises* 259.

a spirit to which such backward looking resignationism and sentimental dreaming were utterly false and foreign.[7]

Undoubtedly Hugh MacDiarmid outgrew Grieve's early English manner, but he did so after exploring the diction he associated with Cairncross.

At significant periods of his creative life Grieve gladly sought out mentors and accepted their advice. For almost twenty years (1911-1930) he corresponded with George Ogilvie, his English teacher at Broughton Junior Student Centre. It was Ogilvie who encouraged Grieve to edit *Northern Numbers* and Ogilvie to whom "A Moment in Eternity" was dedicated. Francis George Scott, who taught English at Langholm Academy from 1903-1912, came back into the poet's life in the 1920s. When "Hugh MacDiarmid" was working in Montrose, he discussed the design of *A Drunk Man Looks at the Thistle* with Scott and dedicated the poem to him in glowing terms. The publication of my own edition of *The Letters of Hugh MacDiarmid* (1984) and the critical debate over Scott's role in *A Drunk Man* have ensured that both Ogilvie and Scott are recognised as men who mattered greatly to MacDiarmid. Cairncross, however, has been forgotten as a force to be reckoned with in any assessment of the evolution of a major poet.

Thomas Scott Cairncross was born on 1 April 1872 in Lesmahagow, a town and parish in Lanarkshire, five miles south-west of Lanark on the river Nethan.[8] He was educated locally, took his Bachelor of Divinity degree at Glasgow University, then completed his theological training by spending a year at the United Presbyterian Hall in Edinburgh. In 1900, the year Cairncross qualified as a minister, the 1,000 parishes of the Free Church joined the 600 congregations of the United Presbyterian Church to form the United Free Church of Scotland. Cairncross's first charge was as minister of Langholm South United Free Church from 1901-1907. These six years cover a formative part of the life of C. M. Grieve who was, as has been stated, eight when Cairncross arrived in Langholm and fifteen when the minister left Langholm to become minister at Old Kilpatrick Church, Bowling, Dumbartonshire.

Grieve's father James, a rural postman, was a follower of the United Free Church: both Grieve's parents, indeed, were "very devout believers and very Churchy people."[9] James

---

7. MacDiarmid, *Lucky Poet* 223.
8. For information about T. S. Cairncross I am indebted to his son-in-law, the Reverend Inglis Finnie.
9. MacDiarmid, *Lucky Poet* 40.

Grieve was a church elder and superintendent at Langholm South United Free Church, and his son, Christopher, attended the church regularly and became a Sunday School teacher at the age of thirteen. Cairncross combined his duties as minister with a passionate interest in literature. He wrote book reviews for the *Irish Times* and introduced Grieve to the work of "many poets (some of whom subsequently became great personal friends of my own), such as T. Sturge Moore, Bliss Carman, Thomas MacDonagh, Joseph Mary Plunkett, Padraic Pearse, Eithne Carberry and many others."[10]

What most impressed Grieve was that the minister, the Reverend Thomas Scott Cairncross, was also a poet, T. S. Cairncross. In 1905, when Grieve was a thirteen-year-old Sunday School teacher in Langholm South United Free Church, Cairncross published (under the imprint Robert Scott of Langholm) his first collection, *The Return of the Master*. The book pays tribute to such favourite writers as "W. E. Henley" and "Bliss Carman" and features "Langholm," quoted above. Cairncross's use of Langholm imagery is sustained in "Saint Thorwald and Whita Well," a poem in dialect Scots beginning:

> There's a well in the Border Country,
> And for miles and miles, roun' and roun',
> There's nane in the Border Country
> Like Whita by Langholm Toun.

"Crying the Fair," a poem alluding to Langholm's annual Common Riding festival (held every last Friday in July), ends:

> For where they dance upon the Castleholm
>   Or throng the Green,
> Or ride the Common, or 'The Langholm' roam,
>   One grief I ween,
>
> Stays as the Thistle and the Bannock proudly pass   thick, flat cake
>   And dims the eye,
> That of the hearth where gay go lad and lass,
>   No child am I.
>
> Yet at your feet I lay my poor wreath down
>   Of withering flowers;
> Knowing that dearer hands than mine shall crown
>   Your fadeless hours.

---

10. MacDiarmid, *Lucky Poet* 222.

MacDiarmid uses the emblems of the Common Riding festival--
"an eight-foot thistle and a barley bannock with a salt herring
nailed to it, with a twelvepenny nail, and all the children carry
heather besoms"[11]--in *A Drunk Man Looks at the Thistle*. The
contrast between Cairncross's gentle quatrains and MacDiarmid's powerfully expressive couplets is startling, showing the
distance between talent and genius:

> Drums in the Walligate, pipes in the air,
> Come and hear the cryin' o' the Fair.
>
> A' as it used to be, when I was a loon   boy
> On Common-Ridin' Day in the Muckle Toon.
>
> The bearer twirls the Bannock-and-Saut-herrin',
> The Croon o' roses through the lift is farin',   crown; sky
>
> The aucht-fit thistle wallops on hie;   eight-foot; gallops
> In heather besoms a' the hills gang by.   brooms
>   (CP 97)

MacDiarmid's exploitation of Langholm imagery is obviously on
a creative level beyond the reach of Cairncross. It is, nevertheless, worth noting that MacDiarmid knew Cairncross's
Langholm poems intimately and was conscious of the topo-
graphical precedent pioneered by the minister. In the early
1930s MacDiarmid projected, as the huge autobiographical first
part of his unfinished *Clann Albann* sequence, a volume called
The Muckle Toon ("the big town," the name by which Langholm
is known in the Borders). *The Muckle Toon* was to discuss,
among other things, "the Church influence which bulked so
largely in my life then";[12] "The Church of My Fathers," a poem
intended for *The Muckle Toon*, suggests that Grieve turned from
the Kirk because he found it "toom" (CP 308], that is, empty.
The Scottish Kirk, the poet increasingly felt, had little in common with the teachings of the Christ with whom he still identified: "I've gane sae faur/(Like Christ) yont faither, mither,
brither, kin" (CP 301).

The young Christopher Murray Grieve probably had
his first serious discussions on socialism with Cairncross, who
was fascinated by the subject. While in Langholm, Cairncross
worked on the essays subsequently assembled as *The Steps of the*

---

11. The Common Riding is an annual festival during which the people ceremonially publicize the
boundaries of the common lands by riding around them. See MacDiarmid, *Lucky Poet* 222.
12. See Bold, ed., *Letters* xii.

Pulpit (1910), his second book. In this discursive work Cairncross considers the relative merits of socialism and Christianity. He is sceptical of socialism as a surrogate religion ready to replace Christianity and certain that spiritual strength is morally superior to economic planning:

> The feeling I have is that Britain to-day is not needing Socialism so much as the Spirit of Christ. Between the choice of having my old clothes patched and a new rig-out I prefer a new suit, if you please. You can have your tickets, and I will keep my individuality if you don't mind. . . . Of course, if the Socialist has a better rule than that one of Christ given in the Sermon on the Mount, "Therefore all things whatsoever ye would that men should do to you, do ye even so to them," if he has a better rule than that, I have an open mind. It was Christ who said that. I go by Him. . . . Even if Socialism comes it is not likely to supersede the need of the gospel of Christ. . . . The defect of much Socialistic pleading today is that it has no Christ.[13]

As we have seen, MacDiarmid never eliminated the figure of Christ from his poems, nor did he abandon the spiritual insights he absorbed as a youngster in Langholm. During his evolution as an artist he ingeniously adapted some of his early beliefs rather than completely rejecting them. I have argued elsewhere[14] that MacDiarmid's intellectual elitism is an extension of the doctrine of the elect so central to the Calvinistic tenets of the Scottish Kirk. It seems certain, too, that he derived from the New Testament his own gospel of salvation through self-sacrifice: this is one of the Great themes of *A Drunk Man Looks at the Thistle*, one of the main contentions of the unfinished epic *Cornish Heroic Song for Valda Trevlyn*. One segment of that sequence, "The Poet as Prophet," projects MacDiarmid as a modern Christ:

> In him were incarnate at that moment
> The liberties and the rights of man asserted in the face of power,
> The independence of the spirit which demands
> That conscience be satisfied
> Even against one who ranks himself higher than its claims.
>   (CP 1376)

That Cairncross's impact on Grieve endured after the minister left Langholm in 1907 is confirmed by the poet's correspondence. Writing to George Ogilvie on 13 February 1918, Grieve enthuses:

---

13. T. S. Cairncross, *The Steps of the Pulpit* (London: Hodder and Stoughton, 1910) 164-66.
14. See Bold, ed., *Letters* viii.

> I have a letter from the Rev. T. S. Cairncross--did I ever mention
> him to you? He has published several volumes of pleasant prose
> and two volumes of poetry. . . . He could not be omitted from any
> adequate anthology of modern Scottish poetry. Several of his ver-
> nacular ballads are wonderfully good. But the great bulk of his
> stuff is still in MSS. He is just back from chaplaining in France and
> is likely to contribute something good to the literature of the War.
> I should like to send on some of his stuff to you--but must wait till
> I get home. I should like your opinion of him. He writes most
> delightful letters.[15]

Another letter, of 28 December 1920 to Ogilvie, mentions an
article Grieve has written on Cairncross: "The thing astounds
me. Did you see it? I haven't a copy--but I can get you one."[16]

From December 1920 to March 1921, Grieve contributed four articles on "Certain Newer Scottish Poets" to the
National Outlook. Inevitably, in the circumstances, he began the
series with a tribute to Cairncross, who is eulogised as the
embodiment of an ideal which Grieve was to attain. Give or take
a few details (substituting, for instance, Candymill, Biggar, for
the Dumbarton Road and the Clyde waterway) the verbal portrait of Cairncross has an uncanny resemblance to MacDiarmid
in his years as Scotland's Grand Old Man of letters:

> Business-like he is--making, for example, a perfect point of reply-
> ing to every letter he receives by return of post. But there is no
> commercial side to his art. Lost in tobacco-smoke and the depths
> of his armchair, covering the single sheets of note-paper he fas-
> tidiously prefers with his extraordinarily minute calligraphy, he is
> lost, too, for all practical purposes, and his pen runs where his
> spirit listeth: and no man in Scotland escapes more cleanly from
> the chaos of modern civilization than this lithe soft-eyed poet
> whose study-window, with a decent interspace of fruit-trees, looks
> down upon the Dumbarton Road and the Clyde waterway.[17]

After saluting Cairncross as "a type of Scottish gentleman surviving with increasing difficulty under modern industrial conditions,"[18] Grieve surveys the man's output in extravagant terms:

> Everything he has written is beautifully coloured, exquisitely fin-
> ished, nowhere inept, and nowhere false. He is a poet for poets
> really, a scrupulous technician, a cunning innovator, a cerebral
> craftsman who chases the polished surface of his thought with rare
> and elaborate designs. His work is full of hints and humours,
> highly allusive, endlessly evocative, fastiduously wrought . . . the

15. Bold, ed., *Letters* 22.
16. Bold, ed., *Letters* 52.
17. Christopher Murray Grieve, "Certain Newer Scottish Poets," in *National Outlook* (Dec. 1920): 120.
18. Grieve, *National Outlook* (Dec. 1920): 120.

spirit of his work is perfectly balanced and ripe without a shadow
of decadence.[19]

That is perhaps not so much an assessment of Cairncross as a
promise by Grieve of the kind of poet Hugh MacDiarmid was to
become.

Two years after publishing that extraordinary
homage to Cairncross, C. M. Grieve created Hugh MacDiarmid
in a successful attempt to remake Scottish poetry in a modernist
image. It was in 1922, the annus mirabilis of modernism, that
Joyce's *Ulysses* and T. S. Eliot's *The Waste Land* appeared and
Hugh MacDiarmid distinguished himself as the author of "The
Watergaw" (*Scottish Chapbook*, October 1922). MacDiarmid the
modernist had no desire to be associated with a Scottish
minister since Scottish ministers were synonymous with the sentimental kailyard school of Scottish writing--as witness the work
of the Free Church ministers "Ian Maclaren" (John Watson,
author of *Beside the Bonnie Brier Bush*, 1894) and Samuel
Rutherford Crockett (author of *The Lilac Sunbonnet*, 1894).
Since leaving Langholm, Cairncross had become minister at
Bowling (his charge for twenty six-years), and he published a
kailyard novel, *Blawearie*, in 1911. At first suppressed because of
its unflattering allusions to easily identifiable Langholm characters, it depicts Grieve's birthplace as a closed community:

> It has always been a mystery to me that Blawearie [that is,
> Langholm] has never loved the stranger, for it is the stranger who
> keeps it alive. He keeps shop for it, finances its mills, heals its sick,
> preaches its gospel, makes its will, and tells of its beauty in story
> and song.[20]

After *Blawearie*, Cairncross published two theological books--
The Making of a Minister (1914) and *The Appeal of Jesus* (1915)--
and two further collections of poetry--*From the Kilpatrick Hills*
(1921) and *The Scot at Hame* (1922). In that last volume he
printed a poem, "Tarras," beginning:

> Oh it's fine to be in Tarras
> When the leaves are comin' oot,
> Where the saughs and elders trimmle,   willows; tremble
> And there's mony a peat-brown troot.   trout

That style of mild dialect Scots was anathema to MacDiarmid
the modernist who regarded his Synthetic Scots as a Joycean lin-

---

19. Grieve, *National Outlook* (Dec. 1920): 121.
20. T. S. Cairncross, *Blawearie* (London: Hodder and Stoughton, 1911) 125.

guistic experiment. MacDiarmid's own poem about Langholm's Tarras Water (which rises in a boggy wasteland known as Tarras Moss) shows how far he wanted to move from Scots sentimentality:

> *This Bolshevik bog! Suits me doon to the grun'!*
> *For by fike and finnick the world's no' run.*   fuss
> *Let fools set store by a simperin' face.*
> *Ithers seek to keep the purale in place*   poor
> *Or grue at vermin--but by heck*   be revolted
> *The purpose o' life needs them--if us.*
> (CP 337)

In Bowling, Cairncross was naturally interested in the celebrity of Hugh MacDiarmid who, as Christopher Murray Grieve, had taken Sunday School classes in his church. There was a family connexion too; MacDiarmid's cousin Bob Laidlaw (1882-1949) was married to Alice, Cairncross's sister-in-law. When MacDiarmid's *Lucky Poet* materialized in print, Cairncross and the Laidlaws were stunned by a reference to

> Thomas Scott Cairncross, who was, when I was a boy, minister of the church my parents attended . . . but who subsequently ceased to be friendly with me because he was of fastidious upper-class temper, while my work from the beginning was Socialistic and anti-Christian, so that any association with it was likely to compromise his chances of ministerial promotion and the degree of D.D., while the fact that from the very outset my work attracted far more attention, and in important quarters at that, than his had ever done, chagrined him sorely and, on the part of a working-man's son, affected him as a piece of intolerable presumption. . . .[21]

It was impossible for Cairncross to accept that passage as an integral part of the polemical protest *Lucky Poet* directed at the world. He was (as his son-in-law confirmed) hurt and horrified by what he regarded as an attack on his integrity. As I discovered when I was editing *The Letters of Hugh MacDiarmid*, Cairncross destroyed the letters he had received from his erstwhile admirer.

MacDiarmid never retracted that attack though he regretted the offence it caused, for when Bob Laidlaw died the poet told a member of the family: "I was sorry [Bob Laidlaw] felt that what I had said about T. S. Cairncross in *Lucky Poet* precluded our being friends."[22] Whereas C. M. Grieve was the

---

21. MacDiarmid, *Lucky Poet* 222.
22. Bold, ed., *Letters* 629.

most courteous of individuals, Hugh MacDiarmid was a formidable propagandist as well as a poet of genius. Sacrificing personal feelings for the cause of a truly radical Scottish literature, MacDiarmid believed there was no place for personal or literary sentimentality in modern Scottish culture. Cairncross was one of the casualties of MacDiarmid's propaganda. Yet, as I hope I have shown, MacDiarmid's poetic development might have been drastically different had he not spent six years of his life learning literary and theological lessons from T. S. Cairncross, who died on 8 December 1961, at Eccles, a hamlet in the Tweed valley.

RAYMOND ROSS

"ONENESS OF CONCEPT":
MacDIARMID AND EMPIRIO-CRITICISM

Hugh MacDiarmid is generally regarded as the poet of perpetual opposition and self-contradiction *par excellence.* He was a nationalist *and* a communist. He declared that Gaelic was Scotland's only true language; but he himself wrote only in Scots and its sister language, English. He was an intellectual elitist who wished to be quoted "in the factories and fields" while (following Shestov) he derided talent as the enemy of genius. He decried obscurantism in life and letters and yet would seem to go out of his own way in order to damn rational consistency. The most famous expression of this romantic egoism occurs in *A Drunk Man Looks at the Thistle* (1926):

I'll ha'e nae hauf-way hoose, but aye be whaur	house; where
Extremes meet--it's the only way I ken	
To dodge the curst conceit o' bein' richt	of being right
That damns the vast majority o' men.[1]	

Yet, four years before the publication of that first great epic, he could write:

Oneness of concept, within the chosen form whatever that may be,
is an essential of great poetry, I think.[2]

It is interesting to note that although the pursuit of that "oneness of concept" spanned his entire poetic career, it is the cult of self-contradiction for which MacDiarmid remains (in)famous. The Whitmanesque cult is perhaps more appealing to the popular notion of a poet as a man of inspiration and passion unbound by any prosaic rationality or commonsense consistency. And MacDiarmid could certainly play to the gallery when it suited.

---

1. Hugh MacDiarmid, *The Complete Poems of Hugh MacDiarmid*, ed. Michael Grieve and W. R. Aitken (London: Martin Brian and O'Keeffe, 1978) 87. All further references to the poems are from this edition.
2. Hugh MacDiarmid, letter to William Soutar, 8 June 1922, National Library of Scotland MS 8506 and *The Letters of Hugh MacDiarmid*, ed. Alan Bold (London: Hamish Hamilton, 1984) 137.

However, it is the striving for that "oneness of concept" which should be the primary focus in understanding MacDiarmid's aesthetic rather than any cult of extremes. This is so because the root of the intellectual or philosophical contradictions which permeate his poetry is to be found in that life-long attempt to express an all-embracing unity which was more than purely formal or structural. With MacDiarmid that "oneness of concept" ultimately concerns nothing less than the meaning of life and death, nothing less than the unity of life and death which reflects a far greater unity of being and purpose "beyond." His belief in that all-embracing unity is based on poetic intuition (as he sees it), and he uses his poetry to express, explore, evaluate, and argue about the meaning and significance of the intuited unity. Thus he writes, in *In Memoriam James Joyce* (1955), in reflective retrospection:

> For one thing I fancy the manner I have allowed
> My natural impulses towards romance and mysticism
> To dominate me has led to the formation
> Of a curious gap or 'lacuna'
> Between the innate and almost savage realism,
> Which is a major element in my nature,
> And the imaginative, poetical cult
> Whereby I have romanticised and idealized my life.
> In this realistic mood I recognise
> With a grim animal acceptance
> That it is indeed likely enough that the 'soul'
> Perishes everlastingly with the death of the body,
> But what this realistic mood, into which
> My mind falls like a plummet
> Through the neutral zone of its balanced doubt,
> Never for one single beat of time can shake or disturb
> Is my certain knowledge,
> Derived from the complex vision of everything in me,
> That the whole astronomical universe, however illimitable,
> Is only one part and parcel of the mystery of Life;
> Of this I am as certain as I am certain that I am I.
> The astronomical universe is *not* all there is.
>   (CP 821-22)

This intuited unity beyond the "astronomical universe" is evoked throughout MacDiarmid's *corpus*. It is symbolised variously (and shiftingly) in *A Drunk Man* (1926) and *To Circumjack Cencrastus* (1930) as the thistle (Scotland's national emblem) which yet will "unite" man and the infinite, a "mony-brainchin' candelabra" which fills the sky; it can be detected in the form and movement of the curly snake and it is "the Unkent God." In

"Lament for the Great Music" (*Stony Limits* 1934) "It is the supreme reality. . .visible to the mind alone." In "On A Raised Beach," from the same collection, it fills the poet "with a sense of perfect form" and

> Is the beginning and end of the world,
> The unsearchable masterpiece, the music of the spheres,
> Alpha and Omega, the Omnific Word.
> (CP 428-29)

In "O Ease My Spirit" (*Second Hymn to Lenin* 1935) it infuses the "terribly illuminating/Integration of the physical and the spiritual"; and in "Diamond Body": (*A Lap of Honour* 1967) the poet tells us:

> Our minds already sense that the fabric of nature's laws
> Conceals something that lies behind it,
> A greater-unity.
> (CP 1086)

Although this "oneness of concept," this "greater-unity" is visible to "the mind alone," and although it can only be intuited through imagination ("romance and mysticism," "the imaginative, poetical cult") and runs counter to a thorough (or "savage") "realism," the poet must nevertheless attempt to give form to his intuition by shuffling the base coinage of language. By definition this unity is beyond language and so language (to borrow from Eliot) must be dislocated into meaning in order to express it. Here, paradox and contradiction are inevitable, not wilful.

Contradictions aside, it is the expression of this intuited unity, its exploration and evaluation, which might be said to be, with MacDiarmid, the ultimate domain of poetry. Therefore, in order to approach an informed appreciation of that domain we must patently try to understand its nature. This is our primary focus.

MacDiarmid saw this unity as intellectual and spiritual (in a non-religious sense) and in many ways his poems can be read as hymns to intellectual beauty. He tried to express the unity in intellectual/spiritual terms either by recourse to symbolism, as in *A Drunk Man, To Circumjack Cencrastus,* and long passages of "On A Raised Beach," or by recourse to that kind of poetic philosophical discourse prevalent in the later work, as exemplified by the above passage from *In Memoriam James Joyce*. He certainly regarded poetry as greater than, if not indeed as a higher form of, philosophy. As he comically laments in *A Drunk Man*:

> . . . I've nae faith in ocht I can explain,   no; anything
> And stert whaur the philosophers leave aff.   start where; off
>   (CP 87)

His poetry is shot through with exhortations in favour of higher forms of "thocht" [thought]. He defined and reiterated many times that the function of poetry is the extension of human consciousness beyond the rational and empirical, beyond even (as he puts it in *Second Hymn to Lenin*) "A' that's material and moral" until we find "oor new state descried."

The Nietzschean notion of developing consciousness beyond good and evil (beyond the "moral") need not detain us here. But the implication that "oor new state" is beyond all that is material is more than pertinent. For that new state must be interpreted as a realm of pure thought, a realm of pure spiritual existence. That this characterises the intuited unity that his poetry tends to is made more explicit in "Third Hymn to Lenin" (*Three Hymns to Lenin* 1957) where he declares that "thought is reality--and thought alone!" Moreover, the poem states that thought "must absorb all the material" in order to produce "The mastery by the spirit of all the facts that can be known."

Therefore, in order for human consciousness to approach the intuited unity, in order to pursue the imaginative hymn to intellectual beauty, we must accept that spirit, mind, or thought can exist in separation from matter; and in order to accept that thought can "absorb" matter we must first accept that matter is dependent on spirit, mind, or thought. In other words, in order to make sense of the "imaginative, poetical cult" and its intuited *given*, we must be prepared to accept (or at least not to gainsay) the poet's idealism. For although MacDiarmid's (philosophical) idealism does not *dominate* his entire poetic *corpus* but is counterbalanced by his "savage realism," it nevertheless does form the basis of his "imaginative, poetical cult." Indeed, his idealism is only of use to him in so far as it feeds that imaginative cult and allows him to express and evaluate his intuitions of spiritual/intellectual harmony. That he sees his idealism within those bounds he makes clear in "The Terrible Crystal" (*A Lap of Honour* 1967) while, incidentally, showing why paradox and contradiction are inherent in any evocation of the all-embracing unity:

> The poetry I seek must therefore have the power
> Of fusing the discordant qualities of experience,
> Of mixing moods, and holding together opposites,
> And well I know that the various facets
> Of sensibility, sensuous, mental, and emotional,
> And its alternating moods
> Cannot be fully reconciled
> Save in an imaginative integrity
> That includes, but transcends, sensibility as such.
>   (CP 1095)

That "imaginative integrity" is itself an expression, or at least a reflection, of the all-embracing unity, for it both includes and transcends ordinary human sensibility. In a similar idealist fashion "Diamond Body" pursues the notion of thought absorbing matter:

> Today we are breaking up the chaste
> Ever-deceptive phenomena of Nature
> And reassembling them according to our will.
> We look through matter, and the day is not far distant
> When we shall be able to cleave
> Through her oscillating mass as if it were air.
>   (CP 1087)

MacDiarmid's poetic intuition by its very nature cannot accept that there are material limits to the extension of consciousness. He stands out against what he calls in "Song of the Seraphim" (*Lucky Poet* 1943) a "narrow materiality":

> This life we have now outgrown.
> It lays the veil of the body over the spirit
> And drags everything down to the level
> Of a narrow materiality.
>   (CP 638)

The purpose of poetry is to overcome this "narrow materiality." As he puts it in *To Circumjack Cencrastus*:

> *It's no the purpose o' poetry to sing*   not; of
> *The beauty o' the dirt frae which we spring*   from
> *But to cairry us as faur as ever it can*   far
> *'Yont nature and the Common Man*   beyond
>   (CP 255)

Its end-purpose is the contemplation and expression of spiritual harmony or intellectual beauty. In "Lament for the Great Music" the intuited harmony is represented by the timeless *Ceol Mor* [the Great Music] of the ancient Celtic pipes:

> Its apprehension an activity of concentrated repose
> So still that in it time and space cease to be
> And its relations are with itself, not with anything external.
>
> It is the supreme reality (not the Deity of personal theism)
> Standing free of all historical events in past or future,
> Knowable--but visible to the mind alone;
> (CP 474)

Thus, all higher forms of art, in MacDiarmid's book, share this intuition of an all-embracing unity; and it must be said that he consciously eschews all forms of religious dogma and quietism.

However, MacDiarmid (or the savage realist within him) always claimed that he was a materialist and that his poetry reflected this. Moreover, he was a dialectical materialist--in short, a Marxist. In October 1941 he wrote to F. G. Scott, the composer who set his early Scots lyrics to music, claiming that he belonged to "the real out-and out materialists, anti-God, anti-all-supernaturalism," and stating: "I have held precisely the same position since my early teens."[3] It is true that there are poems where MacDiarmid does try to weld the extension of consciousness to a materialist outlook, as in "Island Funeral" (*The Islands of Scotland* 1939):

> Yet if the nature of the mind is determined
> By that of the body, as I believe,
> It follows that every type of human mind
> Has existed an infinite number of times
> And will do so. Materialism promises something
> Hardly to be distinguished from eternal life.
> (CP 582)

But when confronted with his "savage realism" it is more usual (in fact, it is a defining characteristic) for the poet to attempt a middle road, as in his presentation of the ideal Renaissance writer ("ideal" in the popular sense of the word) in "The Kulturkampf" (*A Kist of Whistles* 1947):

> All his works provide the clue
> To that kind of consistency in himself
> Which he looked for in others.
> They show that for him
> The most authentic qualities of experience
> Were its unpredictability,
> Its uniqueness, its individual centres

---

3. Hugh MacDiarmid, letter to F. G. Scott, 15 Oct. 1941, Edinburgh University Library Gen. 887, and Bold 487-88.

--Precisely those elements imperfectly recognised
If not denied outright
By the reigning monisms
Of absolute idealism
And mechanical materialism.

(CP 703)

A monism being any theory that denies the duality of mind and matter, it is interesting that the "reigning monisms" that MacDiarmid eschews are the extremes of "absolute" idealism and "mechanical" materialism. The implication is that dialectical materialism can be reconciled with dualism. Here, we are in no-man's-land, the vacuous area of MacDiarmid's "lacunae," the "curious gap" between his realism and idealism.

But throughout his poetry MacDiarmid does attempt to fill that gap in order to identify the more strongly with the intuited spiritual harmony. There is a consistent pattern in these attempts, and a conscious philosophical effort, which can only be understood in terms of empirio-criticism. Let us take an explicatory example, an early Scots poem from *Sangschaw* (1925), "Ballad of the Five Senses."

The poem opens by declaring the beauty of the phenomenal world "That lies forenenst a' men." This beauty seems separate from the world "o' Heaven and Hell" and the private "warl' wi'in mysel.' " From the phenomenal (or material) world the poet wishes to rise and:

As God felt whan he made the warl'	world
I aye socht to feel.	always sought

(CP 37)

Again:

Wi' body and saul I socht to staun'	with; soul; stand
As in Eternity.	

(CP 38)

He then declares that he wishes to be rid of his senses and of thought in order to "face God mysel' "--not a Beatific Vision, certainly, but the notion of "mind" or "soul" existing apart from material conditions. What, in fact, the poet describes, though, is a kind of *spiritualisation* of his senses:

They were like thochts for which a man	thoughts
Can fin' nae words to tell,	find no
Hoo' they compare wi' his ither thochts	how; other
E'en to his ain sel's sel	even; own self's self

(CP 38)

Through these newly developed media he perceives what is "above" or "beyond" the phenomenal world: the all-inclusive unity where

Water for stane micht weel be ta'en	might well; taken
Or Heaven and Hell seem yin,	one
A' differences men's minds can mak',	all; make
Maun end or ye begin. . . .	

(CP 39)

This is the given unity, the intuited spiritual harmony, which cannot be apprehended by reason. These conglomerate sense-thoughts (the paradox is MacDiarmid's) take on a life of their own:

And ilk ane differed frae the neist	each one; next
As ilk ane did frae me:	

(CP 39)

Thus, the perceiver, since they are yet his thoughts, becomes the perceived. For the object of thought here is thought:

And God Himsel' sall only be	shall
As far's a man can tell,	
In this or ony ither life	any other
A way o' lookin' at himsel'.	

(CP 40)

Philosophically, what we have here is a *reductio ad absurdum*, a form of solipsism which claims "divine" overtones. Poetically, it is an expression of MacDiarmid's felt identity with the universal harmony.

In order to present this felt extension of consciousness and its evolutionary momentum (while eschewing the duality of mind and matter), the poet reduces (through his proposed spiritualization of the senses) everything--internal and external phenomena--to pure sensation or pure experience. It is an attempt to evoke what he describes in "Composition" (1934) as

The no-meeting . . . but only change upon the instant . . .
Of spirit and sense; the agile leaping
From the sensual plane to the spiritual,
This straddling of two universes,
This rapidity of movement and back again.
(CP 1070)

or in "O Ease My Spirit" as the "terribly illuminating / Integration of the physical and the spiritual." This reduction to pure sensation or pure experience is what is known as empirio-criticism.

Briefly, empirio-criticism originated with Richard Avenarius (1843-1896) and Ernst Mach (1838-1916) and, as a philosophical compromise between materialism and idealism, it drew a great deal of interest from Bolshevik intellectuals such as Gorky, Bogdanov, Bazarov, Lunacharsky, Berman, and Yushkevich. In the west its main advocates were William James, K. Pearson, Bertrand Russell, and Alfred North Whitehead (whose *Science and the Modern World* MacDiarmid never tired of praising). Avenarius, as the Catholic philosopher Frederick Copleston puts it:

> ... found the immediate data or elements of experience in sensations. These depend on changes in the central nervous system which are conditioned by the environment acting either as an external stimulus or by way of the process of nutrition. Further, the more the brain develops, the more it is excited by constant elements in the environment. Thus the impression of a familiar world is produced, a world in which one can feel secure. And increase in these feelings of familiarity and security is accompanied by a decrease in the impression of the world as enigmatic, problematic and mysterious. In fine, the unanswerable problems of metaphysics tend to be eliminated. And the theory of pure experience, with its reduction of both the outer and inner worlds to sensations, excludes those dichotomies between the physical and the psychical, thing and thought, object and subject, which have formed the basis for such rival metaphysical theories as materialism and idealism.[4]

So, in a similar fashion, does the seminal "Ballad of the Five Senses" reduce both inner and outer worlds to pure sensation or pure experience in order to overcome dichotomies between the physical and the psychical, thing and thought, object and subject, thus allowing the poet to express in a quasi-symbolic intellectual (or philosophical) register his felt identity with the intuited "Absolute."[5]

This is not to say that this, or any, MacDiarmid poem can be reduced to an exercise in empirio-criticism, but it is to say that where his "savage realism" does obstruct his poetic

4. Frederick Copleston, *A History of Philosophy*, 9 vols. (Mahwah, N.J.: Paulist Press, 1975) 7:358-59.
5. The term "Absolute" as used here refers in particular to its use by the "British Hegelians," Bosanquet and Bradley. In *Metaphysics and Poetry* (Hamilton: Lothlorien Publications, 1975) n. pag., MacDiarmid states: "I read them long ago--before I became a convinced Marxist. They are a very fertile influence, a wonderful breeding ground for poets--unlike those who opposed them." For a detailed analysis of MacDiarmid's movement from sensationalism to idealism see his *Lucky Poet* (Berkeley: U of California P, 1972) 283.

intuitions, then he consciously and consistently seeks a compromise between idealism and materialism along what can only be described as empirio-critical lines. His realist and idealist *moods* (as he puts it in that passage from *In Memoriam James Joyce*) do give range and power to his poetry. But when one obstructs or impinges on the other, or when he attempts to conjoin them and inevitable inconsistencies and contradictions arise, then he consciously seeks an empirio-critical compromise because he will not, on the one hand, renege entirely on his declared materialism nor, on the other, wholly embrace a fully comprehensive idealism. There is a continual tug-of-war between these elements in him and the poetry is born out of argument. As he says in *A Drunk Man*:

> The tug-o'-war is in me still,
> The dog-hank o' the flesh and soul--   dog-knot (during mating)

Central to his poetry is an attempt to write out that tug-of-war, to overcome the inconsistencies and contradictions inherent in his ontological and epistemological perspective. At the heart of his poetry is no cult of contradiction. Rather, there is a desire for compromise and reconciliation. The spectre that haunted the poet in MacDiarmid was not the spectre of communism that Marx and Engels declared in the *Communist Manifesto* (1848) to be haunting Europe, but the spectre of the "terribly illuminating/Integration of the physical and the spiritual" with its intuition of a greater unity "beyond." That, perhaps, is a more fitting spectre to be haunting a poet--depending upon your view of poetry.

From a straight philosophical viewpoint there is, of course, no room for compromise with inconsistency. In *Materialism and Empirio-Criticism*: *Critical Comments on a Reactionary Philosophy* (1908) Lenin lambasted the compromise with idealism. As Copleston states:

> Lenin maintained that the phenomenalism of Mach and Avenarius leads inevitably to idealism and thence to religious belief. For if things are reduced to sensations or sense-data, they must be mind-dependent. And as they can hardly be dependent simply on the individual human mind, they must be referred to a divine mind.[6]

This is exactly the difficulty which "Ballad of the Five Senses" attempts to resolve by evoking a sense of what I have termed "divine solipsism":

---

6. Copleston 359.

> And God Himsel' sall only be   shall
> As far's a man can tell,
> In this or ony ither life   any other
> A way o' lookin' at himsel'.
> (CP 40)

Copleston concludes:

> But unless the reduction of things to sensations is interpreted as
> equivalent to the statement, with which not even the most resolute
> realist would quarrel, that physical objects are in principle capable
> of being sensed if there is any sentient subject at hand, it becomes
> difficult to avoid some such conclusion as that drawn by Lenin.[7]

MacDiarmid's "divine solipsism," his symbolic expression of his
felt identity with the greater-unity, is characterized by the drive
to image sense-data as spiritualised. This, naturally enough,
gives rise to paradox, as in "Au Clair de la Lune" (*Sangschaw*
1925) where thought has "keethin' sicht o' a' there is" but
"bodily sicht o' nocht." In "Ballad of the Five Senses" the poet
writes:

> O gin ye tine your senses five,   if you lose
> And get ony o' theirs instead,   any of; instead
> Ye'll be as far frae what ye are   from
> As the leevin' frae the deid.   living; dead
> (CP 39)

The other senses to which he refers here are the conglomerate
sense-thoughts whose number "Ga'ed 'yont infinity" [went
beyond infinity], and this notion leads him to the (idealist) conclusion that:

> . . . daith may only be   death
> A change o' senses so's a man   so that
> Anither warl' can see.   another world
> (CP 40)

The mood, however, we note, remains conditional.

A later, and longer, Scots poem, *To Circumjack Cencrastus*, also attempts the middle road of compromise. This at
times monstrously jumbled poem is marked by an endless circuity of argument about the nature of existence. That this endless
circuity of argument is vitally related to his inability to opt outright for an idealist or materialist ontology is made apparent
near the close of the poem where he tries to reconcile dualism
with an all-embracing monism:

---

7. Copleston 360.

Ah, double nature, distinct yet ane,   one
Like Life and Thocht. For Nature is
A moment and a product o' the Mind,
And no' a Mind that stands abune the warld   above the world
Or yet rins through it like a knotless threid   runs; thread
But coincides wi't, ane and diverse at aince;   with it; once
An eternal solution and eternal problem.
                    (CP 283)

Here MacDiarmid is consciously intellectualising about the nature and relation of the material world to the felt unity "beyond." He tries to temper his acceptance of dualism ("double nature") and idealism ("a product o' the Mind") by eschewing the notion of an Aristotelian Unmoved Mover ("a Mind that stands abune the warld"). But his image representative of the felt unity, that of mind coinciding in unity and diversity with the world, does not resolve the problem that *he* states. For the world remains, nature remains, mind-dependent. MacDiarmid's "eternal problem" is that if nature is mind-dependent, it is either dependent on the individual mind (solipsism) or it must be referred to a divine Mind (religion), and he is unwilling to declare finally for either of these overtly idealist solutions. His poetry is convincing us of his "eternal problem" but not, at the end of the day, of any "eternal solution."

The problem of reconciling materialism with idealism was one that remained with MacDiarmid throughout his whole life. For example, as late as 1975 he states of the supernatural that:

> ... it's essential for life. Human life itself implies a belief in, a desire to participate in, the transcendental. It's inherent in us without reference to any religious belief. ... The transcendental, if I am right, comes out of the seeds of things. It's inherent in the original substance--it's part of the materialism.[8]

While MacDiarmid disputes, and while one may dispute with him, philosophically, there can be no doubt that his intuition of the greater-unity was as real for him as it was for, say, Wordsworth. But with MacDiarmid it is as if there co-existed within him both the Romantic psyche of a Wordsworth and the grimly reductive psyche of James Thomson, author of *The City of Dreadful Night*: uncomfortable bed-fellows, certainly.

MacDiarmid's intuition was for him experiential. The first book he ever penned, *Annals of the Five Senses* (1923),

---

8. MacDiarmid, *Metaphysics and Poetry* n. pag.

consists mainly of self-studies in psychology, varied prose-pieces which approach (but are not finally subsumed under) a "stream of consciousness" style. The book is shot through with vivid illustrations of the spiritualisation of sense-data and of the reduction of internal and external phenomena to one immediate given unity of impression. In "Cerebral," for instance:

> Night and day, city and country, sunshine and gaslight and electric blaze, myriad-faceted existences and his own extraordinarily vivid pictorial sense of his own cranial geography and anatomical activities all co-visible to him, I say, and perfectly composed, without any conflict or strain.

Similarities with the sense-thoughts of "Ballad of the Five Senses" are immediately apparent:

> Nor were any of the elements permanent or passive. All of them lived, and each in perfect freedom, modifying or expanding, easing off or intensifying continually. They moved freely, each in its own particular whim, and they moved also with the unity of one impression.[9]

The subject-mind of *Annals* (this time from "The Never-Yet-Explored") thus rejects the realist conclusion that matter is objective reality existing outside and independent of the perceiving mind:

> She recognised from the outset that to endeavour to arrive at any systemised conclusion as to the reasons for her attitude was bound to prove futile, reminding herself that we cannot concede even to the brute data of sense that fixity and security which a comfortable realism demands.[10]

His intuition demands more than realism or rationalism can provide:

> He was now quite certain that the imagination had some way of dealing with the truth, which the reason had not, and that commandments delivered when the body is still and the reason silent are the most binding that the souls of men can ever know.[11]

As the very titles *Annals of the Five Senses* and "Ballad of the Five Senses" indicate, MacDiarmid had as abiding an interest in the nature, quality, and significance of sensation as did any empirio-critic. And there is (a perhaps indulgent) irony in the fact that the poet displays his "transcendental materialism" in

---

9. Hugh MacDiarmid, *Annals of the Five Senses* (Montrose: C.M. Grieve, 1923) 6.
10. MacDiarmid, *Annals of the Five Senses* 161.
11. MacDiarmid, "A Limelight from A Solitary Wing," *Annals of the Five Senses* 189.

"Hymns" addressed to Lenin, an irony which would not have eluded "lizard eyes"--as MacDiarmid refers to him in "Third Hymn" and elsewhere.

In his concluding chapter of *The Problem of Metaphysics* (1974), D. M. MacKinnon, Cambridge Professor of Divinity, writes:

> If it is insulting to the atheist to speak of him as unknown to himself a religious man, it is permissable to remember that unlike the positivist he allows himself to be concerned with what is, in the very special sense of demanding an unconditional validity for what he says. Hence, indeed, the violence of Lenin's polemics against Bogdanov, for the latter's readiness to substitute Ernst Mach's sensationalism for materialism.... Lenin's *Materialism and Empirio-Criticism* ... is polemic.... Yet it is the sort or work that the philosopher who is concerned with the problem of metaphysics would do well to remember and that not least in the present context as we recall the poetry that MacDiarmid has written in Lenin's honour.[12]

This concern with "what is" on the atheist's part, and his demand for "an unconditional validity for what he says," MacKinnon locates in "On A Raised Beach," a poem which is vital to an understanding of the domain of poetry with MacDiarmid. MacKinnon talks of "the grave atheism" expressed in the poem and argues that "MacDiarmid writes as an atheist and his poem is eloquent testimony that out of an atheist ontology a great poem may spring."[13] This is an interpretation with which MacDiarmid himself agreed.[14]

What concerns MacDiarmid in "On A Raised Beach" is not the existence of God, nor merely the question of life beyond or after death. His "great poem" springs not so much from his "atheist ontology" as from his felt experience of the "terribly illuminating/Integration of the physical and the spiritual" and its inherent intuition of universal harmony.

"On A Raised Beach," forbye linguistic difficulties effectively countered by the use of appropriate dictionaries, must be *conceptually* one of the most difficult poems in the English language, synthetic or otherwise. In the poem, MacDiarmid is constantly shifting ground in an attempt to unravel the very thread of "Being." His conception of the nature or essence of things, his ontology, *is* central. "It is," as he puts it, "reality

---

12. D. M. MacKinnon, *The Problem of Metaphysics* (Cambridge: Cambridge UP, 1974) 168.
13. MacKinnon 167-68.
14. MacDiarmid, *Metaphysics and Poetry* n. pag. See also Ruth McQuillan, "Hugh MacDiarmid's 'On a Raised Beach,'" *Akros* 12.34-35 (Aug. 1977): 91

that is at stake." Here, the extremes are those of "Being and non-being" and they do not so much "meet" as "Confront each other" for reality:

> It is reality that is at stake.
> Being and non-being with equal weapons here
> Confront each other for it, non-being unseen
> But always on the point, it seems, of showing clear,
> Though its reserved contagion may breed
> This fancy too in my still susceptible head
> And then by its own hidden movement lead
> Me as by aesthetic vision to the supposed
> Point where by death's logic everything is recomposed,
> Object and image one, from their severance freed,
> As I sometimes, still wrongly, feel 'twixt this storm beach and me.
> (CP 428)

In "On A Raised Beach" MacDiarmid's realism accepts, as he puts it later in the poem, that "the meaning of life. . .is death." That is, not only is there no "hereafter," but life has no significance beyond itself. But against this conclusion his "transcendental materialism" continues to rebel. The struggle between "Being and non-being" is presented as a war of absolutes. But because "non-being," which we may equate emotionally and intellectually with his savage realism, can win no outright victory, he is led to intuit the possibility of a "higher" unity "beyond" death:

> . . . the *supposed*
> Point where by death's logic everything is recomposed,
> Object and image one, from their severance freed,
> (CP 428; Italics mine)

This cannot be read simply as the reconstitution of matter through decay, for it does not take "fancy" or "aesthetic vision" to achieve that understanding, and nor is that kind of recomposition "supposed." The recomposition MacDiarmid is supposing (or proposing) is of "Object and image," of external phenomenon and internal picture, image or sense-datum. The supposed recomposition is the (re)unification of the external or material with the internal or spiritual. This "Integration of the physical and the spiritual" is here "supposed" in death and "still wrongly" felt in life. The use of "wrongly" suggests the "Lacuna" between his "aesthetic vision" and his "savage realism."

However, the supposed point of "recomposition" is but a short step from the conclusion of "Ballad of the Five Senses":

        . . . daith may only be
        A change o' senses so's a man
        Anither warl' can see.
                    (CP 40)

The movement of the poem is towards closing the gap, towards the idealist-realist reconciliation. Thus, the notion of the supposed unity of object and image leads the poet to demand "Contact with elemental things" and to "go apart" into a "more beautiful and more oppressive world." This "world" he says "fills me with a sense of perfect form" which he posits as the absolute of existence, the absolute of creation:

                . . . It fills me with a sense of perfect form,
        The end seen from the beginning, as in a song.
        It is no song that conveys the feeling
        That there is no reason why it should ever stop,
        But the kindred form I am conscious of here
        Is the beginning and end of the world,
        The unsearchable masterpiece, the music of the spheres,
        Alpha and Omega, the Omnific Word.
                    (CP 428-29)

This unity is not "supposed" but intuited, and the fact that "Few survive" this experience, as the poet has it, suggests that his cosmic egotism is assuming self-identification with the whole of creation, with the all-creating word.

    MacDiarmid's "divine solipsism" is claiming more than an historical world-consciousness. The consciousness he has extended to is that of a "kindred form" which is "the beginning and end of the world," a form which, by any definition, must inhere in a timeless realm of consciousness, an eternal realm of the spirit. Thus, we are taken far beyond the argument of MacKinnon who claims:

        . . . it is indeed a poet's sense of substance as a very condition of
        objectivity that MacDiarmid conveys. . .it is an objectivity which
        meditation on the ancient rocks makes it possible for him to lay
        hold of; he is delivered from a self-regarding anthropocentrism,
        admitted to a serenely accepted atheism by finding in the relatively
        changeless rocky environment which he confronts an eloquent
        reminder of the relativity of human existence, of life itself. It is
        indeed an ontological relativity that he affirms. On the plane of
        being there is that which has been before human emergence upon
        the earth and will survive its disappearance.[15]

---

15. MacKinnon 166-67.

That "sense of substance" could be associated with MacDiarmid's "elemental things" and the "kindred form." But it is difficult to see how the "objectivity" of the poet's "aesthetic vision" can, in reality, be reconciled to an "ontological relativity." Both MacDiarmid and MacKinnon are claiming the best of both worlds. MacDiarmid may be attempting some such reconciliation, but the fact remains that one cannot, at one and the same time, lay claim to objectivity and relativism, unless by objectivity one simply means strict adherence to the limitations of a relativist position--and MacDiarmid's "meditation" or "aesthetic vision" lays claim to far more than that! Moreover, anthropocentrism is not eschewed if one recalls the poet's self-identification with the Omnific Word and his assurance that "our function remains / However isolated we seem fundamental to life as theirs" [the stones'].

The Omnific Word is associated with the stones because "These stones have the silence of supreme creative power, / ...Which alone leads to greatness" (CP 429). The Omnific Word is patently possessed of metaphysical attributes rather than linguistic ones. It is the all-creating Word of which language, infused with thought, is but a pale imitation. For MacDiarmid language springs from thought rather than thought from language. As in *To Circumjack Cencrastus* where he talks of "The consciousness that matter has entrapped" (and many another poem), MacDiarmid is seeing life as determined by consciousness rather than, as all materialists hold, consciousness by life.[16]

What then is the "poet's sense of substance" that MacKinnon takes to be the "very condition of objectivity that MacDiarmid conveys"? To begin with, it is based on the poet's self-identification with the stones which symbolise "the foundation and end of all life," the "beginning and end of the world...Alpha and Omega." Just as "these stones have dismissed / All but all of evolution" so the poet enters the timeless realm, claiming: "I too lying here have dismissed all else" (CP 423). And again: "Already I feel all that can perish perishing in me / As so much has perished and all will yet perish in these stones" (CP 424). Therefore, it is not to "visible substances" or to the "Psychological rhythms and other factors in the case," but

---

16. See S.S. Prawer, *Karl Marx and World Literature* (Oxford: Oxford UP, 1976) 106. Marx states: "Life is not determined by consciousness, but consciousness by life. Those who adopt the first method of approach begin with consciousness, regarded as the living individual; those who adopt the second, which corresponds with real life, begin with the real living individuals themselves, and consider consciousness only as *their* consciousness."

to the felt unity of an underlying substance which the stones represent, to which the poet looks: "Varied forms and functions though life may seem to have shown/They all come back to the likeness of stone" (CP 425). So his "Muse" claims to be at one not simply with human or animal "Psychological rhythms":

> . . . my Muse is, with this ampler scope,
> This more divine rhythm, wholly at one
> With the earth, riding the Heavens with it, as the stones do
> And all soon must.
>   (CP 425)

MacDiarmid's "substance" is what the stones symbolise, a metaphysical unity. Whether or not MacDiarmid can wish to lay claim to a materialist ontology is a moot point, for the unity subscribed to is self-evidently idealist. The "lacuna" has, for him, fallen into desuetude. His hymn to intellectual beauty is now at one with "ordered adjustments / Out of reach of perceptive understanding." His sense of substance derives from that empirio-critical given, that unity of impression, that "Integration of the physical and the spiritual"--and we are not a stone's throw from Wordsworth's *Prelude* where:

> . . . my brain
> Work'd with a dim and undetermin'd sense
> Of unknown modes of being; in my thoughts
> There was a darkness, call it solitude,
> Or blank desertion, no familiar shapes
> Of hourly objects, images of trees,
> Of sea or sky, no colours of green fields;
> But huge and mighty Forms that do not live
> Like living men mov'd slowly through my mind
> By day and were the trouble of my dreams.
>   (Book 1)

Belief in the greater-unity, according to MacDiarmid, is born in us all. As we quoted him above: "Human life itself implies a belief in, a desire to participate in, the transcendental. . . .It's inherent in the original substance." The very use of the term "substance" is a scholastic vestige, and MacDiarmid's "imaginative poetical cult" accepts one of the fundamental assumptions of idealism from the outset: innatism. As he says in "Mind's End" (*The Lucky Bag* 1927), the mighty things that emerge in him were born there before they could ever be nurtured into poetry:

The michty things that kyth in me   mighty; appear
   Were born in me nor fed.
              (CP 174)

Moreover, the comparison with Wordsworth is more than fortu-
itous. Of "great poets" (specifically of Wordsworth and Shelley)
MacDiarmid's favorite empirio-critic, Alfred North Whitehead,
writes in *Science and the Modern World* (published the same year
as *A Drunk Man*):

> Their survival is evidence that they express deep intuitions of
> mankind penetrating into what is universal in concrete fact.[17]

That certainly expresses one of the fundamental concerns of
MacDiarmid's poetry: to seek out a universal consciousness
from the particulars of his own perceptions. The movement of
his poetry is ever outward and upwards towards an apprehension of the greater-unity. As he puts it in *A Drunk Man*:

I love to muse upon the skill that gangs   goes
To mak' the simplest thing that Earth displays,
The eident life that ilka atom thrangs,   busy; each; throngs
And uses it in the appointit ways,   appointed
And a' the endless brain that nocht escapes   all
That myriad moves them to inimitable shapes.
              (CP 117)

His cosmic egotism seeks always to identify itself with the
greater-unity of the *élan vital*:

A mony-brainchin' candelabra fills   many-branching
The lift and's lowin' wi' the stars;   sky; shining with
The Octopus Creation is wallopin'   tumbling, moving fast
In coontless faddoms o' a nameless sea.   countless fathoms

I am the candelabra, and burn
My endless candles to an Unkent God.   Unknown
I am the mind and meanin' o' the octopus
That thraws its empty airms through a' th' Inane.   throw; arms
              (CP 147-48)

This is what he calls in the last movement of *In Memoriam
James Joyce* "participation in self-universal"; and that movement
("Plaited Like the Generations of Men") is another chorus in
his life-long hymn to intellectual beauty, to spiritual harmony; a
movement towards the universal consciousness which was, for
MacDiarmid, the ultimate domain of poetry, the ultimate

---

17. Alfred North Whitehead, *Science and the Modern World* (Cambridge: Cambridge UP, 1926) 122.

domain of all art. "Plaited Like the Generations of Men" is, like
so much of MacDiarmid's poetry, a Song of the Ideal:

> Come, follow me into the realm of music. Here is the gate
> Which separates the earthly from the eternal.
>
> . . .
>
> At first you hear nothing, because everything sounds.
> But now you begin to distinguish between them. Listen.
> Each star has its rhythm and each world its beat.
> The heart of each separate living thing
> Beats differently, according to its needs,
> And all the beats are in harmony.
>   (CP 871)
>
>
> . . .
>
>
> Now you understand how stars and hearts are one with another
> And how there can nowhere be an end, nowhere a hindrance;
> How the boundless dwells perfect and undivided in the spirit,
> How each part can be at once infinitely great and infinitely small,
> How the utmost extension is but a point, and how
> Light, harmony, movement, power
> All identical, all separate, and all united are life.
>   (CP 874)

PETER McCAREY

LEV SHESTOV AND HUGH MacDIARMID

> You believe in a crystal palace that endures forever--so that I won't be able to stick out my tongue at it on the sly or laugh up my sleeve at it. Well, maybe the reason I'm afraid of this palace is because it's crystal, and indestructible, and because I won't be able to stick my tongue out at it even in secret.
>
> --F. M. Dostoevsky, *Notes From Underground*, 1. X.

Even so in these sterile and melancholy days
The ghastly desolation of my spirit is relieved
As a winter wood by glowing moss or lichen,
And the sunk lane of my heart is vivified,
And the hidden springs of my life revealed
Still patiently potent and humbly creative
When I spy again the ancestral ties between Scotland and Wales,
And, weary of the senseless cacophony of modern literature,
Recur to Aneirin's Gododdin, one of the oldest poems
In any European vernacular--far older indeed
Than anything ever produced on the Continent
Outside Greek and Latin; and not only
Note how (great topical lesson for us to-day)
It is not the glory, but the pity and waste, of war
That inspires its highest passages, but realise
That the profoundest cause in these Islands to-day,
The Invisible War on which Earth's greatest issues depend,
Is still the same war the Britons fought in at Catraeth
And Aneirin sings. The Britons were massacred then. Only one
Escaped alive. His blood flows in my veins to-day
Stronger than ever, inspires me with his unchanged purpose,
And moves me alike in Poetry and Politics.
Between two European journeys of Neville Chamberlain's
And two important speeches of Herr Hitler's
I return to the Taliesin and Llywarch Hen poems,

Full of hiraeth, of angry revolt
Against the tyranny of fact . . .[1]

26 March 1938

Shestov is exhausted; he has lost weight and his voice is weak. The political events of these times are taking their toll on him: Hitler's entry into Austria, the persecution of the Jews, the Moscow trials. As ever, these problems posed brutally by reality resound at the very centre of resistance of his philosophy.

"Hitler has entered Austria: I am forced to admit that this *had* to happen, that it *is*. But I am not *persuaded*."[2]

"Jeremiah, too, knew that God does not help us. The Jews knew that perfectly well, with the history of the Maccabees. . . . Jeremiah even said, 'Cursed be the day I was born!' And yet, *in spite of the evidence*, he complains to God; he asks for help; he believes God *can*. . . . I, too, have been unable to surmount this difficulty: I have managed only to struggle."[3]

Such were the respective positions of MacDiarmid and Shestov in the late thirties. Each, in the end, drew on his own tradition for the means to deny an intolerable present.

And above all, Chestov, my master
(CP 622)

And, above all, my great master, Shestov, with his
                 supreme $\tau\acute{o}\lambda\mu\alpha$ daring
His glorious insistence on 'the words that are swallowed up,'
His indeflectible concern with $\tau o\ \tau\iota\mu\iota\acute{\omega}\tau a\tau o\nu$
Plotinus's 'what matters most.'
(CP 745)

Suddenly (my master Shestov's *suddenly*)
(CP 1170)

. . . my favourite philosopher, Leo Chestov . . .[4]

---

1. Hugh MacDiarmid, "On Reading Professor Ifor Williams's 'Canu Aneurin' in Difficult Days," *Complete Poems*, ed. Michael Grieve and W. R. Aitken (London: Martin Brian and O'Keeffe, 1978) 690-91. All subsequent references to the poems are from this edition. Hereafter referred to as CP.
2. Benjamin Fondane, *Recontres avec Leon Chestov* (Paris, 1982) 152. Translation of text by Peter McCarey.
3. Fondane 160.
4. Hugh MacDiarmid, *Lucky Poet* (1943; London: Jonathan Cape, 1972) 28.

> . . . my favourite writers, Rainer Maria Rilke, Charles Doughty,
> Stefan George, Paul Valery in poetry, Leo Chestov in philosophy
> . . .[5]

> I have named Leo Chestov as my master . . .[6]

No one else, except perhaps Dostoevsky in *A Drunk Man Looks at the Thistle*, comes in for this degree of praise, and while Dostoevsky disappears from MacDiarmid's work in 1930, Shestov becomes still more important. MacDiarmid first quotes Shestov in the first issue of the *Scottish Chapbook* (August 1922), referring to *All Things Are Possible* (London, 1920); Harvey Oxenhorn has noted echoes of this book in *A Drunk Man*, and MacDiarmid referred to it as late as 1947.[7] He recommends an earlier book, *Anton Tchekhov and Other Essays* (London, 1916) to readers of the *New Age* (17 December 1925). *In Job's Balances* is central to *Stony Limits and Other Poems*, as Kenneth Buthlay has pointed out.[8] I doubt, in fact, if there is any book, apart from the Bible or his dictionaries, that MacDiarmid quotes or alludes to so frequently in his writing: he is still quoting it and drawing arguments from it in the 1960s, in *The Man of (Almost) Independent Mind* (Edinburgh, 1962). A page of "The Kind of Poetry I Want" and five pages of "Further Passages from 'The Kind of Poetry I Want'" (CP 1033-34, 616-20) are lifted from Shestov's article on Martin Buber.[9] The *Direadh* poems, the last he published, although not the last he wrote, deal with Shestovian themes, as Nancy Gish has pointed out.[10]

In the last year of his life, MacDiarmid gleefully quoted a description of his own thinking as "hopelessly contradictory."[11] This would seem to be the consensus, especially as regards the later poetry. It is hardly surprising, given that we tend either to be overwhelmed by the multiplicity of the sources for the ideas expressed in MacDiarmid's poems or to be dis-

---

5. MacDiarmid, *Lucky Poet* 46.
6. MacDiarmid, *Lucky Poet* 402.
7. Harvey Oxenhorn, *Elemental Things: The Poetry of Hugh MacDiarmid* (Edinburgh: Edinburgh UP, 1984) 78-80. The 1947 reference is in "The Wreck of the Swan": "I am what the guides call *schwindelfrei*," (CP 734). "*Nur für Schwindelfreie*" is the epigraph to the second part of the book, and it is the subject of the last section: "The upper Alpine ways, as any guide will tell you, are *nur für Schwindelfreie*" [only for those who don't get giddy] (244).
8. Kenneth Buthlay, "Some Hints for Source-Hunters," *Scottish Literary Journal* (Dec. 1978): 53. Buthlay has pointed to "examples of MacDiarmid's use of *In Job's Balances* in later poems, notably the 'Ode to all Rebels,' where I have noted fifteen or so as being worthy of attention. . . . MacDiarmid in 'Ode to All Rebels' draws not only on Shestov directly but also upon Shestov's account of, and quotations from, other writers, such as Plotinus, Pascal, Luther and Dostoevsky."
9. Lev Shestov, article in *Revue philosophique de la France et de l'étranger* (11 Dec. 1933).
10. Nancy Gish, *Hugh MacDiarmid: The Man and His Work* (London: Macmillan, 1984) 889.
11. Hugh MacDiarmid, letter to Tom Nairn, 1 March 1978, *The Letters of Hugh MacDiarmid*, ed. Alan Bold (London: Hamish Hamilton, 1984) 889.

tracted from MacDiarmid's ideas by such fascinating figures as Solovyov, or to get lost in search of his place in the Marxist-Leninist tradition.

However, if we approach MacDiarmid's poetry from the metaphysics of his master, Shestov, we can see beneath the logical inconsistencies and beyond the quotations. MacDiarmid's thinking is not the frayed edge of his poetry: it's the source. If we ignore that, then all we will find in his work will be a marvellous variety of conceits, none of which could help the poet, much less his readers, confront the problems of the day.

Elsewhere I have discussed MacDiarmid's references to Shestov in some detail.[12] Here I wish to consider where they agree and where they differ, because salient differences between the two still lead casual readers to overlook the way MacDiarmid's poetry enacts Shestov's metaphysics. When the affinity is established, I hope to show that MacDiarmid's departures from Shestov need not be dismissed as hopeless contradictions. I will concentrate on *In Job's Balances* because, although MacDiarmid had been reading Shestov for ten years before this book appeared in English, and although he read other works by Shestov subsequently (in the *Revue philosophique*), this was far and away his favourite.[13]

Omnitude is the common enemy: ". . . the terrible tyranny to-day of that 'omnitude'--Chestov's word--to which apparently no term can be set and which indeed may destroy civilization altogether. . . ."[14] Shestov defines it thus: "Common consciousness, omnitude, Dostoevsky's principal enemy, is that outside which man cannot conceive of existence."[15] It is a tacit consensus within which people operate, pretending that it is universal truth; it is the "crystal palace" of Dostoevsky's "Underground Man." MacDiarmid defines it repeatedly:

> Anywhere you go in Britain today
> You can hear the people
> Economising consciousness,
> Struggling to think and feel as little as possible
> Just as you can hear a countryside in winter
> Crepitating in the grip of an increasing frost.
> ("The Battle Continues," CP 938)

12. Peter McCarey, *Hugh MacDiarmid and the Russians* (Edinburgh: Scottish Academic Press, 1987).
13. It is appalling that this, one of the greatest works of Russian philosophy, is no longer available in English, even in the rather wooden translation (from Russian via German) used by MacDiarmid that was published in London in 1932, three years after the original. It was reprinted in Athens, Ohio, in 1974, but is no longer available.
14. MacDiarmid, *Lucky Poet* 353.
15. Lev Shestov, *In Job's Balances*, trans. Camilla Coventry and C. A. McCartney (London, 1932) 16.

'Mass suggestion has already reached a stage in England
At which the control of opinion is at least comparable
With that in the totalitarian states.
This typically English fascism depends less
On active force than upon the force of inertia.
The new fascism becomes gradually accepted
As representing order and religion in a shifting world,
Though the ultimate control will not be
In the hands of Catholics, whose beliefs are sincere,
But of hard-bitten men whose religion, at most,
      Is that "of all sensible men."
              ("The Battle Continues," CP 987)

. . . those who mistake blind eyes for balanced minds,
Who practise, in Disraeli's words,
'The blunders of their predecessors.'
People to whom experience means nothing,
Whose strength is the strength of cast-iron, not steel,
Whose souls exist in a state of sacred torpidity,
Prostrated before cold altars and departed gods,
Whose appeal to commonsense is only an appeal
To the spiritual sluggishness which is man's besetting sin.
And in the present unexampled crisis our deadliest peril.
         ("In Memoriam James Joyce," CP 824)

Shestov claims that omnitude builds up from humdrum levels to the heights:

Matter and energy are indestructible, but Socrates and Giordano Bruno are destructible, says reason. And all bow down to the dictum without a word; no one dares even hazard the question: Why has reason decreed this law? Why is it so paternally occupied in safeguarding matter and energy when it has forgotten all about Socrates and Giordano Bruno? Still less do they think of asking another question. Let us admit that reason has proclaimed this revolting law, disregarding all that is sacred to man, τo $\tau\iota\mu\iota\dot{\omega}\tau\alpha\tau o\nu$ [what matters most]: but whence does it derive the strength needful to accomplish this decision? And to accomplish it so perfectly that in no single instance since the beginning of the world has a single atom disappeared completely; that not only no gramme of energy--not a fraction of a Gramme has vanished into space? This is a miracle indeed, the more so because ultimately reason has no actual existence either. Try to find it, to point it out; you cannot. It accomplishes miracles like the most real of beings; but it has no existence. And all of us, who are used to questioning everything, admit this miracle quite easily; for science, created by reason, pays us a good price; out of worthless 'facts', it creates 'experience', through which we become masters of nature. Reason has taken man up into an exceedingly high mountain and shown him all the kingdoms of the world, and has said unto him: All these things I will give thee if thou wilt fall down and worship me. And man has worshipped, and obtained the promised reward (though, to be sure, not fully).[16]

Fondane tells of a meeting between Shestov and Einstein:

Finding himself next to him at table, Einstein asked Shestov to explain to him, in a few words if possible, the philosophy of Husserl.

'But', said Shestov, 'I couldn't explain it to you in a few words. I'd need at least an hour, an hour and a half . . .'

'I've got time', said Einstein.

How to begin? 'If you were able to meet Newton, here or in the next world', said Shestov, what would you talk about? Evidence, proof, truth, or the mass of light, the curvature of the earth, etc.?

'Of the latter', Einstein nodded.

'Well', Shestov replied, 'a philosopher would ask Newton what is truth, whether the soul is immortal, if God. . . . But you, you assume these questions have been answered.'

'Of course', said Einstein.

'But you see', said Shestov, 'these things that are known to you are not known to the philosopher; he asks all these questions as though they had never been answered'.

He then tried to tell Einstein about Husserl's evidence, and even touched on his own polemic against Husserl's philosophy. But Einstein had stopped listening. They met again and Einstein asked Shestov to continue his lesson, but he didn't remember anything Shestov had said on the previous occasion.[17]

And surely Einstein was quite right: if you spend all your time chipping away at the recognized bases of human thought, you will never get round to splitting the atom. You must choose either to play by the rules--and this allows for great virtuosity, as Einstein shows--or to be at best politely ignored. And at worst? Perhaps to come to an isolating madness. No one would choose this, and those who have glimpsed it usually do all they can to escape. And yet MacDiarmid claimed as one of his mottoes Shestov's declaration: "To grasp and admit absolute freedom is infinitely hard for us, as it is hard for a man who has always lived in darkness to look into the light, but this is obviously no objection, the more so as in life there are difficulties which are far greater, simply inacceptable; he who knows these difficulties will not shrink from trying his luck with the idea of chaos."[18] The biographical circumstances of these difficulties

16. Shestov, *In Job's Balances* 33.
17. Fondane 108-09.
18. MacDiarmid, *Lucky Poet* 67.

may be interesting, but they are in the realm of rational explanations we are trying to leave. We should consider, instead, what these problems led to.

The "Ode to All Rebels," as MacDiarmid himself said, is "pure Shestov."[19] It is also pure MacDiarmid. Of all his poems, this is the one that I find changes most from one reading to the next. Initially I was put off by touches of pedantry and banality, the fictional and lyrical voices that didn't fit. Now I have the impression that the strategy of *A Drunk Man* is being used again: begin by lulling the reader into a false sense of banality. But the speaker of "Ode to All Rebels" is not drunk: he is mad; and whereas the drunkenness of *A Drunk Man* was literary (controlled by a sober poetic intent), the madness is, I feel, quite literal: the poet keeps control of the verse, but he progressively, deliberately, relinquishes control of himself.

The narrator presents a cold analysis of his sexual and emotional history. From the start there is an odd split between the dispassionate tone and the strong emotions described. It becomes apparent that the narrator is concentrating on those aspects of his experience that give the lie to commonplaces about sex, love, marriage, and society. It emerges, in fact, that the narrator's intent is not to give an "objective" account of his emotional life but to rattle his complacent readers, to upset omnitude. Eventually he loses patience:

(There's naething ony man ever can think	
Humanity canna accept and hide	
As weemun the ways o' their sex	
And as douce and canty bide,	sweet; cheerful
We rebels maun think the unthinkable then	must
And nocht else and get clean ootside	
Owre faur to hear onybody wheedlin' again	too far
'It looks cauld ootside frae inside.	
Come in by--come in owre the fire'	

    . . .

(CP 494)

This is a change of tactic, and a declaration of intent. After presenting a final, obscene page from his casebook, the narrator drops the dispassionate tone. Following Shestov's injunction to fight the pretensions of reason with any weapon to hand, the narrator drops reason, too, losing his way in the mirror, becoming an idiot/angel, mocking our "horrible wisdom / And integrity." He says:

---

19. Hugh MacDiarmid, letter to Roderick Watson, 20 December 1971, *Letters*, ed. Bold 876.

Keep oot o' a' else except the abyss.	out of all
Rive Joy oot o' Terror's clenched nieve	Tear; fist
Gie't a'e look, syne back again heave.	Give it one; then
You'll no' see it twice. The Beauty that's won	
Frae Terror's aye something new under the sun.	always

(CP 502)

The voice sobers to survey our normalcy, with its "... buildings in ilka toon where daily / Unthinkable horrors tak' place." [ilka toon--each town] If rejection of omnitude is mad, acceptance is wrong. A magnificent call to rebellion supervenes that rises to an impossible pitch, calling for the removal of every stricture of opinion, finance, reason, sanity, law, science, and even language --which would make victory an empty word, as the voice acknowledges. The poem ends:

> *Your song, O God, that none dare hear*
> *Save the insane and such as I*
> *Apostates from humanity*
> *Sings out in me with no more fear*
> *Than one who thinks he has the world's ear*
> *   From his padded cell*
> *--Insane enough, with you so near,*
> *   To want, like you, the world as well!*
> (CP 512)

The situation is almost hopeless. The conclusion is hopeful.

The same could be said of "On a Raised Beach," which is the polar twin of the "Ode": the latter relinquishes reason and pursues human emotion to its extremes, while the former has reason pursue emotion to its extinction, or near it, in philosophical mimesis of the stones. Yet Shestov is still in evidence:

> ... these stones are one with the stars.
> It makes no difference to them whether they are high or low,
> Mountain peak or ocean floor, palace, or pigsty.
> (CP 425)

Compare: "To a stone, even the most precious, it is all one whether it lies on the floor of the sea or on a high mountain, whether it is set in gold or in iron."[20]

> I know there is no weight in infinite space,
> No impermeability in infinite time,
> (CP 432)

---

20. Shestov, *In Job's Balances* 189.

Compare: "Before the face of Eternal God all our foundations break together and all ground crumbles beneath us, even as objects--this we know--lose their weight in endless space, and-- this we shall probably learn one day--will lose their impermeability in infinite time. Not so long ago weight seemed to man an inseparable attribute of things, even as impermeability."[21]

In that part of the book, Shestov observes that the anthropomorphic thinking implicit in ascribing a purpose to nature (that of preserving the organism, for example) is inconsistent with science's pretensions to objectivity. He warns of the temptation "to reduce freedom into an infinite number of infinitely minute elements, of which the decision which determines our action is then composed *imperceptibly*."[22] Shestov's solution is, on the one hand, to drop the pretence of objectivity and, on the other hand, to seize upon "each 'sudden,' 'spontaneous,' 'creative fiat,' each absence of purpose and motive, and screen ourselves with the utmost care from that emasculator of thought, the theory of gradual development. The dominant of life is audacity, $\tau \acute{o} \lambda \mu a$, all life is a creative $\tau \acute{o} \lambda \mu a$, and therefore an eternal mystery, not reducible to something finished and intelligible."[23] MacDiarmid takes Shestov's points-- and elsewhere he is full of praise for Shestov's " $\tau \acute{o} \lambda \mu a$ " and "suddenly"--but in this case he goes in the opposite direction, setting out to eliminate the anthropomorphic element, to gauge the enormity of imperceptible development. Once again, he is led to reject almost all humanity has built. In "On A Raised Beach," however, his lines of communication are never interrupted because he retains a delight in words, and although they are difficult and daunting, we can make them surrender meaning, which sometimes escapes us in the "Ode."

Those who escape the restrictions of omnitude risk disintegration. They can also find themselves incapable of communicating what they find in the abyss with language, which is owned by common consciousness. The words, to quote MacDiarmid's quotation of Shestov's quotation of Job, "are swallowed up": either the poet or philosopher's words make no sense to the rest of us (as in parts of the "Ode") or, much worse, the words make sense and betray the experience:

> The truths that all great thinkers have seen
> At the height of their genius--and then

21. Shestov, *In Job's Balances* 218.
22. Shestov, *In Job's Balances* 198.
23. Shestov, *In Job's Balances* 158.

Spent most of their days denying
Or trying to scale down to mere reason's ken
("Thalamus," CP 413)

This refers to Shestov's comments on Kant's declaration that
Hume had awakened Kant out of dogmatic slumber, prompting
him to write: "That my will moves my arm is to me no more
comprehensible than if someone should say that it could hold
back the moon itself"; Shestov says that "Kant exiled the wonders, in order not to be forced to see them, into the field of the
'thing in itself,' and bequeathed to mankind the *'synthetic a priori*
judgments,' transcendental philosophy, and his three miserable
'postulates.' "[24]

Instead of reacting with unease and fear to things
beyond their reason, Shestov and MacDiarmid were able to
embrace them; and at moments MacDiarmid conveyed a
glimpse of a cosmos that would otherwise have been obscured by
the spurious order of the commonplace. Consider the "false
dawn" section of "Lament for the Great Music," which is particularly relevant:

--Your pibrochs that are like the glimpses
Of reality transcending all reason
Every supreme thinker has, and spends the rest of his life
Trying to express in terms of reason;
Your pibrochs that in the grey life of these islands
Are like the metaphysic of light in the style of Plotinus,
The great one-word metaphors of the Enneads,
Gleaming Godlike in the dry and formal diction,
The light that *has* been on sea and land;
Or as I have seen before the East had begun to brighten . . .
(CP 477)

The section is too long to quote in its entirety. Also, from "The
Kind of Poetry I Want":

And everywhere without fear of Chestov's 'suddenly',
Never afraid to leap, and with the unanticipatedly
Limber florescence of fireworks as they expand
Into trees or bouquets with the abandon of 'unbroke horses,'
Or like a Beethovian semitonal modulation to a wildly remote key,
As in the Allegretto where that happens with a jump of seven
sharps,
And feels like the sunrise gilding the peak of the Dent Blanche
While the Arolla valley is still in cloud.
(CP 1020)

---

24. Shestov, *In Job's Balances* xxvi-xxvii.

Let us now consider where MacDiarmid and Shestov differ, returning to the quotation at the beginning of this article to ask how MacDiarmid's "angry revolt against the tyranny of fact," which is pure Shestov, squares with his poetry of fact, his politics, and his belief in the power of reason to build a better world.

The first thing to remember is that, while Shestov believed in God, MacDiarmid did not. For Shestov, the fight against omnitude had become, by the time of *In Job's Balances*, a struggle to prevent common consciousness--his own, after all, as well as anyone else's--from completely shutting out the metaphysical abyss, the darkness of God: "What we must do is think only of God and the rest will take care of itself."[25] MacDiarmid's task, if not more difficult, was more complicated: he had to subvert omnitude and at the same time (because he was not one for leaving things half done) he had to build something better.

Did the strong Shestovian component in MacDiarmid's work undermine MacDiarmid's own constructs or programmes in politics and poetry? For Shestov, reason, fruit of the tree of knowledge, is part and parcel of the problem. While agreeing with Shestov that every rational support of common consciousness is to be knocked away, MacDiarmid holds that reason may yet be used constructively. In "The Divided Bird," which takes up the Shestovian themes and the imagery of "Thalamus," MacDiarmid concludes:

> The bird is in them all if they'll liberate it
> From the cage of vain reason that holds it yet.
> That is, reason better; for true reason knows
> The abyss it rests on, and distinguishes with fairness
> Between the pseudo-simplicity of perceptual acceptance
> And the genuine simplicity of immediate awareness.
> (CP 720)

Fair enough--so when he praises "the ordered, solvent knowledge" (CP 785) or repeats St. Cadoc's prayer--"Without knowledge, no wisdom, / Without knowledge, no freedom. . ." (CP 1387)--we need not be puzzled. What about the poetry of fact? For if reason is the architecture of omnitude, then facts are its little prefabrications, or fabrications. Here again there is no fatal contradiction, for while common consciousness takes facts as gospel, MacDiarmid subjects them to such aesthetic, philosophi-

---

25. N. Baranova-Shestova, *Zhizn' L'va Shestova* (*The Life of Lev Shestov*), 2 vols. (Paris: 1983) 1. 169. Translation of the text by Peter McCarey.

cal, and imaginative scrutiny that they can never quite be taken
for granted when he has finished with them.

Given that MacDiarmid found it possible to build
something with reason and fact that was not merely an adjunct
to omnitude, there was nothing to prevent him advocating a
political programme although, given the subversive nature of his
metaphysics, we could expect it to be the politics of opposition:

> For I am like Zamyatin. I must be a Bolshevik
> Before the Revolution, but I'll cease to be one quick
> When Communism comes to rule the roost,
> For real literature can exist only where it's produced
> By madmen, hermits, heretics,
> Dreamers, rebels, sceptics,
> --And such a door of utterance has been given to me
> As none may close whosoever they be.
>   (CP 1158)

Let us return, for the last time, to the quotations at the beginning of this article and ask how their respective visions confronted the Europe of 1938. Shestov was spared the Nazi occu-
pation of France. He died, like Job, "an old man and full of
days." Fondane, his disciple, was gassed at Birkenau in 1944.
When Shestov averred that God was omnipotent, he insisted this
meant that God could break the laws of reason, confounding
philosophers and theologians, undoing what had already happened; thus, for Shestov, when Job in the end is given back his
family, it is *the same people*, the ones who were killed, that God
gives him back. Now, nothing else will do.

In some of MacDiarmid's political verse, a strain
emerges that derives not from metaphysical awareness, but from
a different tradition:

> . . . What maitters't wha we kill
> To lessen that foulest murder that deprives
> Maist men o' real lives?
>   ("First Hymn to Lenin," CP 298)

This could have been the motto of many an Empire-building
Scot; and "Lamh Dearg Aboo" (To Stalin) should find a place in
some anthology alongside the famous anthem by James Thomson, another poet from the Borders.[26] Perhaps it's as well that

---

26. MacDiarmid, *Complete Poems* 1323. MacDiarmid provides the following explanation of the term
"Lamh dearg aboo": "Battle-cry of the Scottish and Irish MacDonalds under Alasdair MacDonald and
Montrose at Tippermuir, Inverlochy, etc. Means 'The Red Hand to Victory.'" James Thomson wrote
"Rule, Britannia!"

the strain does emerge: it is, after all, the obverse of MacDiarmid's vision of a new world, and we mustn't ignore it.

Some of his political poems testify to a Dantesque consideration of the place of politics in metaphysics (the Second and Third Hymns to Lenin, the poem to Beatrice Hastings, some of the Glasgow poems). In some places, the different spheres of his thought come into alignment:

> . . . the complete emergence from the pollution and fog
> With which the hellish interests of private property
> In land, machinery, and credit
> Have corrupted and concealed from the sun,
> From the gestures of truth, from the voice of God,
> Hundreds upon hundreds of millions of men,
> Denied the life and liberty to which they were born
> And fobbed off with a horrible travesty instead
> --Self righteous, sunk in the belief that they are human,
> When not a tenth of one per cent show a single gleam
> Of the life that is in them under their accretions of filth.
>
> And until that day comes every true man's place
> Is to reject all else and be with the lowest,
> The poorest . . .
> ("The Glass of Pure Water," CP 1043)

Here we are faced not with a hopeless inconsistency, but with a daunting integration of the metaphysical abyss with the economic depths of poverty, and a programme that combines a Shestovian perception of omnitude with a Marxian urge to change it. This alignment of his metaphysics with his politics might persuade some readers that there is, after all, a seriousness and consistency to MacDiarmid's thought, and yet that alignment is evinced only in a few poems. The issue that informs all of his poetry, and that allies him with Shestov, is the fight against consistent, complacent omnitude--with whatever weapons come to hand.

ALAN RIACH

HUGH MacDIARMID AND CHARLES OLSON

> Limits
> are what any of us
> are inside of
> --Charles Olson, *The Maximus Poems*[1]

> And all who speak glibly may rest assured
> That to better their oratory they will have
> the whole earth
> For a Demosthenean pebble to roll in their
> mouths.
> --Hugh MacDiarmid, *The Complete Poems*[2]

MacDiarmid's dates--1892-1978--span Olson's--1910-1970, but MacDiarmid's most productive years of writing were over by the mid-1950s, whereas Olson's writing career went from the 1940s on until his death. Indeed, much of what MacDiarmid published after 1940 had been written years earlier, so you could say that as MacDiarmid's work closes, Olson's begins. But you would then miss the resonance of MacDiarmid's work in a postmodernist context, and that is what I want to bring out.

Robert Duncan said that Olson was the last possible member of a creative family which rose up from 1882 (the year of Joyce's birth) to 1914. Typical work of this family is *The Waste Land*, *The Cantos*, and *Ulysses*. *The Maximus Poems* is also of that family, but at the same time initiates another. In considering MacDiarmid, you can see how the Scots lyrics and *A Drunk Man Looks at the Thistle* are pretty clearly related to that family. But the overtly political, materialist, and visionary poems of the 1930s effectively reveal a major transition in MacDiarmid's work, through the crisis of "On a Raised Beach." His later poetry (*In Memoriam James Joyce*, *The Kind of Poetry I Want*, for

---

1. Charles Olson, *The Maximus Poems*, ed. George F. Butterick (Berkeley: U of California P, 1983) 21. All further page references to Olson's poetry are from this edition.
2. Hugh MacDiarmid, *The Complete Poems of Hugh MacDiarmid*, ed. W. R. Aitken and Michael Grieve (London: Martin Brian & O'Keeffe, 1978) 431. All further page references to MacDiarmid's poetry are from this edition.

example) seems to me distinctively postmodernist, coming from but projecting beyond that family.

If we are to propose a relation between MacDiarmid and Olson which locates them both in a postmodernist context, we can most happily begin by looking at specific points of contact.

At Black Mountain College, Olson made notes for a tutorial on the Greeks, which included this reference:

> The 3rd cent. BC is also a gallery. For example, there is a lovely homosexual poet (an Alexandrian!) who must date from this century who did a damned fresh poem on Orpheus' death (such Alexandrians have approximately the relation to great Greeks as the Scots do to the English, like that Scot now, and Dunbar etc. after Chaucer).--I am not sure, however, if the 3rd Cent. BC is as relevant overall as the 2nd AD. But Theocritus is enuf to suggest more. Poke around in it.[3]

The notes are dated June 22, 1955. Copies among the papers of Edward Dorn and Michael Rumaker indicate they had been made available to Black Mountain students. George Butterick has noted that the Alexandrian poet was probably Phanocles, author of the *Erotes*, and explains the reference to "that Scot now" as "The poet Hugh MacDiarmid"--but there is no specific reference in Olson. This does suggest, however, that as early as that, Olson had certainly heard of or read MacDiarmid, and that moreover he had arrived at the definite idea that Scottish literature was quite distinct from English. That was a crucial part of MacDiarmid's life's argument, despite the fact that he recognized that "the fraction of readers/For the best work today is: 14,000/300,000,000":

> It means that in each 100,000 souls
> Five are reasonably civilised.
> So our literature cannot be called
> A very national or even racial affair.
>
> (CP 862-63)

This observation comes in MacDiarmid's 1955 volume, *In Memoriam James Joyce*. The only book by MacDiarmid in Olson's library (as George Butterick has informed me) is *In Memoriam James Joyce*, the second impression from 1956. There is no indication how he came to possess it.

---

3. Charles Olson, "Charles Olson, Tutorial: The Greeks," *Olson: The Journal of the Charles Olson Archives* 2 (Fall 1974): 44.

It is uncertain whether they met. MacDiarmid read to considerable acclaim in The Poetry Centre in New York on May 4, 1967, with Norman MacCaig, who also, along with M. L. Rosenthal, introduced him. (Rosenthal, in fact, in his critical work of this period, likens MacDiarmid and Olson.) They both were present at the International Poetry Conference held in London in July, 1967. They were scheduled to read together with John Berryman, Patrick Kavanagh, Anne Sexton and Bella Akhmadulina, introduced by A. Alvarez in the Purcell Room on the south bank of the Thames on July 14th. But Olson read on July 12th. If they did ever talk together, you can imagine any mutual approval being tempered. MacDiarmid was never very complimentary about postmodernist American verse, although he had been one of the first to write about William Carlos Williams in the old *New Age*, and was published himself in the *Massachusetts Review* (Vol. 8, No. 1, in the winter of 1967). The difference he insisted upon between the American poets and himself was expressed in conversation with Duncan Glen in the following year:

> MacDiarmid: I go much nearer Eliot, of course, than I do William Carlos Williams, but my man is Pound, definitely . . . Scottism, (*sic*) that discrimination between the various particles in a given situation and so on is a very different thing [from Sympathetic Magic]. Our opponents, Scottist (*sic*) opponents, are the Thomas Aquinas people who are trying to prematurely synthesise, whereas we are continuing to insist upon the individuality of the elements in a particular context. No, I think where, instead of being sympathetic magic, which after all is pre-scientific, that my attitude to these minute particulars and so on which after all was Blake's slogan--necessity for observing the minute particulars--I think is aligned with another great modern phenomenon in a different sphere altogether and that is the fragmentation of science, the fact that specialisations in the different sciences, once they go beyond a particular point, become unintelligible to specialists in other branches of science. I think it is a general world tendency.

> Glen: You have expressed an admiration for Hopkins and his technical innovations. The variable foot of Williams and those such as Olson who have carried on from Williams--would you not in any way see this as a technical advance comparable to Hopkins' prosody experiments and so forth?

> MacDiarmid: No, I think . . . this is rising out of a different background, different beliefs altogether.

Glen: It's coming out of an animal attitude rather than . . .

MacDiarmid: And a purely aesthetic one instead of a religious and philosophic one.[4]

This should be qualified. MacDiarmid may be doubtful of the emphasis being placed upon the aesthetic element, but he is not rejecting it. He had called Scotland the most backward country in Western Europe aesthetically (in his 1962 introduction to *A Drunk Man*) and in 1950 had written a long essay, *Aesthetics in Scotland*, to demonstrate that it need not always be so.[5] Also, what emerges from the animal and aesthetic elements in post-modernist American poetry--ecological and spiritual concerns-- are of central relevance to his own stance. In a later conversation with Walter Perrie, recorded in 1974, he affirms the supernatural, the larger than life, as something essential for poetry as it is for life. "Human life itself implies a belief in, a desire to participate in, the transcendental. It's inherent in us without reference to any religious belief. . . . The transcendental, if I am right, comes out of the seeds of things. It's inherent in the original substance--it's part of the materialism."[6]

There are even more direct connections between the European philosophical background (the dialectical materialism, Nietzschean metaphysics, and modern scientific aspects of which allow MacDiarmid to assert the simultaneity of spirit and matter) and the Americans. Black Mountain College itself, where Olson was instructor and rector from 1951 to 1956, where Robert Creeley taught and Edward Dorn studied, was founded in 1933 largely through the impetus of exiled artists and teachers from the Bauhaus, whose formation in 1919 Weimar consolidated the legacy of the best in philosophy and ethical teaching to work out a new and more vital kind of art school than had existed for centuries. From 1933 to 1946, Josef and Anni Albers, Xanti Schawinsky, Walter Gropius and others were working at the college, and an important part of the European legacy came down the line to Olson. Compare, for example, Oskar Schlemmer's Bauhaus course on "Man" (1929-1933)[7] with Olson's Black Mountain course "The Chiasma, or Lectures in the New

4. *The MacDiarmids*, interview with Duncan Glen (Preston: Akros, 1970) n. pag.
5. Hugh MacDiarmid, *Aesthetics in Scotland*, ed. Alan Bold (Edinburgh: Mainstream Publishing, 1984).
6. Hugh MacDiarmid, *Metaphysics and Poetry*, interview with Walter Perrie (Hamilton: Lothlorien Publications, 1975) n. pag.
7. Hans M. Wingler, *The Bauhaus Archives Berlin, Museum of Design*, trans. Mary Hhocker (Braunschweis: Westermann, 1983) 70-71.

Sciences of Man" (1953). It was Albers himself who, in 1948, invited Olson to give a series of lectures at the college. To carry it home, a project was set up run jointly by the Richard Demarco Gallery and the University of Edinburgh in association with the North American Students Association in 1972 called *Edinburgh Arts*. This was a residential, summer university in which a gallery of creative teachers, experts on history, art, architecture, sculpture, fine arts, dance, mime and literature worked together with students on a daily basis. The 1973 Prospectus describes the project (which continued for ten years) as neither a summer school nor an Arts Symposium but "about the *dialogue* which exists in the ideal University--'the University under a tree'-- where the poet or philosopher speaks in a human dimension to those who wish to share a dialogue with him. It is also the Renaissance idea of the Workshop, the Artist's studio where Master and apprentice worked together to produce art and art artifacts." Other Scottish poets involved included Sydney Goodsir Smith, Edwin Morgan and Ian Hamilton Finlay. The whole project was, in Richard Demarco's words, based on and inspired by Black Mountain College, and by Demarco's decision, MacDiarmid, as the greatest living poet, was to have been head poet, reading and lecturing in a position of authority (though obviously without any of the administrative responsibilities) thus clearly related to Olson's. MacDiarmid's attitude was one of enormous enthusiasm, and he took part with zeal and commitment.

The pedagogic dimension evident in this is crucial to the stance of both poets, and is related through their work to a vision of civil society informed and motivated by critical thought and political consciousness. To a certain extent, this was shared by the one poet both men regarded as a mentor and master: Pound.

MacDiarmid corresponded with Pound in the early 1930s. They both contributed to A. R. Orage's *New Age* and its successor, the *New English Weekly*. They had a number of acquaintances in common, particularly regarding Major C. H. Douglas's social credit proposals. Pound gets an extremely favourable mention wherever MacDiarmid can manage it. He valued *The Cantos* more highly than almost any twentieth-century long poem, and refused to consider the liability of Pound's fascism. His essays on Pound come back to three themes: (1) that the long poem or epic work is the necessary form for these times, being the only kind capable of getting it all in, (2) that economics is a good subject for great poetry, and (3) that an élitism of the keenest intellects is a desirable discipline.[8] They met finally in 1971 in Venice:

> . . . I had a long talk with him about mutual friends, especially Messrs T. S. Eliot, C. H. Douglas, A. R. Orage and Peter Russell.
>
> We subsequently went out and had lunch together, and then we crossed the Grand Canal in a vaporetta and walked in St Mark's Square and had coffee in Florian's Cafe. Mr Pound was in good trim and walked very briskly. He had some affection of the throat and his speech was not very clear, but he was very animated and discussed economics and other matters very connectedly and incisively.[9]

This is from a letter to *The Scotsman* (an Edinburgh newspaper) dated November 3, 1972, refuting the report that Olga Rudge had been the only person Pound had talked to for years before his death. More personal letters recounting the meeting are not much more revealing. In 1973, MacDiarmid wrote of Pound, "he was the most lovable man I ever met and I was happy to know that my affection for him was reciprocated."

What a difference from Olson, whose notes on the visits he made to Pound at St. Elizabeths in the 1940s spot Pound's stance exactly. "His sense is not social, but societal . . . he's got a 200 year *political lag*. . . ." To Olson, Pound's desire for a "purity" in the Republican ideal reflected an ignorance of "the coming into existence of the MASSES," and in 1946 resulted in Pound's naive opposition to immigration, and conflicted profoundly with a realistic grasp of economics. (Having worked in Roosevelt's government, Olson could at least claim that.) The science of the masses, Olson says, is economics, and Pound is confronted and frustrated by the economic necessities which underlie the revolution in society and in politics. "In language and form he is as forward, as much the revolutionist as Lenin. But in social, economic and political action he is as retrogressive as the Czar."[10] Whatever Olson took from Pound--and there is a lot, in the poems of *Archaeologist of Morning*, or in Pound's help with publishing *Call Me Ishmael*, for example--he gave, in those visits, much in return. "Olson saved my life," Pound said. But Olson, closer in a literal sense than MacDiarmid, involved in a more intimate, intimating relation

8. Hugh MacDiarmid, "The Return of the Long Poem," *Ezra Pound: Perspectives*, ed. Noel Stock (Chicago: Henry Regnery, 1965) 90-108.
9. Hugh MacDiarmid, letter to *The Scotsman*, 3 Nov. 1972, *The Letters of Hugh MacDiarmid*, ed. Alan Bold (Athens, Georgia: U of Georgia P, 1984) 837.
10. Charles Olson, "Encounters with Ezra Pound," *Antaeus* 2 (Spring 1975): 76.

(as son is to father, rather than as a younger cousin to a loved but distant elder), goes out on a line to criticize Pound, as MacDiarmid never does. Olson values the potential of feeling, the discreet emotions of Williams ("Uncle Bill") more highly than the emotional egosystem of "Canto Man." Robert Creeley describes the situation as it was for them precisely, in a letter to Olson dated October 3, 1950:

> You can't renounce Ez, you can only leave him sitting in the dust, which is where: exactly where, he should be left. A reaction, simply, against Ez is going to throw you back to the Georgians, to that thinking, or granted we can't go back, to such, is going to mean, again, looseness, etc. The alternative is what, exactly what you plot.[11]

And yet, is not what happens through *The Maximus Poems* the gradual disjunction of Maximus, the metal, the builder of the nest, the vast sensibility of cosmic authority, and a tragically smaller figure, the Olson whose last losses are the final poem:

> my wife my car my color and myself (*Maximus* 635)

The response to Pound is perhaps as much the gauge and the key to the triumph as it is to the tragedy of *The Maximus Poems.* Earlier in 1950 (in a letter dated May 25) Olson had written to Creeley:

> at bay? and who isn't, *what* force of man isn't--even those who are not quite intelligent and not wholly stupid?
>
> agreed, the weapon *is* the real one, agree, it must, *forever*, fight,
>   stay
> cornered, like a Texan keep its shoes on and
> its back to a wall
>
> agree its dance, among syllables, is
> the ultimate necessity
>
> yet, 35 yrs out, we are not, no longer are we
> REFORMERS, we
> are too dry
> for dreams, we
> are not as hard as youth, we
> are as hard as
> anything can be made to be

---

11. Robert Creeley, letter to Charles Olson, 3 Oct. 1950, *Charles Olson and Robert Creeley: The Complete Correspondence*, ed. George Butterick, 8 vols. (Santa Barbara: Black Sparrow Press, 1981) 3: 75.

((h melville wrote for the whole of his
later life with, over his desk, this:
"keep true to the dreams
of thy youth"

bah, him, bah
Ez: each,
to his time))

which goes for us, too, i mean the time,
not
the dream

Is it not rather handsome, and gain, that we have lowered
the sights?[12]

It is an important advance, for postmodernist poetry, this recognition that from Pound, the sights must be lowered, and that the results of this can be gain. We will come back to it.

One other figure excited in both Olson and MacDiarmid a mutual regard of significant consequence. The relevance of Herman Melville to the respective careers of both poets should be emphasized here not only because Melville is one of the major writers to have been a harbinger of the literature of this century but also because of what both men find in him: a cosmological understanding of inexhaustibility and human limitation directly related to the workings of economic history.

Olson spent years working on material directly related to his study of Melville and produced, first, an MA thesis on "The Growth of Herman Melville, Prose Writer and Poetic Thinker" (1933), then a paper on "*Lear* and *Moby-Dick*" (1938); finally, having traced and explored Melville's own library, he wrote *Call Me Ishmael* in 1945 and saw it published two years later. Melville was of continuous importance to him, through his personal experience of the sea (the three-week fishing trip for swordfish in 1936, for example), his dance-play of Ahab and Ishmael, *The Fiery Hunt* (1948), and on to the "Letter for Melville 1951." But *Call Me Ishmael* is unique in its sustained power, closeness of attention, detailed and useful discoveries, and revelatory methodology. Melville and *Moby-Dick* produced three "great creations" for Olson: Ahab, the Pacific, and the White Whale. If there is less personal identification in MacDiarmid's understanding of Melville's greatness, there is an

---

12. *Charles Olson and Robert Creeley: The Complete Correspondence* 1:45.

equally powerful and imaginative response taking place, well before the business of Melville scholarship had seriously begun to get underway. That understanding runs viscerally through *A Drunk Man* (1926). He sees the sea's serpent coil:

> *In mum obscurity it twines its obstinate rings*
> *And hings caressin'ly, its purpose whole;*   hangs caressingly
> *And this deid thing, whale-white obscenity,*   dead
> *This horror that I writhe in--is my soul!*
>   (*CP* 94)

As Kenneth Buthlay has observed, this is a transcription of a translation from Zinaida Hippius's poem "Ona" ("She").[13] The one most striking image--the "whale-white obscenity"--does not occur in Hippius's poem. And the white whale surfaces more than once and for more than one reason. In *A Drunk Man*, MacDiarmid makes full use of the salient images of whale and octopus, and Melville's presence recurs. MacDiarmid even quotes from Melville's *Clarel* in a parenthetical aside preceded by a near-acknowledgment:

> Melville (a Scot) kent weel hoo Christ's   knew well how
> Corrupted into creeds malign,
> Begotten strife's pernicious brood
> That claims for patron Him Divine.
> (The Kirk in Scotland still I cry   The Church
> Crooks whaur it canna crucify!)   where it cannot
>   (*CP* 135)

The reference is even more bitterly powerful when you consider the context in Melville's long poem, a vitriolic diatribe on those "Mammonite freebooters" the Anglo-Saxons:

> Old ballads sing
> Fair Christian children crucified
> By impious Jews; you've heard the thing:
> Yes, fable; but there's truth hard by:
> How many Hughs of Lincoln, say,
> Does Mammon in his mills to-day
> Crook, if he do not crucify?[14]

Referring to *A Drunk Man* itself, MacDiarmid then goes on to say that it may be of some help to a Scottish reader, and uses Melville in another way to make his point:

---

13. Kenneth Buthlay, *Hugh MacDiarmid* (Edinburgh: Scottish Academic Press, 1982) 46.
14. Herman Melville, *Clarel: A Poem and Pilgrimage in the Holy Land* (London: Constable, 1924) 192-93, vol. 15 of *The Works of Herman Melville*.

And never mair a Scot sall tryst,   more, shall meet
Abies on Calvary, wi' Christ,   Except, with
Unless, mebbe, a poem like this'll   maybe
Exteriorise things in a thistle,
And gi'e him in this form forlorn
What Melville socht in vain frae Hawthorne. ...   sought, from
(CP 135)

But Melville is a stronger, deeper, and more resonant presence in the poem than these examples show. He is the "sea-compelling man"

Before whose wand Leviathan
Rose hoary-white upon the Deep,
(CP 139)

He can cast and help MacDiarmid cast for what lies beneath to rise, and he leads the drunk man on to Dostoevsky, the second great teacher of the poem.

In *Contemporary Scottish Studies* (1925-1927), *Moby-Dick* is said to exemplify Scottish literature in one of its most distinctive forms, as opposed to what the reading public regard as Scottish. MacDiarmid quotes Raymond Weaver: "the dull and decent Philistine, untouched by Platonic heresies, justifies his sterility in a boast of sanity. The America in which Melville was born and died was exuberantly and unquestionably 'sane.' Its 'sanity' drove Irving abroad and made a recluse of Hawthorne. Cooper alone throve upon it. And of Melville, more ponderous in gifts and more volcanic in energy than any other American writer, it made an Ishmael on the face of the earth." MacDiarmid comments: "That America was largely Scottish."[15] (And MacDiarmid's earliest reading was largely American: he claimed to have read a staggering array of American writers as a boy.[16])

In 1930, MacDiarmid saw published *To Circumjack Cencrastus*. In Jamieson's *Etymological Dictionary of the Scottish Language*, "to circumjack" is given as "to agree to, or correspond with. -Lat. *circumjac-ere*, to lie round or about," and "Cencrastus" is given as "a serpent of a greenish colour." But the title is meant to imply the task and intention of the poem: to come to enclose, to get the better of, the mythological serpent which circles the world with its tail in its mouth. In the poem,

15. Hugh MacDiarmid, "Newer Scottish Fiction (I)," *The Scottish Educational Journal* 25 June 1926, rpt. in *Contemporary Scottish Studies* (Edinburgh: Scottish Educational Journal, 1976) 109.
16. Hugh MacDiarmid, *Lucky Poet: A Self-Study in Literature and Political Ideas* (1943; London: Methuen, 1972) 9-11.

MacDiarmid quotes Dante's *Inferno*, Canto 26, 112-20, where Ulysses is relating to Virgil how he exhorted his crew to go beyond the Pillars of Hercules. MacDiarmid identifies himself with Dante's Greek; he is sailing the Pequod of his own imagination through the empty ocean of his own country, crying to his fellow Scots with the obsessive ardour of an Ahab and the hopeless isolation of an Ishmael. These are also the lines quoted in translation by Olson at the climax of *Call Me Ishmael*. They describe, in Olson's view, the central one of three Odysseys which parallel 3,000 years of economic history. The first was that of Homer's Odysseus, with the hero pushing against the limits of Anaximander's map, the closed circle of Oceanos ("like a serpent with tail in mouth," says Olson--which is Cencrastus), seeking a way out. "Homer gave his hero the central quality of the men to come: *search, the individual responsible to himself.*"[17] Then Dante's Ulysses, in 1400, again prospective, an Atlantic man, a Columbus. The Pillars, the entrance to the West, is the one spot on earth's surface Dante recognizes from the seventh sphere of the *Paradiso*. And then the third "and final" Odyssey-- Ahab's. When West returned to East, the Pacific marked the end of the UNKNOWN and the end of the individual responsible only to himself. Such an understanding of the cosmic totality MacDiarmid wanted. To circumjack Cencrastus is to get on the outside of the serpent, the River Ocean, to swallow the world, to announce the end of, and end, UNKNOWN.

But it does not, finally, climatically, happen. Neither in that poem nor in MacDiarmid's life work. That tropic desire is, triumphantly and joyously, surrendered. The sights are lowered. And that results in gain, in ample gain.

From *Sangschaw* (1925) to *A Drunk Man* (1926) MacDiarmid creates a world he cannot call to heel, and comes himself to be wheeled round in Juggernaut. After *Cencrastus* (1930), the poetic persona turns into a more modest, though still formidable and unique, force in Scotland. In "Harry Semen" he re-examines the themes of the divine (or artistic) creation (or procreation), looking back to his own cosmogony. The cataclysm has become the arbitrary blash of sperm "frae which I was born." *Stony Limits and Other Poems* reflects and represents a crisis MacDiarmid went beyond.[18]

---

17. Charles Olson, *Call Me Ishmael* (London: Jonathan Cape, 1967) 109.
18. This movement in MacDiarmid's work has been examined in detail and depth by Peter McCarey in *Hugh MacDiarmid and the Russians* (Edinburgh: Scottish Academic Press, 1987).

Dostoevsky had dropped from MacDiarmid's *oeuvre*
as a seminal figure at just the time when Lenin was marching in,
but Melville remained a point of reference. He is mentioned
twice in *In Memoriam James Joyce*; in the section "Plaited Like
the Generations of Men" MacDiarmid announces as the poet's
task what Olson, in the very first of *The Maximus Poems*, exhorts
his Gloucester-man to do. "At this moment when braidbinding
as never before, / The creation of the seamless garment, / Is the
poet's task." MacDiarmid adds a note from *Moby-Dick*: "The
warp seemed necessity; and here, thought I, with my own hand I
ply my own shuttle, and weave my own destiny into these unal-
terable threads" (CP 876n). And in the earlier section, "The
Snares of Varuna," MacDiarmid says, in a long parenthesis, that
he has often told his angling friend Norman MacCaig:

> If I went fishing I could not be content
> With salmon or brown trout.
> My heart would be set on an oar-fish,
> 'King of the Herrings,' with its long tapering tail,
> Continuous scarlet dorsal fin,
> Scarlet erectile crest, and pelvic fins,
> Placed far forward, transformed
> In long slender oar-like blades.
> And then I'd have dorado,
> The golden fish of the Alto Paraná,
> The giant wels or sheat-fish which runs
> To 600 lb in the Volga,
> The African tiger-fish,
> 'The fiercest fish that swims,'
> Sail-fish, marlin, wahoo, tarpon, tuna,
> Sword-fish in New Zealand, and the great mako shark,
> And largest of the true giants of the sea,
> Largest of living animals indeed,
> The blue rorqual . . . and even then
> I'd remember with Herman Melville
> That behind Leviathan
> There's still the kraken,
> And no end to our 'ontological heroics.'
> And MacCaig has laughed and said
> 'Let me see you catch anything yet
> Big enough not to throw in again.'
>   (CP 851)

Nothing is that big. The thistle, Europe, even the egoistic self:
nothing is set over against that plenitude as greater than it (least
of all an immanent God). This sense of wealth runs through all

the later poetry: Scotland is the place it starts from; the poet gives it his energy, and the poetry keeps its usefulness.

If this demonstrates the relation of the poet and cosmology, we should now look more closely at the poetry itself. In Olson's terms, "Projective Verse" signifies an energized and immediate, instant-by-instant response to reality, coming from the physical being of the poet through the precise formulation of the poem to the reader:

> But breath is man's special qualification as animal. Sound is a dimension he has extended. Language is one of his proudest acts. And when a poet rests in these as they are in himself (in his physiology, if you like, but the life in him, for all that) then he, if he chooses to speak from these roots, works in that area where nature has given him size, projective size.[19]

This is from the second part of Olson's 1950 essay, "Projective Verse." The term is more widely and challengingly applicable than might be expected from the painstakingly exact specifications in the first part of the essay, explaining the significant balances of head and heart, ear and breath, syllable and line. Technically, Olson innovates in the most subtle ways, and MacDiarmid, in his general observation of a rhythmically regular verse-line, his acceptance of (and adaptability to) stanza forms of a wide variety, his use of Biblical-rhetorical modes of address often in tune with Old Testament wisdom, even in his quite strict adherence to the rule of the margin, may seem at first glance not to be, technically, relatable to Olson at all. This would be a mistake. In rhythmic subtleties in the Scots poems, he has at least as much to command and does it as well. If Scots, like any other language, is "synthetic," then it is still being employed in these poems by a man who will later address "Speech" as "All men's whore. My beloved!" (CP 838). Increasingly, however, as more and more sources come to be used in his poetry, as the nature and function of the work change, there is a sense in which his technical control of subtle expression is surrendered to a more demanding input of energetic expansiveness. MacDiarmid's sense of membership of the "*sodaliciis adstricti consortiis* / Of all the authors who have been, are, or will be" (CP 738) offsets his sense of isolation. He is, consequently, not strident (as rectorial Olson sometimes is) but

---

19. Charles Olson, "Projective Verse," *Human Universe and Other Essays*, ed. Donald Allen (1965; New York: Grove, 1967) 60.

compelling, compulsive, occasionally fanatical. He wants "A poetry in keeping with the human nervous system" (CP 782).

"Projective," however, does have other senses than the technical. It is closely connected with both the kind of teaching and the view of history Olson espoused. It is a term used in its most general sense to describe a progressive dynamic mobilization of forces:

> For what I despair a little at making absolutely clear, is, that a certain homogeneity of instruction in *all* the arts is possible today to a degree that I don't think was so possible just a short while back, here, or in any college. That is, one of the reasons why just what is happening here does happen--the bringing in of *active* education--is because a growth of *action* in art itself is noticeable. I would put it--have put it--that PROJECTION, with all its social consequences, is the mark of forward art today. And it is one of the best ways we find out the kinetic secrets of projective art--the very way we do it--is to put art *in action*, to join the arts *in action*, to break down all stupid walls, even the wall of art as separate from society![20]

In that more general sense, MacDiarmid's later work is certainly projective. It is a poetry given to advocacy, the explicit and encouraging expressions of human desire in a world both creatural and political, and therefore directly related to the speech of its first person singular. The subtlety of the relations between the poetry's first person singular, the words of the text and its social and political context creates a fine and potent tension. The "centre" is no longer the poet, or the work, or society. Rather, there is a constant play of intertextual reference, which demands the reader's recognition and participation as a motor force. What I have elsewhere called MacDiarmid's "epic" poetry keeps on insisting that these references be experienced as consciously as possible. But in the dynamic of its forward push it does not allow more than temporary relaxations, momentary closures, and tactical decisions. In that, the contrast lies with the tremendous relaxation and finality in the last *Maximus* volume.

"Projective Verse," in Olson's terminology, describes a methodology, a way of acting to be used *by the poet*. Applied to MacDiarmid, the term can be better directed towards the poem itself, or the kind of poetry it is, which also involves the stance of the poet: it becomes a critical tool for the *reader* to use. In that relationship the political and social dimension of MacDiarmid's

---

20. Charles Olson, letter to W. H. Ferry, 7 Aug. 1951, *Olson: The Journal of the Charles Olson Archives* 2 (Fall 1974): 13.

project should be evident and the projective value of its dynamic directly brought into the present and future debate.

   If we want to characterize more closely the technique MacDiarmid employs in demonstrating that "Projection," we might call it "Synaptic Verse." The words on the page are like the progression of an impulse-instruction going along the neurological paths of a body. When the impulse-instruction arrives at the nerve-end, it must leap to another one, make a synaptic connection with at least one of a number of possible nerve-ends. It thus progresses by a number of such synaptic connections until its course is run. These synaptic leaps are most often found in the poetry where MacDiarmid seems about to make an analogy. He uses words and phrases which, while they act as hinges, also make evident that what follows will be different from what has gone before. For example, between pages 759 and 764 of *The Complete Poems*, we find the phrases: "And so on to . . .," "And to . . .," "Even as . . .," "Even as we know how . . .," "Even as we know that . . .," "Even as we delight in . . .," "And even as we know . . .," "Even as we know . . .," "Or even as we know . . .," "And rejoicing in all . . .," "Or even as . . .," "Or like . . . ." While within the verse-paragraphs (referring to considerations of grammar, dialect, specific vocabularies and languages, etc.), we are also treated to a "philological parenthesis" on the world history of dance, and an extended simile likening "our" knowledge of abstruse languages to the perspicacity of the farmer who, surveying his fields, can easily distinguish between the crops in each one, while an untrained eye would merely see them all alike. The effect of this simile is that we are taken further and further from the awareness that it is a simile and are held by the depiction itself, until we are suddenly reminded of the poem's procedure by yet another "Even as we know. . . ."

   If this describes the progress of the words down page after page, there is implied in my analogy an organic body which houses the neurological system thus represented. This body is never fully visible--"since ecdysis is never complete"[21]--but it is implicit from and around the text, as the city of Dublin in *Ulysses* is never described but always present. Part of the exhilaration of reading *In Memoriam James Joyce* is in the discovery that as you proceed that body can never finally be realized. Apotheosis--Cencrastus circumjacked--is no longer a single and apocalyptic goal.

---

21. Ecdysis is the act of sloughing, the process of casting off and renewal, from the Greek *ek*, out of, and *dyein*, to put on. The line is from *In Memoriam James Joyce*.

Melville's hunt takes place in the confluence of economic and cosmological histories. The book--*Moby-Dick*--blasts notions of the novel from any formal bases. Similarly, the kinds of poetry both Olson and MacDiarmid evolved, though very distinct, have this in common. They are intended to shake the formal conceptions of verse from static comprehension. The gain resulting from what Olson called the lowering of the sights includes a sense of historical distance which even *The Cantos* does not "contain." This sense is evident not only from the verse itself but from the speculative prose of both writers, and it calls out their pedagogic authority. Olson's directions to his students at Black Mountain confronting Homer and the Greeks were: "Take both backwards," to get out of the European box. This is another aspect of what MacDiarmid did, moving from the reflection in *A Drunk Man* that Europe was far enough afield for him, to "A Vision of World Language"--which is what the Joyce poem was said to have come from. His key reference in the historical sense, however, came as early as 1931, in the essay "English Ascendancy in British Literature" (first published in *The Criterion*--then edited by T. S. Eliot). He says that the "most romantic of all movements, the search for a new classicism today, is not a quest for any mere neo-classical formalism but an effort to get down to *Ur-motives*--to get back behind the Renaissance!"[22] He wants to inherit and embody a dynamic that existed in Europe before the whitening of youthful national European cultures by the Renaissance, and beyond that even, to pre-Christian times. The linguistic importance of Gaelic and the spiritual importance of the Gaelic Idea MacDiarmid adumbrated in the early 1930s was deeply related to this prospect. A curious set of correspondences suggests the relevance of the Gaelic Idea here. The earliest formulation of a well-known phrase from Olson's "Projective Verse" essay occurs in a letter to Olson from Creeley dated June 5, 1950:

> Again: abt 'instruments . . .' ('becoz he is instrument, & uses all available instruments only to dominate 'em, not his fellow cits. . .'): you will know of all the blah: abt possible 'audiences' in the case of both prose & poetry / you will also know: absolute bull/shit. That is: the intelligence that had touted Auden as being a technical wonder, etc. Lacking all grip on the worn & useless character of his essence: thought. An attitude that puts weight, *first*: on form

22. Hugh MacDiarmid, "English Ascendancy in British Literature," *The Uncanny Scot*, ed. Kenneth Buthlay (London: MacGibbon & Kee, 1968) 133.

/ more than to say: what you have above: will never get to: content. Never in god's world. Anyhow, form has now become so
useless a term / that I blush to use it. I wd imply a little of
Stevens' use (the things created *in* a poem and existing there . . .)
& too, go over into: the possible casts or methods for a way into /
a 'subject': to make it clear: that form is never more than an *extension* of content. An enacted or possible 'stasis' for thought. Means
to.[23]

In Olson's hands, this becomes the *principle* of Projective Verse:
FORM IS NEVER MORE THAN AN EXTENSION OF
CONTENT.

Now, in an essay on Ronald Johnson, Guy Daven-
port has described the particular significance of this phrase thus:

"Every force," said Mother Ann Lee of the Shakers, "evolves a
form." For the poet this is the opposite of supposing that a form
can be filled with a force. The sentiments aroused by the moon
painted by Ryder can be accommodated by a sonnet, but it is the
sonnet in the end which is being accommodated, not the moon. . . .
What has happened is that the force of the subject matter has
been allowed to shape the poem.[24]

This recalls in a peculiarly apposite way, MacDiarmid's reflections upon the houses, now abandoned, of the old Gaels of the
islands of Scotland, in "Island Funeral":

There are few and fewer people
On the island nowadays,
And there are more ruins of old cottages
Than occupied homes.
I love to go into these little houses
And see and touch the pieces of furniture.
I know all there is to know
About their traditional plenishing
And native arts and crafts,
And can speak with authority
About tongue-and-groove cleats,
The lipped drawer, and the diameters of finials.
But I know them also in their origin
Which is the Gaelic way of life
And can speak with equal authority
About a people one of whose proverbs
Is the remarkable sentence:
'Every force evolves a form.'

(CP 578-79)

---

23. *Charles Olson and Robert Creeley: The Complete Correspondence* 1: 78-79.
24. Guy Davenport, "Ronald Johnson," *The Geography of the Imagination: Forty Essays* (London: Picador, 1984) 193.

Remarkable indeed. The suggestion that the Gaels are a people outside Europe, in a sense, unrelated to the central focuses of the European Renaissance in any other than an oblique or tangential way, also throws a line from MacDiarmid's contemporary place into the backward vault of time. And this draws up meanings of immediate social significance (*The Islands of Scotland*, where "Island Funeral" first appeared in 1939, contained numerous practical proposals for specific reforms) while it draws attention to the linguistic peculiarity of the Gaelic situation. The sense of history which MacDiarmid evinces is pervasive, as Olson's also is. A special view of history runs through all their work, the long, didactic poems, the prospective prose, and their commitment to education. Edward Dorn remarked upon it in 1960, with particular reference to the individual ego: "*Maximus* returns to a pre-Christian ordering of the ego," he wrote, "or, however, comes forward to a non-Christian ordering."[25] Olson says that he wants to open

> the full inherited file
> of history
> *(Maximus* 367)

In *In Memoriam James Joyce*, the references range from Herodotus to Korzybski, from Varuna to Valéry, from Marlowe to Malraux, from "Koraina in the third century A.D." to "Pirandello's treatise in German on the Sicilian dialect," from Amos Tutuola to the Eddic "Converse of Thor and the All-Wise Dwarf," "Existing in its present MS form / Over five centuries before Shakespeare" (which MacDiarmid found in E. A. Waddell's *The British Edda*).

> We must respond maximally
> To the whole world we can.
> (CP 798)

What stance MacDiarmid has in this epic work, his poise, is (exactly in accordance with Olson's essay) the result of the poetry, the kind of poetry it is. Without a logocentric, lyric moment to achieve, without an anthropocentrically committed ethos, it contrasts strongly with *The Maximus Poems*, where the fusion of Whitehead's notion of process and a Herodotean idea of history is mediated through the voice in Gloucester, a man standing in a particular corner of America, astride the Cabot

---

25. Edward Dorn, "What I See in *The Maximus Poems*," *Views*, ed. Donald Allen (San Francisco: Four Seasons Foundation, 1980) 42.

Fault. MacDiarmid's Scotland, in a way, affords more than Olson's Gloucester could. Edward Dorn once commented that he would not want or need to visit Gloucester; his attitude is recognizable and a complement to Olson's. Place, in itself, does not justify celebration. Dorn notes in "Success?":

> I never had to worry about success
> Coming from where I come from
> You were a success the minute you left town[26]

Departure and residence might not be such simple factors though. Either option can present problems. But the degree of commitment to understanding the difficulties implicit in Dorn's iconoclasm, and in the subtlety of recognitions evident in his poetry, can be read alongside Olson's singular grandness, as a useful balance.

As Guy Davenport has it, "Olson's argument throughout his poetry is that awareness is an event caused by multiple forces, setting multiple forces in action. No force is ever spent. All events are lessons. No event can be isolated." So, structurally, any attempt to argue this out is bound to be demonstrative at least to some degree, just as MacDiarmid, in *The Kind of Poetry I Want*, is bound to attempt to bring onto the page what he so well describes as desirable. ("I dream of poems like the bread-knife / Which cuts three slices at once" (CP 1005). There will be the inchoate, the inconsequential, half-formulations, abortive grapplings, near-incoherencies, none of which, ultimately, are very damaging. Endless or almost endless sentences, semantic difficulties, opening and opening parentheses, are all carried by a live dynamic.

MacDiarmid wants:

> A poetry throwing light on the problems of value
> --Deriving its stimulating quality, its seminal efficacy,
> Not from the discovery, as old as the Greeks,
> That moral codes are relative to social factors,
> But from the nice and detailed study of the mechanisms
> Through which society
> Determines attitudes in its members
> By opening to them certain possibilities
> By induction into objectively recognised statuses
> While closing quite effectively other possibilities
> --A poetry, not offering a compromise between naïve atomism
> Giving an utterly unrelated picture of social phenomena,

---

26. Edward Dorn, *Yellow Lola: Formerly Titled Japanese Neon* (Santa Barbara: Cadmus editions, 1981) 105.

And the unrealistic conception of a mystical social *Gestalt*,
The defining quality of which is intuited by transcendental means
(That growing danger, as a reaction from the bankruptcy
Of the atomistic approach, of a mystical
Organismic approach instinct with anti-rationalistic obscurantism),
But seeking to do justice to the discrete
As well as to the organically integrated aspects of society,
To the disruptive as well as to the cohesive forces.
                              (CP 1023)

The language of the pre-Socratic Greeks made no distinction between *logos* and *muthos*. They both meant "what is said"--necessarily the absolute arbiter in a pre-literate culture. During the fifth century B.C., *muthos* came to mean "fictitious narrative" and *logos* to mean "the controlling principle, the Word" as it is in the Gospel of John. In his *Preface to Plato*, Eric Havelock argues that the *Republic* should not be read as an essay in utopian politics but as a document in the power struggle between the oral poets and the literate philosophers for the control of Greek education.[27] Now, Olson, who said that poets were the only pedagogues left to be trusted, seems to have believed that Plato got men thinking of eternity and Socrates got them thinking of truth. Combined, you get Western man's self-concept as separate from objects confined to durational time and whose framework of "abstract" thought is a void. And that all this is pretty villainous. He blames Socrates (as Nietzsche does) for abandoning the sensuous apprehension of the concrete for the rational pursuit of the abstract. The moral code of the old discourse is the old humanism which arrogantly insisted on an anthropocentric universe and which MacDiarmid also vigorously rejected. The moral code of the new discourse more modestly declares man but one in a world of forces declaring itself as force. As Maximus proclaims this, it is ironic that his stance can be seen as heroic.

      MacDiarmid's more discursive voice rounds on the familiar theme as well:

Alas! the thought of ninety-nine per cent of our people
Is still ruled by Plato and Aristotle
Read in an historical vacuum by the few
From whom the masses receive
A minimum of it but along with that
A maximum incapacity for anything else.
                              (CP 662)

---

27. Eric Havelock, *Preface to Plato* (Cambridge: Harvard UP, 1963).

He also takes every opportunity to make centripetal references to cultures outside the Western-Hellenic, showing a concern for Oriental as well as Occidental languages and literatures in inverse proportion to his mastery of them.

> And I do not forget
> The old Red River dialect,
> That curious patois born
> Of the union of Scots pioneer with Cree,
> Now dying out, with *apeechequanee*
> Meaning head over heels, and *chimmuck*,
> The sound of a rock falling perpendicularly into a lake,
> . . . Or loch!

(CP 1035)

There is a continual sense of the world being within MacDiarmid's orbit, although there is none whatsoever of his having fully conquered it. It remains far from exhausted. (Thus the epigraphs to this essay.) His sense of his own limitations is brought out a number of times in *In Memoriam James Joyce*, but it is carried in a context of breathless and invigorating reference, which in its turn is charged by a priceless humor and tempered by a political pragmatism. The kind of poetry MacDiarmid wants is essentially itself various and contradictory, but it is also a poetry aware of its own value in the field of literary practice:

> --If the book's ultimate realisation
> Is the impotence of language
> In the face of the event,
> This abdication is announced
> With a power of words wholly inaccessible
> To those never overpowered and speechless.

(CP 776)

There is an immediate, daily sense of reality coincident with a sense of global consequence in MacDiarmid's later poetry, which is, I take it, a coincidence whose material demonstrability has been a characteristic of the world since 1945.

> Poetry of such an integration as cannot be effected
> Until a new and conscious organisation of society
> Generates a new view
> Of the world as a whole
> As the integration of all the rich parts
> Uncovered by the separate disciplines.
> That is the poetry that I want.

(CP 1025)

These separate disciplines arise in studies begun upon the bases of various and often contradictory experiences. Their effective organisation and integration must begin with the concrete analyses of the heterogeneous processes of identification in particular fields of activity and struggle.

The great works of Modernism, by declaring their own artistic processes of construction, entered into a social and hence political and critical relationship with their readers or audiences. Postmodernism may be usefully thought of as involving a stance towards reality, as well as text, willing to take advantage of both the primordial and the latest understandings, taking that political and critical relationship into an immediate present. That development, for Olson as for MacDiarmid, is made though the poet's intervention.

What limits the range of that act of intervention is a fixity of identity. If poets are Promethean, they must learn also to be Protean. And what they show, ultimately, is that if the inevitable identities of class, race, age, and sex impose daily, it is not because of some necessary "natural" features of biology or of the means of production which also establish such identities. It is because of the practices and discourses which mobilize these biologies and these means in particular ways. It is the high distinction of postmodernist poetry that it is wakefully and deliberately addressing itself to the question of how these practices and discourses change, can be changed.

And within that context, MacDiarmid is distinct in his own commitment to changing them towards Communism, from Scotland out.

Hugh MacDiarmid reading poems on the Polish vessel, Batori,
en route for Gdynia in the Baltic.
Photo used courtesy of Michael Grieve.

KENNETH BUTHLAY

ADVENTURING IN DICTIONARIES

My decision to restrict the scope of this essay to some examples of MacDiarmid's writing in Scots was made as what I felt to be a much needed response to the principal statement about his practice in this respect which is made in a study of his poetry from 1920 to 1934--that is, the period in which he produced all his main work in Scots:

> While MacDiarmid claimed that he found in dictionaries like Jamieson's, lost elements of dialect and used these in his early lyrics, he also asserted that he wrote out of a living language and stated that the success of his work was due to the fact that he used colloquialisms and idioms which he heard all around him.[1]

This seems a strange way of describing the situation: MacDiarmid "claimed" that he found "lost elements" of Scots in dictionaries like Jamieson's *Etymological Dictionary of the Scottish Language*--as if no one had examined the evidence of what he did, and as if the poet were eager to make such a "claim" regardless of the weight of critical opprobrium directed against what was contemptuously called his "dictionary-dredging" by more than one generation of critics. Over thirty years ago, when I first spoke to MacDiarmid about his use of Jamieson, he was not at all pleased to have the subject raised. I remarked to him then that children read dictionaries because they are interested in words, and that it seemed natural to me that poets should continue to do so since they are life-long word-fanciers and dictionaries are where the words are. He responded to that with some relief--and it was not long before he was saying something similar himself, in print.

The critical study from which I have quoted above passes over some very basic facts. In 1922, at the age of thirty, Christopher Murray Grieve unexpectedly turned his hand to writing in Scots instead of the English in which he had established a considerable reputation. He produced two poems that

---

1. Catherine Kerrigan, *Whaur Extremes Meet* (Edinburgh: James Thin, 1983) 66.

were constructed around a number of Scots expressions which he happened to find in James Wilson's *Lowland Scotch as Spoken in the Lower Strathearn District of Perthshire*. When printing the poems in a newspaper article, he himself explained that they had been produced in that way, but he concealed the fact that he was the author of them.

One of the poems, "The Watergaw," was then reprinted in his magazine, *The Scottish Chapbook*, attributed to "Hugh MacDiarmid" and commended by the editor, C. M. Grieve. In the same issue of the *Chapbook* (October 1922) one can find the earliest specimen of his Scots prose, "Following Rebecca West in Edinburgh." This is filled with obsolete or obsolescent Scots words, the great majority of which begin with the first three letters of the alphabet. And if anyone doubts the statement I made many years ago,[2] that MacDiarmid had acquired this vocabulary from the ABC of Jamieson's dictionary, let him reflect on the provenance of a dozen quotations embedded in this piece of prose. All of these appear in the same section of Jamieson, as illustrative examples.

So much for MacDiarmid's earliest writing in Scots. If we look at some of his work in *Scots Unbound* (1932), the last collection before he returned to writing (with very few exceptions) in English, it is not hard to find examples of a similar procedure in operation there. The first part of "Water Music" draws its extremely strange Scots vocabulary from the first three letters of the alphabet; the second part turns to minding its P's and Q's, R's and S's. And sections of other late Scots poems such as "Tarras," "Depth and the Chthonian Image," "Scots Unbound," and "Balefire Loch" take to an ultimate extreme the *reiving* of the dictionary that had been evident in his early long poem in Scots, "Gairmscoile," the title of which was originally "Braid Scots: An Inventory and Appraisement."

There are plenty of examples, too, of short lyrics which carry a considerable weight of Dictionary Scots, assembled regardless of all historical and geographical demarcations; and the success of these can hardly be attributed to his use of "colloquialisms and idioms which he heard all round him." Readers of one of the most justly admired of MacDiarmid's short poems, "The Eemis Stane," have to be persuaded to overcome their resistance to what they inevitably feel to be "dictionary-dredging" when confronted with its lexical

---

2. Kenneth Buthlay, *Hugh MacDiarmid* (Edinburgh: Oliver and Boyd, 1964) 23.

"uncouthness"--to use the word in its old, dictionary-preserved sense. But it was not just words as so many lexical items that MacDiarmid took from the dictionary, but images, metaphors, sounds, patterns of rhythm. No doubt he was attracted to *how-dumb-deid* ("the hollow centre of the dead of night") by its semantic compression, but his use of it in "The Eemis Stane" immediately suggests that its sound is at least as important. And it was not the word itself he took from Jamieson but a phrase which he altered slightly to its form in the opening line of his poem--"I' the how-dumb-deid o' the cauld hairst nicht" [cauld hairst--cold harvest]--a phrase which Jamieson had found in a piece of prose in *Blackwood's Magazine* (November 1820), and which now supplied the poet with a suggestive sequence of sounds in a powerful verse-rhythm. There is a fine irony about the artistry with which MacDiarmid exploited that rhythm in his opening line to help create the atmosphere he wanted for his image of the Earth as a loose stone (*eemis stane*) drifting through space. A. R. Orage cited an example of that very rhythm as being self-evidently ludicrous in effect. It occurred in a report by the London *Times*'s military correspondent of a ceremonial visit to the Fleet, beginning as follows: "When the grey grim forms of the King's Grand Fleet...." "There's a grand opening for you," said Orage: "diddi dum dum dum, diddi dum dum dum. It is like the prelude to a recitation by Mr. G. R. Sims."[3]

It is useful to know something about the principal dictionary which MacDiarmid drew upon for his Scots. Although not an efficient dictionary by modern standards, Jamieson's is a highly readable one. It is packed with illustrative material, much of it in verse, since the development of Scots prose was effectively aborted to facilitate the political absorption of Scotland by its greatly more powerful neighbour, England. Jamieson offers the browser an anthology in miniature of literary samples chosen to illustrate linguistic usage--appropriate fare for a writer like MacDiarmid belatedly endeavouring to enlarge his grasp of the language, an attenuated dialect of which was his own mother tongue, though the educational system had taught him to disparage it in deference to English. And Jamieson was by no means interested only in words. He was concerned with Scottish culture in a wide general sense. So that, for example, of the dozen quotations I mentioned above as having been used by MacDiarmid in his first piece of Scots prose, five are taken from what is from

---

3. A. R. Orage, *The Art of Reading* (New York: Farrar and Reinhart, 1930) 97.

the linguistic point of view a prolonged digression by Jamieson
on the old Scottish customs and celebrations associated with the
Abbot of Unreason or Lord of Misrule. The same general point
is illustrated by the following short poem:

Reid E'en	The Eve of Rood Day
Ilka hert an' hind are met	every hart
'Neath Arcturus gleamin' bonnie,	
Bien the nicht owre a' the warl'.	snug; all the world
Hey, nonny, nonny!	
But my hert sall meet nae maik	heart; no mate
This reid-e'en or ony.	any
Luve an' a' are left behind.	
--Hey, nonny, nonny!4	

Even such a simple lyric as this, with its mock Tudor English
refrain, owes its existence to a piece of little-known Scots folk
tradition in Jamieson. The *Reid E'en* referred to was the evening
prior to the *Reid Day* about the middle of September before
which the wheat was generally sown, and it was believed to be
the one night of the year when hart and hind met for copulation.
Jamieson adds a nice touch of pathos by noting that "if the
evening is cold, the hart is said to cry all the ensuing day"--which
is presumably what led MacDiarmid to specify that on this particular occasion the night was *bien* (with the basic sense of
"warm").

No one is likely to miss the pun on the word *hert*, sig-
nifying both the animal and the centre of human passion. Less
obvious is the function of the reference to Arcturus, which also
came from Jamieson. He quotes Pliny to the effect that "hinds
begin to goe to rut after the rising of the starre Arcturus, which
is much about the fifth of September."

The sexual reference has a special interest here,
because sex is an important aspect of experience which MacDi-
armid felt he was inhibited from expressing in English, but not in
Scots. This is one of the main factors behind his remark in 1923
that he had been struck by a *moral* resemblance between
Jamieson's *Dictionary* and James Joyce's recently published
*Ulysses.*5 He made a similar point in "Following Rebecca West in
Edinburgh" when he said that it would take a Scottish Joyce to

4. Hugh MacDiarmid, *The Complete Poems of Hugh MacDiarmid*, ed. Michael Grieve and W. R.
Aitken, 2 vols. (Harmondsworth: Penguin, 1985) 26. All subsequent references to the poems are from
this edition.
5. Hugh MacDiarmid, "A Theory of Scots Letters-I," *Scottish Chapbook*, 1, (1923): 183.

do justice to the seamier side of life there, and it could only be done in Scots.

In this connection there is a Scots word used several times by MacDiarmid that can only be elucidated properly by reference to Jamieson. The word is *nesh*, basically meaning "sensitive," which MacDiarmid uses with a specially sexual connotation, for example in his poem "Love." The point of the poem rests on the precise meaning he gives to this word in the closing lines: "Till clear and chitterin' and nesh/ Move a' the miseries o' his flesh."

When faced with the problem of putting *nesh* into English for the glossary of his collection *Penny Wheep*, in which "Love" appeared, MacDiarmid supplied the meaning "full of awareness"; and twenty years later, in a "literal rendering" of the poem for an American selection of his work, he translated as follows: "clear and quivering and raw move all the miseries of his flesh."[6] The associations of "rawness" make the sexual impact stronger in one sense. But it is still worth knowing that *nesh* acquired its particular sexual significance for him through the word *neeshin* in Jamieson, who sends one to *eassin* and *eisin* ("to be on heat sexually")--a word which the poet remarks on elsewhere as being specially potent because it suggests the primitive sense of smell which modern man has largely bowdlerised out of his language.

I want to deal now with a very different sort of example: a poem into which readers nowadays project a sexual meaning that I suspect was not intended:

Servant Girl's Bed

The talla spales	tallow (of candle) curls over
And the licht loups oot,	leaps out
Fegs, it's your ain creesh	faith!; fat, grease
Lassie, I doot,	fear, suspect
And the licht that reeled	
Loose on't a wee	short time
Was the bonny lowe	flame
O' Eternity.	

(CP 65)

Alexander Scott is in no doubt that this poem is to be understood in sexual terms: he puts it into the section entitled "Eros Exultant" of his anthology, *Scotch Passion*.[7] And Walter

6. Hugh MacDiarmid, *Speaking for Scotland* (Baltimore: Contemporary Poetry, 1946) 76.
7. Alexander Scott, *Scotch Passion* (London: Robert Hale, 1982).

Perrie has published a detailed reading of the poem in which he interprets the guttering of the candle as the ejaculation of semen, and says that the "protagonist" (as he sees the speaker of the poem) is "primarily interested not in the girl at all but in his own experience of being in bed with her." This "somewhat brutal approach" ends in post-coital depression, since *"omnia post coitum tristae sunt."*[8] Thus for Perrie also the poem is devoted to Eros, though no longer Exultant.

      Now, Perrie consulted Jamieson about the verb *reeled* in line 5, and came up with a meaning supplied for the noun: "violent or disorderly motion." This satisfied him presumably because the idea of violent motion seemed to accord with the brutal sexual activity he attributed to the "protagonist," though I am not convinced that the poet intended anything more than the unsteady movement he suggested elsewhere by the phrase "reelin' and imperfect licht."[9] But suppose Perrie had persevered in Jamieson as far as *spale*, and *deid-spale*, which is defined as follows:

> That part of the grease of a candle, which, from its not being melted, falls over the edge in a semicircular form; denominated from its resemblance to the shavings of wood. This, by the vulgar, is viewed as a prognostic that the person to whom it is turned will soon die. By the English it is called a *winding-sheet*.

Does this foreboding of death not suggest a satisfactory interpretation of the poem's imagery without any call to translate it into sexual terms? And is there no other likely reason for the poet in 1926 associating a candle with a servant girl's bed than Perrie's assumption that he would only think of such a scenario in terms of rampant phallicism? Maybe Eros was not only not Exultant but not present at the scene.

      Let me, however, invite him back for the next poem, "Scunner"--the meaning of the title-word to be discussed presently:

Your body derns	hides
In its graces again	
As the dreich grun' does	drab ground
In the gowden grain,	golden
And oot o' the daith	death
O' pride you rise	
Wi' beauty yet	

---

8. Walter Perrie, "Notes on a MacDiarmid Lyric," in *Out of Conflict* (Dunfermline: Borderline Press, 1982) 55-60.
9. See *A Drunk Man Looks at the Thistle* in MacDiarmid, *Complete Poems* 146.

For a hauf-disguise.   half-

The skinklan' stars   twinkling
Are but distant dirt.
Tho' fer owre near   far too
You are still--whiles--girt   sometimes
Wi' the bonnie licht
You bood ha'e tint   should have lost
--And I lo'e Love   love
Wi' a scunner in't.
(CP 64-65)

I do see the situation presented in this poem as a post-coital one, with the girl resuming a more romantic aura--and no doubt a more graceful posture--after suffering the "death of pride" in the gross animality of copulation. The second stanza is reminiscent of Heine's remark in *The Romantic School*: "It may be that the stars of heaven appear fair and pure simply because they are so far away from us, and we know nothing of their private life." But it is the crucial function of the word *scunner* in the poem that I want to draw attention to here.

Scunner is still a quite widely current Scots expression which in some people's usage has come to mean nothing much stronger than "irritation" or "boredom." Consulting Jamieson would provide them with a useful reminder of how strong its older meaning was, conveying a sense of "loathing, abhorrence" for which he quotes examples associated with actual spewing. MacDiarmid himself glossed the word as meaning "disgust" (which would be extended to "a shudder of disgust" in the last line), and one must accept this as being in his view the closest English equivalent available. An important distinction is made, however, by J. B. Montgomerie-Fleming in his *Desultory Notes on Jamieson's Dictionary*, which MacDiarmid is likely to have seen:

> "Disgust" is too strong. Scunner and Scumfish are two Scotch words illustrative of the benefit of maintaining the Scotch language, for their meaning cannot be expressed in English. "Disgust" implies something serious and permanent, not to be got over. "Scunner" implies only a sort of temporary disgust, that may pass away, or be got over.[10]

Now, the psychological point of MacDiarmid's poem is that an element which from one angle appears disgusting or repugnant

---

10. J. B. Montgomerie-Fleming, *Desultory Notes on Jamieson's Dictionary* (Glasgow: William Hodge, 1899) 134.

may from another angle prove to be the very element which gives its special savour to the human experience of sexual love. And *scunner* is exactly the right word for this. Even his feelings about the word itself--which incidentally he noted as being strongly onomatopoeic--may be taken as reflecting the ambivalent nature of the experience he wanted to convey. *Scunner* is typical of the sparse Scots vocabulary that survived in the speech of people taught by the established educational system to despise their native tongue as vulgar and uneducated. However successful the system was in persuading them that the only proper, educated language was English, they were liable to retain a sneaking affection for certain "disreputable" Scots words such as this one. And the resulting mixture of feelings about the word are highly appropriate to the mixture of feelings conveyed in the poem about the "disreputable" side of sexual experience--so much so that one can hardly conceive of the poem without the word.

To illustrate the more specific relevance of Jamieson to MacDiarmid, I shall quote a few more of his shortest poems and comment on them from that point of view.

Locked

The folk a' yammer that they've never seen	all clamour
A corpse thraw owt like thine;	twist in agony
But e'en alive ye were byordinar thrawn	extraordinarily obstinate
As we ken fine.	know very well
They've wide-flung ilka door and ilka drawer	every
But syne ye thraw like mad.	then
Nowt's lockit i' the hoose abies my hert.	except
--*Thraw on, my lad*!	

(CP 51)

For the opening of this poem, consider Jamieson's illustration of the word *yammering* by a quotation from Bellenden's *Historie and Cronikles of Scotland* (1536): "The hyllis, valis and lesuris [pastures] resoundit all the nicht with maist terribyl spraichis [screams] of yammeryng pepyll in the deith-thraw." And for the rest of the poem, here is Jamieson's comment on the *deith-thraw* or *deid-thraw*, the agonies of death:

> The superstition is pretty general in Scotland, that the soul of a dying person cannot escape from its prison, how severe soever the agonies of the patient, as long as anything remains locked in the

house. It is common, therefore, among those who give heed to such follies, to throw open drawers, chests, &c.

And he goes on to quote from Scott's *Guy Mannering*:

Wha ever heard of a door being barred when a man was in the dead-thraw? How d'ye think the spirit was to get awa' through bolts and bars like thae?

This suggests that the raw material of the poem was provided by Jamieson. What MacDiarmid does with it is to give it the form of a dramatic monologue which includes the sardonic comment that in this case the only thing remaining locked is the heart of the speaker.

There are also a couple of linguistic curiosities in the poem. Readers are liable to misread *owt* in the second line as meaning "out." It is actually a Southern Scots form of *ocht*, equivalent to "aught," "anything," "in any such way." (Cf. *nowt*, "nothing," in the penultimate line.) And *abies* does not normally mean "except," as rendered by MacDiarmid, but "in comparison with" or "in addition to." The *Scottish National Dictionary* (not available to MacDiarmid when he wrote these poems) notes that "except" "seems a recent extension" of the meaning, and MacDiarmid's is the earliest example of that usage recorded there. In fact, the only other example cited is from J. G. Horne in 1928, and he may well have picked it up from MacDiarmid, whose attribution of the meaning "except" to *abies* was perhaps the result of confusing it with the word *beis*, which has that meaning as noted by Jamieson.

Whip-The-World

Mountains and seas	
Birl under his wings	spin
Till a' gaes in a kink	all goes
O' skimmerin' rings.	twinkling
He lays on wi' his sang,	
The wullie wee chap,	sturdy
Till he gars earth bizz	makes (compels to); buzz
Like a dozened tap.	top spun so fast that its
	movement is hardly discernible
Syne he hings sidelins	hangs sideways
Watchin' hoo lang	
It tak's till it staggers	
Oot o' his sang.	

Aye it tak's langer,
And ane o' thae days   those
"I'll thraw't in a whirl
It'll bide in," he says.   stay

(CP 35)

The term "whip-the-world" is not in Jamieson or any other dictionary I have consulted. I think, however, that MacDiarmid probably invented it on the model of *Willie-Whip-The-Wind* in Jamieson. This was a Scots name for the kestrel, otherwise know as the *Wind-vanner*, the *Windcuffer* in Orkney, the *Windhover* of Hopkins's celebrated poem, and (until the seventeenth century in England, when they seem to have thought better of it) the *Windfucker*.

MacDiarmid's bird imagines that it whips the world into a spin not only with its wings but with its song. *Lays on*, in the 5th line, has the sense of "plies the lash," as though the song were a whip for a humming top.

The *kink* of line 3 is not, I think, just a "twist." *Gaes in a kink* retains a suggestion of the phrase *to gae in ae kink*, explained by Jamieson as meaning "to go off in a convulsive laugh."

Skimmering is a gem of a word for a poet to find. Not only does its sound simultaneously recall the English words "skimming" and "shimmering" but, as Jamieson explains, the Scots term actually possesses these two distinct senses. Applied to light, it means "flickering," and it also conveys the skimming movement of a swallow over the surface of smooth water.

While drawing attention to what the poet owed to Jamieson, I should not neglect to add that for MacDiarmid Scots was above all "a quarry of subtle and significant sound,"[11] which is not an aspect of words to which any particular attention is given in a non-pronouncing dictionary like Jamieson's. From the point of view of sound, the most potent words in the poem are *birl* and *whirl*, for which you need "a Scots tongue in your heid": they are what MacDiarmid called "shibboleths o' the Scots."

In MacDiarmid's first collection of Scots poems, *Sangschaw* (1925), there is a "suite" of four lyrics entitled "Au Clair de la Lune" which is prefaced with an epigraph from John MacTaggart's *Scottish Gallovidian Encyclopedia* (1824), via Jamieson: "She is yellow, / And yawps like a peany" (cries like a pea-hen or female turkey). This came from a poem by a writer

---

11. Hugh MacDiarmid, "A Theory of Scots Letters - II," *Scottish Chapbook*, 1, (1923): 210-11.

identified only as "The Miller o' Minnieive," and was directed at a woman whom he abhorred in every respect--a fact that Mac-Diarmid surely did not know, being acquainted only with the lines as quoted by Jamieson. Otherwise it is hard to believe that he would have applied these lines to the Moon as she appears in the poems that follow.

I. Prelude To Moon Music

Earth's littered wi' larochs o' Empires,	foundations of ruined buildings
Muckle nations are dust.	mighty
Time'll meissle it awa', it seems,	waste it imperceptibly away
An' smell nae must.	no
But wheesht!--Whatna music is this,	hush!; what sort of
While the win's haud their breath?	winds hold
--*The Moon has a wunnerfu' finger*	
For the back-lill o' Death!	hole at back of wind instrument

(CP 23-24)

The first stanza of this poem was produced by applying to the Earth and world history a saying quoted by Jamieson: "It is said of one with respect to his money, *He meisslit it awa, without smelling a must*; He wasted it, without doing any thing to purpose." Against this is juxtaposed, with startling effect, the image produced in the second stanza by applying to the Moon and Death a tribute to a piper quoted by Jamieson from Walter Scott's "Wandering Willie's Tale" (*Redgauntlet*): "He had the finest finger for the back-lill between Berwick and Carlisle."

In addition to his response to the metaphorical content of the saying about smelling no must, rendered so inadequately by Jamieson, MacDiarmid brings to the poem a characteristic slant whereby imagery with "hamely" vernacular associations is given a suggestively cosmic dimension. When this is combined with a fine ear for fresh and effective sound-patterns, the result is stylistically unmistakable MacDiarmid. But it remains a fact that the whole poem owes its existence to material which the poet encountered in the dictionary.

II. Moonstruck

When the warl's couped soon' as a peerie	sound asleep as a spinning top
That licht-lookin' craw o' a body, the moon,	crow of a person
Sits on the fower cross-win's	four
Peerin' a' roon'.	

She's seen me--she's seen me--an' straucht	straight away
Loupit clean on the quick o' my hert.	leapt
The quhither o' cauld gowd's fairly	touch of cold gold
Gi'en me a stert.	start

An' the roarin' o' oceans noo'	
Is peerieweerie to me:	tiny
Thunner's a tinklin' bell: an' Time	thunder
Whuds like a flee.	whisks; fly

(CP 24)

MacDiarmid commented on the first stanza of this poem as follows:

> Attempting a straight translation we get: "When the world is dozed like a top at the height of its spin, that light-looking crow of a creature, the moon, sits on the four cross-winds, peering all round." The line I have underlined is nonsense in English--light-looking and crow seeming a contradiction in terms, and crow a most inapt epithet to apply to the moon. I can find no passable equivalent for the phrase in English at all--no means of conveying its quality--but in Scots it is (if I may say so with all modesty) a marvellously effective description.[12]

Later--perhaps on reflection that even a Scots *craw* (or for that matter the *peany* of the epigraph) is not all that readily accommodated with the moon--he added:

> I can think of no English equivalent which can bring out, at once insubstantial and disreputable looking, radiant and yet dark with sinister influences.[13]

The "disreputable" quality he sees in it comes partly, I think, from *licht* in *licht-lookin'* having the same sort of moralistic cast that "loose" used to have when applied to a woman. (Cf. *licht-farrant*, meaning "flighty," "frivolous.")

MacDiarmid's source, however, was Jamieson, who found the word *peanerflee* ("one who has the appearance of lightness and activity") in the *Gallovidian Encyclopedia*, a loosely lexicographical work of notable loquacity, where, as Jamieson remarks, "it is oddly defined in these words: '*Peanerflee*, a light-looking craw o' a body.'" It is not surprising that Jamieson is so vague about the meaning of the expression, since MacTaggart says merely that it applies to "one like Auld Ned," a local worthy whose main distinction appears to have been his drinking

---

12. Hugh MacDiarmid, letter to M. Wollman, 20 July 1934, *The Letters of Hugh MacDiarmid*, ed. Alan Bold (London: Hamish Hamilton, 1984) 506.
13. Hugh MacDiarmid, Note. *A Treasury of Modern Poetry*, ed. R. L. Megroz (London: Pitman, 1936) 117.

prowess. (MacTaggart himself doesn't seem too sober to me.) If MacDiarmid's moon *yawps like a peany*, however, there may be some ground for comparing her with Auld Ned, who used to *scraich oot* his favourite song, quoted by MacTaggart as follows: *tarr ar a, tautra bubus, big bull waggie, bow, bow, bow*. *Peaner* is defined by MacTaggart (and hence Jamieson) as "a cold-looking, naked, trembling being--small of size." This may conceivably have put MacDiarmid in mind of *a quhither o' the cauld*. The *flee* in *peanerflee* duly turns up at the end of his poem.

Its starting-point was a quotation on the same page of Jamieson from Andrew Wilson (end of 18th century):

Auld Saunders begoud for to wink,	began
Syne couped as sound as a peerie	fell asleep in a sitting position

Again, MacDiarmid's characteristic twist is to translate the image from the context of a local worthy to that of the world in space.

Quhither (in the seventh line) is an older Scots spelling of *whither*. For over forty years the poet left the reader to make what he could of this word, as I have done in the gloss above. If, as is probable, it was MacDiarmid who then supplied the meaning "beam" for it in the glossary of the revised edition of his *Collected Poems* in 1967, he simply invented that meaning to suit himself. What he had actually encountered in Jamieson was the following: "*Quhidder*. A slight and transient indisposition, pronounced *quhither*; *a quhither of the cauld*, a slight cold."

Whuds in the last line is so much admired by Catherine Kerrigan that she singles it out as *the* example of MacDiarmid's ear for the right word--"a synthesis of sound and meaning."[14] Granted that one's response to sound-effects is bound to be subjective, I must say nevertheless that this instance seems to me a rare case of the poet having slipped up by using the wrong one of the alternatives offered by Jamieson: *quhid* (*whid*) or *whud*. It is to *quhid* that Jamieson gives the nominal sense of "a whisk, or quick motion, as the course or sweep of a fly"; and specifically on the matter of sound he says that the verb *quhid* is nearly allied to *quhidder* ("to whiz"), which is "used to denote the sound which is made by the motion of any object passing quickly through the air." When the object is in fact a fly, *whids* strikes me as clearly preferable to *whuds*, glossed by MacDiarmid himself as "dashes, thuds by, down, etc." and used

14. Kerrigan 64.

by him more appropriately for somewhat heavier creatures than flies:

> The West whuds doon
> Like the pigs at Gadara.
> ("Somersault")
> (CP 48)

But we must let that flee stick tae the wa'.[15]

III. The Man In The Moon

The moonbeams kelter i' the lift,	undulate; sky
An' Earth, the bare auld stane,	old stone
Glitters beneath the seas o' Space,	
White as a mammoth's bane.	bone

An', lifted owre the gowden wave,
Peers a dumfoun'ered Thocht,
Wi' keethin' sicht o' a' there is,
An' bodily sicht o' nocht.
(CP 24-25)

The metaphysical or at any rate extra-terrestrial suggestiveness of this little poem was conjured up by applying on a cosmic scale a distinction which Jamieson notes as being observed by fishermen:

> *Keething sight*, the view a fisher has of the motions of a salmon, by marks in the water, as distinguished from what they call a *bodily sight*.

The imagery of the "seas" of space is enhanced if MacDiarmid's glossing of *kelter* ("undulate") is expanded by reference to Jamieson, who adds that "eels are said to kelter in the water when they wamble." Another sense of the word is, he says, "to struggle violently, as a fish to release it self from the hook."

IV. The Huntress And Her Dogs

Her luchts o' yellow hair	locks
Flee oot ayont the storm,	beyond
Wi' mony a bonny flaught	flame
The colour o' Cairngorm.	a yellowish semi-precious stone

Oot owre the thunner-wa'	thunder-wall
She haiks her shinin' breists,	hoists
While th' oceans to her heels	

---

15. "To let that flee stick to the wa'" signifies "to say no more about that particular subject."

Slink in like bidden beasts.

So sall Earth's howlin' mobs	shall
Drap, lown, ahint the sang	hushed in the wake of
That frae the chaos o' Thocht	
In triumph braks or lang.	breaks ere long

(CP 25)

In the third line of the above poem, MacDiarmid's glossing of *flaught* as "flame" has sufficient support in Jamieson. However, it is *flaught* with the meaning of "a handful" that Jamieson illustrated by quoting the phrase from a ballad, "a flaught o' his yellow hair." This supplied a link with the first line of the poem, which also came from Jamieson in the form of a quotation from James Hogg's *Three Perils of Man*: "Wha ever saw young chields [men] hae sic luchts o' yellow hair hinging fleeing in the wind?"

It is appropriate enough that MacDiarmid should give his moon-goddess, Diana, the yellow hair featured so often in the traditional Scots ballads, since that is the colour he repeatedly associates with the moon in the poems of this period. It is also typical that the image triggering off the poem should have been encountered in Jamieson.

There are numerous other examples of this among MacDiarmid's short lyrics. The opening line of "Thunderstorm," "I'se warran' ye're rawn for the yirdin,' " is a quotation explained by Jamieson as meaning "I can pledge myself for it that you are afraid on account of the thunder." "There's no' a ressum to the fore," the first line of "The Currant Bush," is Jamieson's illustration of *ressum* ("a small fragment"), and MacDiarmid duly follows up Jamieson's suggestion that "the phrase may have been borrowed from a ruined house of which there was not a beam or wattle left standing." "Blind Man's Luck" is built on a phrase quoted by Jamieson from a historical drama, *Mary Stewart*: "O how he turn'd up the whites o' his een, like twa oon eggs" (eggs laid without shells). And the little poem "Morning" consists of a cosmic image formed from the definition of *paddle-doo* in Jamieson: "The frog that used to be kept among the cream (in the 'raim-bowie' or 'raim-pig' [cream-basin]) to preserve the luck."

Not that Jamieson was by any means the only lexicographical source used by the poet in this way. George Watson's *Roxburghshire Word-Book* (1923) supplied the phrase "a clud on the cantle [summit] o' Wheel-rig" which set MacDiarmid's poem

"Wheelrig" in motion. The poet built up the imagery of "Overinzievar" from words and phrases in Watson, with inventive touches of his own, such as *crottled* (from *crottle*, "a breadcrumb") and the neologism *dullery* (to supply a rhyme for the invaluable term *hullerie* ("with ruffled feathers"). The opening lines of "Ex Vermibus," with the imagery developed throughout the poem and most of its vocabulary, came from the same source. And this is true also of "The Sauchs in the Reuch Heuch Hauch," the opening line of which is a linguistic illustration which Watson got from the great lexicographer, James Murray, of the *Oxford English Dictionary*. It was not only the *sauchs* (willows) in that formidably-named field near Hawick that MacDiarmid acquired in turn from Watson. The image of the willows being "yoked in a whirligig" had the same provenance, though it was originally a foal that was thus yoked (in a poem by Andrew Scott, 1808).

But the crucial aspect of this last-mentioned poem is its *sound*, as is indicated by the fact that the original sentence supplied by Murray--"They're teuch sauchs growin' i' the Reuch Heuch Hauch"--was designed to illustrate the use of a particular variety of the velar fricative which is a distinctive feature of Scots but not English speech: another "shibboleth o' the Scots."[16] By a remarkable coincidence, it is also a near-perfect specimen of that same rhythm, scorned by Orage in English, which MacDiarmid used so effectively for the opening line of "The Eemis Stane."

Sound is of fundamental importance to the stylistic implications of what MacDiarmid described as his "conversion" to Scots from English. It is the aural appeal of his *tour de force*, "Water Music," for example, which triumphs over the extreme unfamiliarity to the reader of the vast majority of the words in the poem. Specifically, it is the poet's rhythmical verve which carries this off, rather than any use of colloquialisms and idioms which he heard around him, as posited by Dr. Kerrigan. However, there is one point in "Water Music" where something of that sort may be felt to come into operation. It is at a juncture where the streams of words emanating from Jamieson's dictionary--and easily looked up since so many of them begin with the same letters of the alphabet--are suddenly checked and there is a strong suggestion of direct, spontaneous reminiscence of boyhood memories. A change in stanza-form and the use of italics

16. I have discussed this aspect of MacDiarmid's poetry at length in "Shibboleths of the Scots," *Akros*, 12. 34-35 (1977): 233-47.

further encourage the reader to make a mental shift and take this as a vividly recalled experience from MacDiarmid's actual boyhood, expressed in the language he and his mates used then:

But a tow-gun frae the boon-tree,	pop-gun with tow wadding; elder tree
A whistle frae the elm,	
A spout-gun frae the hemlock,	pop-gun
And, back in this auld realm,	
Dry leafs o' dishielogie	tussilago (coltsfoot)
To smoke in a 'partan's tae'!	crab's claw

(CP 335)

This seems to me to work very successfully in the manner suggested--no doubt because in origin it was indeed a direct account of actual boyhood experience. But not MacDiarmid's:

The elder furnished a boon-tree gun or tow-gun, the elm a whistle, the hemlock a spoot-gun, while the brown, withered leaves of the tussilago or colt's-foot--"dishie-logie" it was called--were eagerly utilised as a substitute for tobacco, and smoked, "with diffeeculty," in a "partan's tae."

The above is a recollection by James Colville of his childhood in a Fifeshire village about the middle of the nineteenth century.[17]

Colville's book is not of course a dictionary, but it contains glossaries, and a great deal of his writing is in fact an elaboration of the lexicographical material which he indefatigably collected. Incidentally, I am reminded here of a fine passage of MacDiarmid's Scots prose in "Holie for Nags" where he recalls the names of various marbles he says he played with as a boy: "clay-davies, doolies, hard-hacks, mavies, cracksie-pigs, cullies."[18] One wonders if it is pure coincidence that these names had been collected from elsewhere in Scotland, along with another term used by MacDiarmid, *crancrums* ("things hard to be understood") and the name of the game "Holie for Nags" itself, in the word-lists published as *Transactions of the Scottish Dialect Committee* which were among the fore-runners of the *Scottish National Dictionary*.[19]

In a long passage in *To Circumjack Cencrastus* which leads to a list of children's games, another suggestion of nostalgic memories is reinforced by an echo of T. S. Eliot's lines in *Ash-Wednesday*:

17. James Colville, *Studies in Lowland Scots* (Edinburgh: William Green, 1909) 123.
18. Hugh MacDiarmid, "Holie for Nags," *Scots Observer* (22 Sept. 1928): 5.
19. *Transactions of the Scottish Dialect Committee*, Nos. 2 and 3 (Aberdeen: Bon-Accord Press, 1916 and 1919).

And the lost heart stiffens and rejoices
In the lost lilac and the lost sea voices.

MacDiarmid, however, is ostensibly rejecting such memories. (In the quotation which follows, words which are not glossed in the margin will be discussed below.)

                        I hear
        Its sailors like a sparrow's scaldachan

                        . . .

They micht as weel bide in the Islands whaur	stay
. . . fishermen can ha'e the undeemis stars	countless
Like scorlins roond their thowl-pins ilka nicht	
Or ony gudge look through his window-bole	
Past nettles, dockens, apple-ringie, heather reenge	
And think they're on his rizzar bushes there,	

                        . . .

My hert'll stiffen and rejoice nae mair	no more
In the lost lilac and the lost sea-voices,	
Whaup's cry or goose's gansel o' mankind	curlew's
. . . but haud	hold
The warld a photo o' me as a loon	boy
I canna mind o' haen been at a'	remember
A state I put awa' wi' spung-taed pranks	
Wi' nae precociousness.	
A state removed, as "Little Goodie" yet	
Nae doot'll dae awa' wi' a' the stars.	
For Nature's like grown men and wimmen thrang	busy
Wi' hi-spy, smuggle the geg, crawflee, and tig,	
Merry-my-tanzie, and beds o' Edinburgh.	
(CP 259-60)	

For the children's games, compare Colville:

There was the usual round of games--hi-spy, smuggle the gag (never geg), tig, craw-flee. . . . Girls chose the quieter sports of merry-my-tanzie, jing-ga-ring, or the ever-entertaining palall, the "beds" of Edinburgh, and the peevor . . . of Lanarkshire.[20]

That this was MacDiarmid's source is confirmed by his misreading of Colville. He took the name of the last-mentioned game to be "beds o' Edinburgh," whereas what Colville meant was that "beds" was what it was called in Edinburgh, "peevor" in Lanarkshire. It is a form of hopscotch, still commonly known as *peever*.

---

20. Colville 127.

Little Goodje is explained by Colville as "sun spurge," which was "plucked for its astringent, milky juice, infallible against warts." MacDiarmid supplied the reference to warts in a note, but neither he nor his source observed that the strange-looking name *Goodje* (transformed into *Goodie* in Colville's glossary) seems to come from "Goodyear," a name applied to the Devil, the plague, etc., in Shakespeare.

If one looks now at the above passage from the beginning, it will soon become apparent how useful it is to know of its source in Colville--not least because MacDiarmid seems to have forgotten the source, or failed to check it, when many years later he supplied glosses for some of his more out-of-the-way vocabulary.[21] For example, he glosses *scaldachan* (in the second line) as "chattering," but Colville gives its meaning as "unfeathered nestlings." The word was used in a poem, "Flory Loynachan," written in "a curious blend of Celtic and Saxon" such as was said to have been in common use in Campbeltown in the early nineteenth century, and glossed by a native of the place. *Scorlins* and *thowl-pins* came from the same poem. The first of these means "slimy, cord-like seaweed" (as MacDiarmid somewhat vaguely recalled), and the other (which he evidently forgot) means "rowlocks, oarlocks." *Gudge* MacDiarmid glossed as "a stupid fellow," though Colville had informed him that it was the Aberdeenshire word for a farm labourer--but that may have sprung from the animus against Aberdonians which the poet reveals elsewhere.[22]

MacDiarmid gives the meaning of *apple-ringie* as "wood-ruff" and leaves *heather reenge* unglossed, but there can be no doubt that he took these terms from Colville, who explains them in the following passage:

> The back walls of the houses . . . had their window-boles looking out on these silent neighbours through a screen of nettles, dock-ens, apple-reengie, and heather-reenge, as the fragrant southern-wood and showy hydrangea were called.

Colville refers to "rizzar (currant) bushes" a couple of pages later, but before that he has a description of the nearby beach which suggests why MacDiarmid was reminded of Eliot's "lost sea-voices" and linked them with the whaup's cry:

---

21. See Hugh MacDiarmid, *More Collected Poems* (London: MacGibbon and Kee, 1970) 24-25.
22. MacDiarmid resented criticism of his early Scots poems in the Aberdeen press. He retaliated against the Aberdonians in, for example, *A Drunk Man Looks at the Thistle* (*Complete Poems* 145).

> The swish of the white crests as they broke mingled with the moan
> of the bar when the turn of the ebb brought in the rush of billowy
> foam to hide the mussel scaups and lagoons, dear to the flounder
> and the heron, the mussel-picker and the whaup (Oyster-catcher
> and Greater Curlew).

Colville is useful, too, in correcting MacDiarmid's glossing of
gansel as "nonsense-talk" and in supplying the missing gloss for
spung-taed pranks. Gansel, he says, from being originally a garlic
sauce for goose, was used in his day only figuratively for a saucy
remark by a child. *Spung-taed pranks* he disowns in the following
passage about his boyhood in Fife:

> We never were Herods, such as the Border herd-boys with their
> "spung-hewet" or spung-taed (toad) pranks, which consisted in
> placing a frog or toad or young bird on one end of a stick balanced
> on a stone, then striking the other end smartly, so as to send the
> victim high up into the air, to fall neatly cleft in two.[23]

There are of course other Scots poems by MacDi-
armid of very much greater lexical difficulty than anything I have
looked at here. One of them is the long poem. "Scots Unbound,"
which contains passages of what he characterised as "an exercise
in delight in the Scots sense of colour."[24] However, it is not so
much colour that interests him but rather colour-words. He
pushes to the extreme a tendency which Havelock Ellis noted in
Keats:

> His colour-words are not epithets of colours he has seen; they are
> words that have appealed to his ear, that he has found in books
> and brooded over, vague exotic colour-words that no one would
> think of using in the presence of actual colour.[25]

The lengths to which MacDiarmid goes in this direction are well
beyond my scope here. In what space I have left, I would like to
comment on one passage in "Scots Unbound" where his interest
In colour-words leads him to what he sees as some of the ancestral roots of his language. (Again, difficulties in the passage
which are not glossed in the margin will be discussed below.)

Syne let's begin	then
If we're to dae richt by this auld leid	language
And by Scotland's kittle hues	tricky
To distinguish nicely 'twixt sparked and brocked,	
Blywest and chauve, brandit and brinked,	

23. Colville 123, 116, 113, 115, 65, 119, 121, 136, 125.
24. MacDiarmid, Footnote. (*Complete Poems* 458).
25. Havelock Ellis, "The Colour-Sense in Literature," *Contemporary Review* 69 (1896): 714-29.

And a' the dwaffil terms we'll need
    To ken and featly use,   fittingly
Sparrow-drift o' description, the ganandest gait,
Glaggwuba, ἀκριβῶς , to dae as we ocht,
Bring oot a' the backward tints that are linked
Frae purpie to wan in this couthless scene   purple; black; cold
    --You see what I mean!
English is owre cauld-casten-to
For the thochts that Scotland should gar us brew.   make
        Warth skura windis mikila,
        Withondans haubida seina.
        Trudan ufaro waurme.
        Krimi, carmine and crimson:
        κόκκος, cochineal, vermis, vermillon.
        Bestail, grains, vins, fruictz.
           Haithi, timrjan, thaurnus, blowans.
           Fani, hugs. Hwaiwa us siggis?
              Silence, come oot o' him!
              Keep oot, che vor' ye!
        (CP 340-41)

In the fifth line, *blywest* and *brinked* are examples of words the meaning of which Jamieson did not know but guessed. He supposed that *blywest* perhaps refers to colour, and may mean "the palest." And as for *brinked*, or rather *brinkit*, "if this be not, as Lord Hailes conjectures, an error of some transcriber for *bruikit*, it may signify bronzed, blackened with heat." MacDiarmid, however, implies that hidden behind such dubious meanings were fine distinctions conveyed by the original use of the words, somewhat as two of his other examples, *brocked* and *chauve*, indicate different patterns or gradations of black and white. *Sparked* is "spotted" and *brandit* is "reddish-brown, as if singed," according to Jamieson.

    I do not think that MacDiarmid uses his Dictionary Scots with much distinction here. He had some support in Jamieson for using *dwaffil* in the sense of "pliable," but the rendering "limp" or "feeble" might seem more appropriate to the poet's actual use of the terms which follow: *sparrow-drift* ("the smallest kind of shot") and *the ganandest gait* ("the shortest road, or the easiest to travel"). However, at least one of his finds provides him with a metaphor which he employs in a lively, epigrammatic way: "English is owre cauld-casten-to/ For the thochts that Scotland should gar us brew." *Brew* gives a clue to the meaning of *cauld-casten-to*, which metaphorically extends, in the sense of "lifeless, dull, insipid," a term used in the brewing of beer. "If the wort be *cauld casten to* the barm," says Jamieson, "i.e. if the wort be too cold when the yeast is put to it, fermentation does not take place, and the liquor of course is vapid." The beer is flat--and, in MacDiarmid's view, that is what happened when the Scots adopted English in place of their native tongue.

The link between Scots and the strange language which follows it in italics is suggested by the word *glaggwuba*. This is a Gothic ancestor of the Scots *glegly*, and MacDiarmid's inference is that if his countrymen were to revive their native roots they would express themselves *glegly*, in lively, acute, and (as the Greek word suggests) accurate language.

At this point I would ask the reader to recall the Scots word *whud*, used in "Moonstruck" (p. 12) where *whid* seemed to me to be preferable. Colville comments on *whid, whidding* as "expressing a rapid movement" and links it with the Gothic *hwithon*, "to shake." Now, the second of the italicised lines in the "Scots Unbound" passage, *Withondans haubida seina*, is Gothic for "wagging their heads," and the other mysterious expressions also come from Colville's discussion of the phonology of Gothic in relation to Scots. *Warth skura windis mikila* means "a muckle shoor of wind arose." *Trudan ufaro waurme* means "treading on serpents"; and it is from Colville's comments on *waurme* that the next lines were extracted:

> The word has its original sense of dragon, "monster of the prime," as in the Welsh cape, christened by the Norsemen Great Orme's Head. The original is *hwaurms*, which again is the Sanskrit krimi, and this, through early Arab traders, has given us carmine and crimson. Greek translated the Arabic *kermes* by κόκκος , hence our cochineal, the Romans by vermis, hence vermilion.

The line of French, from Rabelais, presents little difficulty (apart from the question of what it is doing there). For the Gothic words which follow, the relevant information is found in a passage where Colville says:

> It is possible to construct a Gothic landscape out of the words of that far away time, words perfectly intelligible still. . . . All round lies the open heath (*haithi*) and the woodland (timrjan, to build), with thorns (thaurnus) and wild flowers (blowans haithjos = lilies of the field) . . . deep in mire (fani, fen = mud). . . . In moist hollows one sees the fields (hugs, Scots haugh land).

Hwaiwa us siggis needs to be corrected to *siggwis*. (MacDiarmid's editors have not kept up their Gothic. Nor do they seem to be aware that the "Wufilic Gospel" appearing in a note to this phrase should be "Wulfilic.") The phrase itself means "How singest thou?" and is a curious translation of Christ's words in the synagogue at Nazareth: "What is written in the law? How readest thou?" Colville suggests that "singest" is an allusion to intoning the lessons. He goes on to quote Christ's words to the unclean spirit that possessed the poor man-- "Silence! come out of him"--and Edgar's bit of Somerset dialect in *King Lear*, "Keep out, *che vor' ye*" (meaning "I warn you"), which he relates to the Gothic *ik warja thuk*.[26]

So there it is: all crystal clear to Moeso-Gothic buffs or those who know their Colville. The rest of "Scots Unbound" is by no means so easily traversed. But readers who survive those Promethean heights should then be ready for the "Vision of World Language" which awaits them in the later MacDiarmid:

> We fumble along with partially bandaged eyes
> Our reindeer-skin kamiks worn into holes
> And no fresh sedge-grass to stump them with.
> We come on ice-fields like mammoth ploughlands
> And mountainous séracs which would puzzle an Alpine climber.
> That is what adventuring in dictionaries means,
> All the abysses and altitudes of the mind of man,
> Every test and trial of the spirit,
> Among the débris of all past literature
> And raw material of all the literature to be.[27]

---

26. Colville 32, 13, 14, 23, 27, 31, 38.
27. MacDiarmid, *In Memoriam James Joyce* (*Complete Poems* 823).

HARVEY OXENHORN

FROM SANGSCHAW TO "HARRY SEMEN": THE POET'S LANGUAGE AND THE POET'S VOICE

> The act of poetry is not an idea gradually
> shaping itself in words, but deriving entirely
> from words--and it was in fact in this way
> that I wrote all the best of my Scots poems.
> Hugh MacDiarmid, *Lucky Poet*

Hugh MacDiarmid's early Scots lyrics were written in part as demonstrations of a theory. In simplest terms, this theory held that Scottish writers could redeem and integrate what lay unrealized in their consciousness only by writing in their native tongue; that by doing so they would express certain values, and achieve effects, which were unobtainable in English; that the style thus forged by making precedents of lapsed traditions matched, in practice, the emerging modes of modern poetry.[1]

In addition to being demonstations of a theory, these lyrics are, of course, poems. This point is self-evident, but worth repeating for two reasons. First of all, although one must understand the language and context in order fully to appreciate these poems, in order to relate them to our own experience of more mainstream work we must stick primarily to the questions we would ask of *any* verse. These include: Does it move us? Is it beautiful? Does it have something necessary, interesting, and fresh to say--not just to those who share its cultural context, but to readers anywhere? Secondly, MacDiarmid himself pushed this experiment to its limit, and abandoned it a few years later. Thus, if we tie our responses to these poems too closely to polemical intentions (as this poet often asked us to), we'll be forced, each time those intentions change, into inconsistencies and special pleading.[2]

---

1. See C. M. Grieve, "Causerie," *Scottish Chapbook* 1.3 (Oct. 1922) and "Causerie," *Scottish Chapbook* 1.8 (March 1923).
2. This is especially true of comments on the long late poems, which often address the poetry itself less than what it "says," or MacDiarmid claims it says, or wants to say.

On the other hand, if we think less in terms of the language MacDiarmid used, and more about the way he used that language, we may learn how and why his voice outlived the idiom in which it was first expressed. We'll be better able to trace continuities throughout his work, and suggest what is common to the best of it, in either tongue, in any phase.

With that goal in mind, this essay will first discuss three "wee bit sangs" from *Penny Wheep* and *Sangschaw*. It will then look in depth at "Harry Semen" to explore how what flowered in the early lyrics bore fruit, ten years later, in a major poem.

II

Most of the poems in *Penny Wheep* and *Sangschaw* present an intimate human drama against the backdrop of indifferent nature. Typically, they begin with a clash of contrasts: unity and multiplicity; the humble and the cosmic; what is big with what is vulnerable, and small. Then they somehow reverse the conventional relationship of these paired terms, or deny the dichotomy altogether. Categories are confounded and transcended by means of lacunae, paradoxes, radical shifts of voice, chronology and scale, and through the evocative use of individual Scots words. MacDiarmid establishes this pattern right at the start, in *Sangschaw's* opening poem:

The Bonnie Broukit Bairn

Mars is braw in crammasy,	handsome; scarlet
Venus in a green silk goun,	
The auld mune shak's her gowden feathers,	golden
Their starry talk's a wheen o' blethers,	lot of nonsense
Nane for thee a thochtie sparin'	
Earth, thou bonnie brouki bairn!	dirt-streaked
--But greet, an' in your tears ye'll droun	weep
The haill clanjamfrie![3]	crowd

MacDiarmid here personifies the planets in order to distinguish "Earth" (i.e. human existence, with its needs and sorrows) from the beauty of a universe indifferent to those needs. In a sustained conceit, the earth is a neglected child; the rest of the cosmos, those proud old gossips who ignore it. At first, it is they

---

3. Hugh MacDiarmid, *Complete Poems*, ed. Michael Grieve and W. R. Aitken (London: Martin Brian and O'Keeffe, 1978) 17.

who demand and receive our attention. But then the kind of love a suffering child requires dispels our fascination with more distant matters, makes them seem trivial and vain.

So much for English paraphrase. The Scots poem owes its resonance less to an extractable idea than to the suggestive powers and music of its language. The poem opens on a note of mythic grandeur. "Crammasy" is an archaic word whose heraldic sound recalls the heroic past. "Venus in a green silk goun" maintains the tone of elevated allegory, yet lowers it slightly with a touch of homeliness. Then, the balladic "auld" mune adds further familiarity. This effects a transition from the first two lines, which seem urban, to the language of farm and bothie, where nature is a source of values. [Bothie--bunkhouse for farm servants.] "Starry" now becomes an ambivalent term, ascribing fatuous irrelevance to distant glamour. "Blethers" means idle prattle, nonsense. From third person descriptions the poem now jumps without warning to the second person singular. The effect of introducing an intimate pronoun before its antecedent is further heightened by the diminutive "thochtie" and the direct address to "Earth," which makes its name sound like a term of endearment. Then alliteration (as in nursery rhymes) completes the change of tone. Though we can translate "broukit" simply as "neglected," the Scots word principally means "streaked" or "soiled," and originally described the sooty kettles on peasant hearths. Nothing could be more removed from "crammasy"; that is why Earth must "greet."

But the very act of weeping possesses an immediacy and capacity for growth (reflected in the poem's only enjambed line) beside which conventional pride and inanimate beauty have less value. The Scots "clanjamfrie," meaning a mob or rabble, and "frequently used to denote the purse-proud vulgar," underscores the change in affections. Characteristically, the poem closes in an unanticipated outburst which at first seems to contradict what preceded, but on careful examination can be seen to have been inherent in it.

As a whole, "The Bonnie Broukit Bairn" suggests a reorientation of values, a progression from myth to nature, from the realm of literary gods and abstract aesthetic value to that of humane sympathy. On another level, it is a social-political statement which professes more interest in the neglected indigenous culture than in all the "starry talk" of Anglophile Scotland. Last, and most important, it is a poem that does not discuss, but rather demonstrates the right and wrong uses of language, embodying a growth from the diction of the opening, once serviceable but now stilted, into language which serves life.

A similar poem, "Empty Vessel," owes its effect less to Lallans words than to skillful adaptation of traditional verse rhythms. [Lallans--Scots, the language of Lowland Scotland.] Here again we have the cosmos and a child juxtaposed, and a radical shift of scale, only this time we start out small:

I met ayont the cairney	beyond; small cairn
A lass wi' tousie hair	tousled
Singin' till a bairnie	to
That was nae langer there.	

(CP 66)

These lines quote from "Saw Ye Jenny Nettles," a traditional song which begins:

I met ayont the Kairny
Jenny Nettles, Jenny Nettles
Singing till her bairny,
Robin Rattle's bastard . . .[4]

The original is almost all plot. MacDiarmid's first stanza contains two notable changes. For the proper name, he substitutes a physical description to enhance the realism and increase our sympathy. For the remainder of the traditional song (which portrays Jenny seeking out Robin and exhorting him to make an "honest woman" of her), MacDiarmid substitutes the simpler, more suggestive line, "That was nae langer there." Details are thus left to the reader's imagination. Stark treatment of the tragic intensifies our interest. Was the bairnie taken from her? Did it die, or has she abandoned it? All are possible, and each makes us want to find out more.

But the next stanza leaps unpredictably to this:

Wunds wi' warlds to swing	winds; worlds
Dinna sing sae sweet,	don't
The licht that bends owre a' thing	
Is less ta'en up wi't.	

As in "The Bonnie Broukit Bairn," the entire universe is suddenly juxtaposed to a minor human incident, and in comparison, found wanting. (Similarly, the phrase "tak up," which connotes church hymns as well as infatuation, may suggest that the mother's song is at least as sanctified as more formal

---

4. This song can be found in Ramsay's *Tea Table Miscellany* (1724) and was later included in David Herd's anthology as well.

worship.) The leap is audacious, signalled by a metric change from iambic to the stressed first syllable "wunds." It rests once again on the precise use of strong language. "Bends" equally describes a mother hovering over her child and what happens to the "licht ... owre a' thing" as it enters our atmosphere. The metrically staggered chiming sounds of "swing," "sing," and "thing" hold all parts of the poem in relation even as we learn what makes each unique.

Along with the rhythms of old Scots songs, MacDiarmid's strongest Lallans poems share something of their sensibility. As Edwin Muir noted, Scottish ballads in particular possess

> ... Terrific simplicity and intensity, an intensity which never loosens into reflection. There is nothing in the ballads but passion, terror, instinct, action: the states in which soul and body alike move most intensely; and this accounts for the impression of full and moving life which, stark and bare as they are, they leave with us. ... It is their absence of reflection which distinguishes them from English ballads. ...
>
> This sense of life and death, pleasure and sin, joy and loss, not thrown out lavishly but intensified to one point, to a breaking point where a flame springs forth: that is the sense which had inspired the greatest Scottish poetry.[5]

As a twentieth-century writer, MacDiarmid is more introspective than his folk antecedents. But his best short lyrics have that same stark volatility. In reading them one gains the sense of reticence barely containing tremendous feeling. Dignity and self-restraint intensify emotion; the effect is simultaneously passionate and austere. It can be felt most strongly in the best of the Lallans poems, "The Eemis Stane":

The Eemis Stane

I' the how-dumb-deid o' the cauld hairst nicht	dead middle; harvest
The warl' like an eemis stane	unsteady
Wags i' the lift;	sky
An' my eerie memories fa'	fall
Like a yowdendrift.	gale-driven snow
Like a yowdendrift so's I couldna read	could not
The words cut oot i' the stane	
Had the fug o' fame	moss
An' history's hazelraw	lichen

---

5. Edwin Muir, "A Note on the Scottish Ballads," *Latitudes* (1924; New York: Viking, 1972) 19, 17.

No' yirdit thaim.   buried them

(CP 27)

    The poem comprises some sort of hallucination and encompasses radical shifts of vision. Let us first establish, more or less, what is being described:

> The observer sees the earth like an unsteady, tottering stone, but is it a tombstone on which the record and significance of its own past are somehow inscribed, if only we could read the inscription, or is it more like a logan-stone whose very precariousness and seeming defiance of the laws of survival are its main attraction? The desire for knowledge and the appeal of strangeness, opposite as they are, are knit together. Subjectivity ('my eerie memories') as well as the apparently more objective comments of fame and history succeed only in adding layer upon layer of interposition on between us and the real.[6]

    As Edwin Morgan's comments indicate, this poem about the inaccessibility of meanings is itself remarkably resistant to analysis. Its power and (to my mind) nobility come from the way its diction and phrasing suggest countless secondary meanings without confirming any. First of all, there are the connotations of the Lallans words. "Eemis" (variable, uncertain), related to the Old Norse "ymiss" and Icelandic "yms," likens the world to a rocking-stone, a huge boulder borne along by the ice-sheet, to come to rest, at last, perilously poised on a hillslope. The resulting backdrop of extinct or vanished civilization prepares us, subconsciously, for the transformation of earth to tombstone five lines below. As George Bruce has written, the portentous Shakespearean sound swell of the first two lines is deflated instantly by the stressed verb, "wags." Once brought down to this human level, what follows can acquire dignity and mystery.[7] Even more remarkable is the way the opening long lines balance on the short line that begins with "wags"; the very structure of the verse is an image of what it describes.

    As a syntactic unit, "warl ... wags" is matched by "memories fa'." The verb sequence "wags-fa'" sticks in the mind, to imply, but not state, an equivalent fate for the two verbs' subjects. Successive pauses required by "lift" and "fa'" (whose broad "a" recreates the windy hush of a blizzard) liken the earth's situation in interstellar space to that of the speaker in (perhaps) a human graveyard. Then, the silence that both

---

6. Edwin Morgan, *Hugh MacDiarmid* (Harlow, Essex: Longman, 1976) 8.

7. George Bruce, "Between Any Life and the Sun," in *Hugh MacDiarmid: A Festschrift*, ed. K.D. Duval and Sidney Goodsir Smith (Edinburgh: K.D. Duval, 1962) 62.

inhabit is filled by the onomatopoeic "yowdendrift" in a phrase whose pitch falls like snow.

But immediately the same phrase is repeated on a rising pitch. Why? Because as it reaches our level the snow doesn't simply come to rest; it is picked up by the wind again, and then settled again in smooth piles of snow called "yirddrift." "This isn't just a fanciful comparison," MacDiarmid says, "I want you to think about the obliterating process."[8] The emotional effect of this sound swell is like that of resisting burial alive.

"Yowdendrift" is introduced in the first stanza as a simile for subjective memories. Now, when repeated, it becomes part of an actual setting in which new metaphors (for fame and history) arise. In like manner, the "stane" which previously described the world and its fate now becomes a tombstone marking man's own. That inscription might be like the laws God gave to Moses, perhaps, or the Logos, or "the word" in John. No matter; even if man weren't blinded by his own drifting memories, objective circumstance would thwart his understanding. The sense of doom is reinforced as the two alliterative pairings ring--like a chisel on stone.

In utilizing the language of a countryman, MacDiarmid risked throwing into high relief the sophisticated technical effects he favored. In poems like "The Eemis Stane" he solved this problem, paradoxically, by refining those techniques still more, to a point where they don't obtrude. Note how when line seven's "words . . . stane" echoes line two's "warl' . . . stane," the extra stress in "cut oot" suits the transition from drift into fixed doom. Similarly, in each stanza an assonantal end rhyme (nicht-lift, stane-fame) ossifies into standard masculine rhyme at the close.

Moreover, if one looks at the poem as a structure alone, one sees a progression from a very long opening line to short lines, to a moderately long line to a very short one. In dynamic terms, it moves *forte* to *piano* to *mezzo forte* to *pianissimo*. Metrically, one is forced to observe an *accelerando* at the start of each stanza; a *ritardando* in the middle. In meticulous modulation, "The Eemis Stane" sways, falls, drifts upward, and then settles, very slowly, down. The cosmic bang with which the poem begins becomes, in the end, a human whimper.

---

8. Morgan 8.

"The Eemis Stane" is clearly a more profound and accomplished poem than the others we've examined. I think that's because in this poem the poet is not just observing a piece of country life, the plight of others, but expressing, in images taken from it, his own condition. He is speaking not only for a "bairn" but almost *as* a bairn, for what's most vulnerable in himself.

In an essay from this period, MacDiarmid argued that "the value of Doric lies in the extent to which it contains lapsed or unrealized qualities which correspond to unconscious elements of distinctively Scottish psychology."[9] Reading the best Lallans lyrics, one senses that the wellspring of their feeling, and source of emotional integration, is indeed the language.

Is this because Lallans is the language of MacDiarmid's childhood? No. He himself explained that he found most of the words in dictionaries.[10] And as David Murison has demonstrated in detail, the language of the early poems is not spoken Langholm, but a hodgepodge of regional Scots, Norse, and literary sources.[11] Nevertheless, for our present purpose that's beside the point. We don't have to buy all MacDiarmid's claims for Scots to appreciate what it meant to him, and as a non-Scot in the 1980s I care less about Lallans *per se* than the imaginative use the artist made of it.

That language was MacDiarmid's *vehicle*. Whatever its intrinsic merits, the very process of reformulating it unearthed something dark and fertile in this poet's experience. Synthetic or not, Lallans helped him to forge a technique, lay claim to his cultural sources, and thereby discover his own voice.

*   *   *   *   *   *

In *Penny Wheep* and *Sangschaw* that voice has three technical hallmarks. First, there are the frequent images of slithering, teeming, quivering--of randomness--counterposed against those of whiteness, vastness, empty space, or stone. Second, there is the motif of a man alone (at night/in snow/on a hill/on a beach), firmly situated in a rural landscape, speaking directly to no one in particular. This motif will recur in nearly all of the

---

9. Grieve, "Causerie," *Scottish Chapbook* 1.3 (Oct. 1922): 62-63.
10. See Hugh MacDiarmid, *Lucky Poet: A Self-Study in Literature and Political Ideas* (London: Methuen, 1943) 84. Also, see a BBC broadcast quoted by Walter Keir in Duval and Smith 14.
11. David Murison, "The Language Problem in Hugh MacDiarmid's Work," *The Age of MacDiarmid*, ed. P. H. Scott and A. C. Davis (Edinburgh: Mainstream Publishers, 1980) 83-99.

most deeply felt and fully realized poems. Finally, there is the tight relationship of image and language. This verse has very little ornament; what images there are are relevant and spare. They achieve their effects not by argument, but through association and suggestion. Yet the language which allows this is itself deliberately unromantic and astringent; sculptural, strongly cadenced, and precise.

As with imagist verse of the time, this style's strengths comprise its limitations. Like Williams and Pound, MacDiarmid soon moved on to forms which allowed more extended statement. For him, this also meant a change of language and less reliance on lexical surprise. The question thus arises whether techniques derived from Lallans would translate, successfully, into conversational Scots, or Scots-inflected English.

I believe that they could and did. Were space available, I would pick up the thread with thirties poems such as "Whuchulls," "Milk-Wort and Bog-Cotton," "Charisma and My Relatives," "Water of Life," and "On the Ocean Floor."[12] As is, I will jump straight to where the method culminates in MacDiarmid's greatest poem.

III

"Harry Semen" was written in 1934, nine years after *Penny Wheep* and *Sangschaw*. It is written not in a print vernacular, Lallans, but rather in a blend of English and colloquial Scots such as any Scots speaker then (or now) might use. The full text is as follows:

Harry Semen

I ken these islands each inhabited
Forever by a single man
Livin' in his separate world as only
In dreams yet maist folk can.
Mine's like the moonwhite belly o' a hoo   dogfish
Seen in the water as a fisher draws in his line.
I canna land it nor can it ever brak awa'.
It never moves, yet seems a' movement in the brine;
A movin' picture o' the spasm frae which I was born,
It writhes again, and back to it I'm willy-nilly torn.

---

12. See Harvey Oxenhorn, "Water Music: Wordsworth, MacDiarmid and Frost," *Southern Review* 20.2 (April 1984): 265-78 for a discussion of the latter two poems.

A' men are similarly fixt; and the difference 'twixt
    The sae-ca'd sane and insane   so-called
Is that the latter whiles ha'e glimpses o't   sometimes; have; of it
    And the former nane.

Particle frae particle'll brak asunder,
Ilk ane o' them mair livid than the neist.   each one
A separate life?--incredible war o' equal lichts,
Nane o' them wi' ocht in common in the least.   aught
Nae threid o' a' the fabric o' my thocht
Is left alangside anither; a pack
O' leprous scuts o' weasles riddlin' a plaid   short erect tails
    Sic thrums could never mak'.   ravelled threads
Hoo mony shades o' white gaed curvin' owre   went
To yon blae centre o' her belly's flower?   blue
Milk-white, and dove-grey, wi' harebell veins.   Scottish bluebell
Ae scar in fair hair like the sun in sunlicht lay,   one only
And pelvic experience in a thin shadow line;
Thocht canna mairry thocht as sic saft shadows dae.   do

Grey ghastly commentaries on my puir life,
A' the sperm that's gane for naething rises up to damn
In sick-white onanism the single seed
Frae which in sheer irrelevance I cam.
What were the odds against me? Let me coont.
What worth am I to a' that micht ha'e been?
To a' the wasted slime I'm capable o'
Appeals this lurid emission, whirlin' lint-white and green.
Am I alane richt, solidified to life,   alone right
Disjoined frae a' this searin' like a white-het knife,
And vauntin' my alien accretions here,
Boastin' sanctions, purpose, sense the endless tide
I cam frae lacks--the tide I still sae often feed?
O bitter glitter; wet sheet and flowin' sea--and what beside?

Sae the bealin' continents lie upon the seas,   festering
    Sprawlin' in shapeless shapes a' airts,   in all directions
Like ony splash that ony man can mak'
    Frae his nose or throat or ither pairts,
Fantastic as ink through blottin'-paper rins.
But this is white, white like a flooerin' gean,   wild cherry
Passin' frae white to purer shades o' white,
Ivory, crystal, diamond, till nae difference is seen
Between its fairest blossoms and the stars
Or the clear sun they melt into,
And the wind mixes them amang each ither
Forever, hue upon still mair dazzlin' hue.

Sae Joseph may ha'e pondered; sae a snawstorm
Comes whirlin' in grey sheets frae the shadowy sky

And only in a sma' circle are the separate flakes seen.
White, whiter, they cross and recross as capricious they fly,
Mak' patterns on the grund and weave into wreaths,
Load the bare boughs, and find lodgements in corners frae
The scourin' wind that sends a snawstorm up frae the earth
To meet that frae the sky, till which is which nae man can say.
They melt in the waters. They fill the valleys. They scale the peaks.
There's a tinkle o' icicles. The topmaist summit shines oot.
Sae Joseph may ha'e pondered on the coiled fire in his seed,
The transformation in Mary, and seen Jesus tak' root.
                              (CP 483-85)

This poem embodies the perfection of techniques and culmination of thematic concerns we have noted in early poems. To see how these elements merge here, we may begin with technical matters.

"Harry Semen" is written in rhymed free verse stanzas, each consisting of three abcb quatrains, with a couplet inserted between the second and third.[13] Some stanzas (the second for instance) employ the truncated cut-lines of Habbie Simpson metres and much of Burns, whereas others are elliptical and Whitmanesque: "White, whiter, they cross and recross as capricious they fly." While the individual line lengths thus vary greatly--from four to eleven words--the rhyme scheme is regular. The resulting blend of loosely structured discourse and tightly woven form serves MacDiarmid well. From the start, the tone is uniquely MacDiarmid's own, yet the rhymes, analogies (such as "belly o' a hoo") and metre of the first stanza's final quatrain help keep that individual tone in contact with a representative voice; they place his complicated statement in an approachable, inviting context.

In the second stanza, the first four lines are again unmistakably MacDiarmid. Their hint of apocalypse and fear of fragmentation (reflected in a broken question and reversal) recall the middle section of *A Drunk Man Looks at the Thistle*:

Particle frae particle'll brak asunder,   break
Ilk ane o' them mair livid than the neist.   each one
A separate life?--incredible war o' equal lichts,
Nane o' them wi' ocht in common in the least.

Then the quatrain that follows again lowers the rhetoric, domesticates and humanizes the declamation:

---

13. Except for stanzas four and five, where the couplet is missing. I have not been able to locate the manuscript for this poem, but if it becomes available it may reveal whether the two couplets were somehow dropped, or simply never written.

> Nae threid o' a' the fabric o' my thocht
> Is left alangside anither; a pack
> O' leprous scuts o' weasels riddlin' a plaid
>   Sic thrums could never mak'.

Among the fine Scots words, "thrums" warrants special attention. Literally, "thrum" means "thread" and by extension a pervasive thread or streak in one's character. "Thrum" is also a technical term for the warp thread in the end of a loom, a shred or scrap of no value. Kin to weavers, the poet certainly would have known this usage, as well as its slang derivatives: "thrum cutter"--a derogatory name for weaver--and "thrum descent"--of lowly origin. To convey his marginality MacDiarmid reaches into the common language; the words which concede how he doesn't "fit" paradoxically reaffirm how he does.

In its next lines the poem asks:

> Hoo mony shades o' white gaed curvin' owre
> To yon blae centre o' her belly's flower?
> Milk-white, and dove-grey, wi' harebell veins.
> Ae scar in fair hair like the sun in sunlicht lay,
> And pelvic experience in a thin shadow line;
> Thocht canna mairry thocht as sic saft shadows dae.

The mystery here is not what is happening--the speaker is beginning to excite himself--but now this relates to what just preceded. True, there is the vaguest association of "her" belly with "the belly o' a hoo" in line five, and with his own, now presumably exposed. But by and large, the jump is inexplicable. What's going on? The connection may be deliberately obscure; perhaps the poet is having a small joke on those whose critical seriousness leads them to ask. He knows that the baffled reader will want to marry thought to thought, to "make sense" of this, yet mischievously leaves us baffled. Thus unaccounted for, the memory inaugurates a feeling of frustration and irrelevance, which expands in the following stanza:

> Grey ghastly commentaries on my puir life,
> A' the sperm that's gane for naething rises up to damn
> In sick-white onanism the single seed
> Frae which in sheer irrelevance I cam.
> What were the odds against me? Let me coont.
> What worth am I to a' that micht ha'e been?
> To a' the wasted slime I'm capable o'
> Appeals this lurid emission, whirlin' lint-white and green.
> Am I alane richt, solidified to life,
> Disjoined frae a' this searin' like a white-het knife,

> And vauntin' my alien accretions here,
> Boastin' sanctions, purpose, sense the endless tide
> I cam frae lacks--the tide I still sae often feed?
> O bitter glitter; wet sheet and flowin' sea--and what beside?

Two points should be made about this writing. First of all, let us not pretend to more shock, amusement, or disdain than we feel. Of course the speaker is masturbating as he thinks. The movement of the stanza as a whole expresses the act described, and those who admire the Nausicaa section of *Ulysses* need not quail at MacDiarmid's similar intention.[14]

Secondly, we need not project, as one critic does, "revulsion from the flux of living," and "desperate disgust at sexual experience, not resolved by the rationalizing and fleering humour that he brings in to handle the revulsion."[15] "Harry Semen" is not about sexuality *per se*. It is about creation and conception in the broadest sense, and uses sexual frustration to dramatize intellectual and spiritual waste.

We may most usefully approach the poem as one expression in a long line of others of MacDiarmid's fascination with necessity and probability, how spirit "solidifies" to flesh-- the relationship of what is to "what micht hae been" and to what might be. That question figures largely in *A Drunk Man*, and in "Kinsfolk," his most nearly confessional poem, where MacDiarmid says of his father:

> Gin he had lived my life and wark micht weel   if
> Ha' been entirely different, better or waur,   worse
> Or neither, comparison impossible.
> It wadna ha' been the same. That's hoo things are.
> (CP 1148)

Viewed in this light, the "irrelevance" from which Harry Semen "cam" does not connote self-hatred, just an admission that nothing in human experience--not even our own identity--has the logical inevitability we might wish to ascribe to it. The "odds against me" (my becoming *me*, as I've turned out) are of course incalculable, as are the odds that any particular sperm will achieve conception. By offering rhetorically to "coont" those odds, the speaker brings home the incapacity of such reckoning-- "sanctions, purpose, sense"--to provide the answers which we so desire.

---

14. The stanza's last line is a well-known schoolboy's sendup of a Victorian poem.
15. David Craig, *The Real Foundations: Literature and Social Change* (London: Chatto and Windus, 1973) 238.

In this regard we must bear in mind that the stanza just quoted constitutes only one step in a dramatic monologue which is moving *through* bafflement and solipsism toward some other resolution. Far from being merely "fleering humour," the multiple meanings of "marry," "rises up," and "coming" foreshadow that resolution, as shall be seen. By forcing himself, and the reader, to acknowledge the extent to which our personal realities are randomly determined, the poet prepares us to recognize and acknowledge still larger mysteries. The speaker next declares:

> Sae the bealin' continents lie upon the seas,
>> Sprawlin' in shapeless shapes a' airts,
> Like ony splash that ony man can mak'
>> Frae his nose or throat or ither pairts,
> Fantastic as ink through blottin'-paper rins.

By this point "Harry Semen" as a whole seems almost a compendium of favourite MacDiarmid devices first used in the lyrics: fish seen under water, "moon-white" bellies, imagery of weaving, sunlit erotic memories, slime, off-colour humour, the self as tide. While familiar, these are nevertheless interwoven with refreshing subtlety. For example, wasted sperm is described as "lint-white," the colour of flax and of sloughed-off waste fabric. Black ink in blotting-paper (waste words that won't be printed) is analogized with white sperm (blotted in a wet sheet) that won't achieve conception. And a continent's "shapeless shape" can only be described in terms of what it came to be, what "tides" have made it. In short, the poet's imagination is at full force.

Despite its paraphrasable content, we would be hard pressed, after forty-two lines, to say what this poem is "about." Its development appears to be essentially associative and random, its only logic the "logic" of imagination, leading where it will. But if this development is not ordered in the usual sense, neither is it uncontrolled. Images are not flung about with cacaphonous abandon, but gently introduced and folded into one another, like ingredients in self-rising batter. Despite the poem's constantly expanding scope, the speaker's tone remains, if not at ease, good-natured; his avuncular cosmology rubs off on us. The result is compelling, yet not threatening; within a "shapeless shape" the poem's evocative details are handled beautifully--paced, and yet primed to explode.

The "explosion" of meaning is prepared in the penultimate stanza's final lines, as all the preceding images begin to
cohere:

> But this is white, white like a flooerin' gean,
> Passin' frae white to purer shades o' white,
> Ivory, crystal, diamond, till nae difference is seen
> Between its fairest blossoms and the stars
> Or the clear sun they melt into,
> And the wind mixes them amang each ither
> Forever, hue upon still mair dazzlin' hue.

A word about "crystal": at various stages of his career, MacDiarmid's poems show an uncanny identification with particular
"elements" in the classical sense. In *First Hymn to Lenin and
Other Poems* and in *Scots Unbound,* nearly half the poems use
water to embody memory, movement, connection, change. In
Stony Limits ("I must get into this stone world now"), a half
dozen stone poems express isolation and finitude, and equate
explicit definitions with lost possibility. In "Harry Semen" we
find both the watery hope and stony fear in one representative
substance, clear as water, hard as stone--in crystal.[16]

Let us look at these last five lines again. Notice how,
with the introduction of this new imagery, the imaginative flow
itself now crystallizes. Each word, each stressed metrical unit--
ivory, crystal, diamond--lifts the vision and makes it more definite. Line endings that sound like closures one instant ("sun,"
"stars," "into") are immediately run-over, taken up in the line
that follows. The movement of this verse replicates that of wind-
blown crystals at the start of a snowfall. In the final stanza, this
becomes a veritable storm:

> Sae Joseph may ha'e pondered; sae a snawstorm
> Comes whirlin' in grey sheets frae the shadowy sky
> And only in a sma' circle are the separate flakes seen.
> White, whiter, they cross and recross as capricious they fly,
> Mak' patterns on the grund and weave into wreaths,
> Load the bare boughs, and find lodgements in corners frae
> The scourin' wind that sends a snawstorm up frae the earth
> To meet that frae the sky, till which is which nae man can say.
> They melt in the waters. They fill the valleys. They scale the peaks.
> There's a tinkle o' icicles. The topmaist summit shines oot.

---

16. Crystal appears increasingly in MacDiarmid's later visionary poems, such as "Crystals like Blood,"
"At Lenin's Tomb," "The Monument," "The Terrible Crystal," and "Diamond Body." Along with
passing references to the "poetry of knowledge," the last title suggests a possible interest and reading
in tantric buddhist sources--some worth looking into.

Sae Joseph may ha'e pondered on the coiled fire in his seed,
The transformation in Mary, and seen Jesus tak' root.

The power of this vision, the marvelous verse movement, the graceful introduction and repetition of "Sae Joseph" and the shining conclusion are all self-evident. Less apparent are two little words which unobtrusively determine that conclusion, and may reveal its full significance.

The first is "frae," i.e. "from." Throughout most of "Harry Semen's" first four stanzas, the word "frae" denotes a backward glance lamenting waste or separation, as in "the sperm frae which I was born"; "particle frae particle'll brak asunder"; "the seed frae which in sheer irrelevance I cam"; "disjoined frae a' this searin' "; "the endless tide I cam frae"; "the splash that ony man can mak' frae his nose" (etc.). However, with the onset of snow and whiteness in the fourth stanza, "frae" suddenly acquires the forward sense of progression--of "passin' frae white to purer shades o' white." And in the final stanza, where the word appears four times in eight lines, it begins to confound directions altogether; snow falls "frae" the sky, "frae" the wind, "frae" the earth, thereby blurring distinctions between hill and valley, ground and sky ... just as the Incarnation blurred distinctions between earth and heaven, man and God.

With the other little word, "sae" (or "so"), we seem at last on the verge of an explanation, or causal connection. But it does not materialize. What we get instead are two sets of implied correspondences for which we have not been consciously prepared.

The first set of correspondences is visual--between the "grey commentaries" of "whirlin' " seed and the snowstorm "whirlin' in grey sheets," between the alien accretions of sperm and the "capricious" accumulations of "separate flakes."[17] The second correspondence is linguistic--between the descent of snow and of Christ, whose advent also temporarily transfigured the visible world. Here the visual echo of a snowy Christmas morning is reinforced by connotative language. Flakes "cross and recross"; though akin to thrums, they are nevertheless woven into "wreaths"; they find "lodgement" on earth much as, in folklore, the Holy Family seeks lodging at the inn.[18] That god-

17. In her touring show called "U.S.A.," performance artist Laurie Anderson projects overlapping images of snow and sperm. Hearing the audience respond as she intones "Which one will make it?" one is tempted to cry out: "It's been done already ... fifty years before!"
18. Reminiscent of the "roofless ingles" which the snow seeks out in "Hymn to Dostoyevsky" in *A Drunk Man Looks at the Thistle*. In addition, the flooerin' gean (cherry tree) may recall the well-known

head should emerge in one humble child, crystallize, as it were, in one flake among all the countless and apparently meaningless millions, cannot be explained by the conventional union of Mary and Joseph, any more than thought can *marry* thought (stanza two) to explain the "coming" of Harry Semen. This inadequacy of literal, causal explanation brings with it a third correspondence. Any human child could have been made the Christ. If Christ came "randomly" as any snowflake in a storm, and snowflakes are analogous to blizzards of wasted sperm, then "Sae Joseph," forced to contemplate the coming of the one, may have "pondered" just like Harry, searching for the meaning of the other.

In the biblical account of Christ's birth, all that is specified about Joseph's feeling is his concern for Mary: "When she was found to be with child, her husband, being a just man and unwilling to put her to shame, resolved to divorce her quietly" (Matt. 1.19). Similarly, in their consuming interest for the virgin birth *per se*, most authors who have made use of it were (and are) concerned only with its divine protagonist(s). Hugh MacDiarmid is the only poet who comes to mind who addresses the Incarnation from Joseph's point of view, first in "O Wha's the Bride" from *A Drunk Man* and then here, in "Harry Semen."[19] Harry is the modern Joseph. Baffled, surrounded by improbable, indeed miraculous, events which he himself cannot determine or explain, he finds his own role limited, at best, to testimony. And yet, to look on in the proper spirit, to appreciate and strive to understand, *is* to participate in a fully human way. Such witness is ... sufficient. He accepts it. He does not find peace. He affirms by having seen.

This shift from imitation of Christ (as in "On a Raised Beach") to identification with Joseph links MacDiarmid's ripened recognition of the common life, and kinship, with his earliest, and truest voice. Significant for MacDiarmid personally, it has broader implications for modern poetry.

Hugh MacDiarmid was a declared atheist. He was also a deeply spiritual man. Like many of his contemporaries who had rejected the specific content of their parents' faith, he yet employed the Christology, its mythic and fictive power, to nourish the preternatural self, and sustain his hopes for the

ballad of that name, in which the cherry trees bow down their heads so that Joseph may gather fruit for Mary.
19. One does get Joseph's point of view in the medieval mystery cycles, and, though not about Joseph, Hardy's "The Oxen" and Yeats's "The Magi" voice similar concerns.

race's spiritual evolution. Re-imagining the Christ story from Joseph's point of view at once renounces doctrinal certitudes and restores the primitive sense of wonder. Compared to this, the "fire and rose" of Eliot, the *Anathemata* of David Jones, seem (to this reader's mind) cold compilations of ecclesiastic symbols; they predicate belief upon received, elaborate definitions.

By comparison, MacDiarmid's secular wonder is a manger faith. In "Harry Semen" he asserts no explanation, expects no arbitration, discounts no possibility. Looking "sae that nae difference is seen," he comes as close as a writer can to purging himself of preconceptions. The result is neither confessional nor impersonal, but *objective*: the cosmological vision of the early poems retained, yet tempered by social experience-- cleansed, for a little while, of crankiness, and pride--and fear.

IV

Looking back on his own career in 1967, MacDiarmid compared it to another poet's, noting that

> It took Heine years of agonised effort to find the form he needed, and his later work, in which he did find it, never won a measure of esteem like that secured by his early work. So it is in my case. But poems like "Wauchopside" and "Whuchulls" succeed, I believe, in realizing the sort of poem in Scots I wanted when I ceased to write the kind of short lyric on which my reputation was at first based.[20]

One difficulty faced by an American critic trying to broaden that reputation is that even the finest poems have many unfamiliar elements. These require much explanation, and in offering it one runs the risk of treating poetry as discourse. But that is precisely what poems like "Harry Semen" are *not*. They cannot be either "contradicted" or "agreed with." This is what separates them from more discursive work and connects them--imaginatively, with the late Scots verse MacDiarmid mentions; technically, with the early Lallans poems.

Earlier in this essay I identified three hallmarks of those poems: phono-, logo-, and melopoeic qualities which taken together reveal not just a style but a genuine and integrated voice. This is the voice of MacDiarmid's best poems, regardless of their language. It is, above all, a *lyric* voice. Used sparingly,

---

20. Hugh MacDiarmid, "Prefatory Note" in *A Lap of Honour* (London: MacGibbon & Kee, 1967) 11.

words act as a brake on his utterance, to refine emotion. Used suggestively, they become the source of memory and synthesis; words themselves embody the feeling they redeem.

By contrast, the synthesis in MacDiarmid's so-called "poetry of knowledge" is willed, not discovered. The poet is so intent on proclaiming truth that he forsakes the means by which he had best explored it. Reverting to non-colloquial diction, he forgets the lessons which Lallans taught about suggestion, music, and restraint, and thereby severs the roots of his own feeling. Whatever the intellectual interest of these writings--and it is in spots considerable--they do not succeed *as poems*.

Using the lyric voice as a touchstone thus requires us to reject what is false in much of MacDiarmid's writing. At the same time, we may realize that his *true* achievement is less discontinuous than we once believed. We may affirm that any poem's value lies not in a given set of words, but in the quality of feeling words give access to. And we'll know a little better why this poet, compared with his contemporaries, is most tender when most grand.

RENA GRANT

SYNTHETIC SCOTS:
HUGH MacDIARMID'S IMAGINED COMMUNITY

I wish I kent the physical basis	
O' a' life's seemin' airs and graces.	
It's queer the thochts a kittled cull	tickled testicle
Can lowse or splairgin' glit annul.	loosen; splattering slime
Man's spreit is wi' his ingangs twined	spirit; entrails
In ways that he can ne'er unwind.	
A wumman whiles a bawaw gi'es	scornful glance
That clean abaws him gin he sees.	abashes; if
Or wi' a movement o' a leg	
Shows'm his mind is juist a geg.	deception
I'se warrant Jean 'ud no' be lang	
In findin' whence this thistle sprang.	
Mebbe it's juist because I'm no'	
Beddit wi' her that gars it grow! . . .[1]	makes

Here and elsewhere in *A Drunk Man Looks at the Thistle* a woman confronts the protagonist as the interpreter of his imaginative work, an interpreter whose understanding of that work's object seems to be biologistic and reductive. The poem closes with the same gesture: the protagonist's apocalyptic (or utopian) "Yet ha'e I Silence left" is answered "'And weel ye micht;/Sae Jean'll say, 'efter sic a nicht!' '" It is not an unusual gesture, particularly for Scottish literature, which has represented woman in terms of a bathetic or abject "realism" as far back as Dunbar's "The Twa Mariit Wemen and the Wedo" and Henryson's *The Testament of Cresseid*. The direct allusion here, however, is to Burns's "Tam o' Shanter," where Kate, the wife waiting at home,

---

1. Michael Grieve and Alexander Scott, eds., *The Hugh MacDiarmid Anthology* (Boston: Routledge and Kegan Paul, 1972) 41. (All subsequent references to the poem are from this edition.)

represents a sober antagonist--and reader--who stands as a hinge between our common-sense disbelief in the poem's narrative and our involvement with its representations, and who mediates, as a "sensible" person caught up in the poem's nonsensical action, between the phantasmagoria of Tam's "adventure" and the narrator's distanced and "picturesque" retelling of it.

In *A Drunk Man*, however, there is no split between narrator and protagonist, and Jean, here, does not frame the poem by allowing an identification with her sensible behavior or by allowing the narrative to be placed as a quasi-anthropological tale of life and manners. MacDiarmid has burned his bridges with literary-critical authority and with what he describes as "sensible poetry"; indeed, in the "Introduction" to *A Drunk Man*, which is written in the high English that traditionally marks the Scots intellectual and that here must be taken as at least to some extent parodistic, he asserts that critics who are not used to drunkenness themselves will find his work incomprehensible.[2]

This apparently self-sabotaging gesture has its rationale, however: *A Drunk Man*, in resisting traditional and essentialistic concepts of the (national) subject, raises vital questions for twentieth-century Scottish culture. The central problem of *A Drunk Man* is its position as a national epic in a time when the valencies of nationalism are uneven and questionable, and for a country which has not been a nation-state since before the time when the concept of the nation-state arose, so that a poem can only very problematically "retrieve" the essentially Scots--and although many of the writers of the Scottish Renaissance, not least MacDiarmid himself, tried to do just this, the project is struck with inescapable contradictions.

Some of the contradictions arise just after the passage I quoted above. The evocation of Jean as the stereotype of the canny wife (an extremely common representation in Scottish literature, even to the "Chris Caledonia" of Gibbon's *A Scots Quair*) leads into one of the eeriest passages in modern British literature, and MacDiarmid's most celebrated and anthologized piece of writing:

---

2. Hugh MacDiarmid, *A Drunk Man Looks at the Thistle*, ed. John C. Weston (Boston: U of Massachusetts P, 1971).

   I use the term "high English" here rather than Standard English, Queen's English, BBC English, English English, Received Pronunciation, etc., because it seems to me to mark more clearly the class coding of language mode in the British Isles. The connotation of *high* as *rotten, evil-smelling*, is also in this context one which I enjoy.

O lass, wha see'est me
As I daur hardly see,   dare
I marvel that your bonny een   eyes
Are as they hadna' seen.

Through a' my self-respect
They see the truth abject
--Gin you could pierce their blindin' licht
You'd see a fouler sicht! . . .

O wha's the bride that cairries the bunch
O' thistles blinterin' white?   gleaming
Her cuckold bridegroom little dreids
What he sall ken this nicht.   shall know

For closer than gudeman can come   husband
And closer to'r than hersel',
Wha didna need her maidenheid
Has wrocht his purpose fell.

O wha's been here afore me, lass,
And hoo did he get in?   how
--A man that deed or I was born   died ere
This evil thing has din.   done

And left, as it were on a corpse,
Your maidenheid to me?
--Nae lass, gudeman, sin' Time began
'S hed ony mair to gi'e.

But I can gi'e ye kindness, lad,
And a pair o' willin' hands,
And you sall ha'e my breists like stars,
My limbs like willow wands,

And on my lips ye'll heed nae mair,
And in my hair forget,
The seed o' a' the men that in
My virgin womb ha'e met . . .
(41-42)

These verses seem to repeat the preceding passage's,
and *A Drunk Man's*, reduction of an eerie effect to a straightforward physicality, or to suggest a new physicality in terms of,
as Catherine Kerrigan puts it, "a vision of transcendence . . .
inseparable from material origins,"[3] but the two last stanzas
should, I think, be read as at least a little horrifying to the

---

3. Catherine Kerrigan, *Whaur Extremes Meet* (Edinburgh: Mercat Press, 1983) 127.

poem's protagonist, and as parallel to MacDiarmid's earlier poem "Scunner,"[4] where he questions (presumably male) desire by evoking disgust and boredom:

Your body derns	hides
In its graces again	
As the dreich grun' does	desolate
In the gowden grain	golden
And oot o' the daith	death
O' pride you rise	
Wi' beauty yet	
For a hauf-disguise.	
The skinklan' stars	gleaming
Are but distant dirt	
Tho' fer ower near	far too
You are still--whiles--girt	
Wi' the bonnie licht	
You bood ha'e tint	should; lost
--And I lo'e Love	love
Wi' a scunner in't.	in it

(14-15)

The trajectory of *A Drunk Man* is to suggest how desire, whether as sexual or as sublimated into imaginative or political enterprises, works against its own abjection; to ask what strategies one might use to speak from a place that, on the one hand, has been written as the picturesque (Scotland as the wretched object of eighteenth-century travel narratives and their literary descendants), and, on the other hand, has been claimed as laudably conformist (the paradigm of the "canny Scot," and the myth of the docile Scots worker).[5]

One of the problems of twentieth-century Scots culture, then, is that several hundred years on the margins of English society has made it fragmentary; the obvious discontinuity of *A Drunk Man*--its shifts in tone and its logical contradictions--is not, I think, only an effect of MacDiarmid's maverick personality, but on the one hand reflects the impossibility of presenting Scottishness as a coherent and singular identity; on the other hand this discontinuity is used in *A Drunk Man* to reevaluate the project of Scottish literature and to suggest a radically new concept of the aesthetic in its political context.

---

4. *Scunner* is a difficult word to gloss: it expresses both acute disgust and irritated or exhausted boredom. It can act either as noun or as verb (the adjectival form is *scunnert*).
5. For a valuable examination of this myth, see James D. Young, *The Rousing of the Scottish Working Class* (London: Croom Helm, 1979) 165-88.

By the beginning of the twentieth century, the Scottish literary tradition, under the pressure of an English hegemony which rendered it either invisible or merely supplementary to high literature, had split into two antithetical tendencies: that of the Kailyard (kitchen-garden) school of sentimental writing, and that which existed--often orally--in popular culture, most relevantly in the Bothy Ballads, songs sung by ploughmen and other itinerant farm laborers in the bothies (bunkhouses). Both of these traditions openly and unproblematically declared themselves to be parochial, simply naturalistic, and marginal or external to the high literary tradition. The Kailyard school produced several successful novels and plays--Barrie's *A Window in Thrums* and *The Little Minister* are paradigmatic--whose effects rely on a banal, winsome and exploitative portrayal of Scottish life and manners, usually set in small farming communities at the time of the narrator's extreme youth. The best efforts of the Kailyard school are those which perform their elegies to a vanishing culture without also attempting to make that culture sweetly amusing, and even then they scarcely rise above the level of individualistic nostalgia:

There was a sang;	
But noo, I canna mind it.	now; remember
There was a star;	
But noo, it disna shine.	does not
There was a luve that led me	love
Thro' the shadows--	
And it *was* mine.[6]	

The Bothy Ballads--which I will take here as paradigmatic of Scots popular culture because MacDiarmid uses them centrally--are mostly straightforward accounts of the experience of farming life, which rely on bawdy humor rather than pathos, but which make no claim to belong to the official literary canon: the most famous is probably "The Ball o' Kirriemuir," which is also current in the United States as "The Village Ball":

There were Campbells there and Camerons, MacDougalls and o'Rourkes	
Ye cudna see the barn flair for bottles wantin' corks	floor
Singin' fa'll dae it this time, *fa'll dae it noo*	who'll
The anes that did it last time canna dae it noo	

---

6. Helen Cruikshank, "There Was a Sang," *The Penguin Book of Scottish Verse*, ed. Tom Scott (London: Penguin Books, 1970) 427.

> Farmer Tamson he was there, and man he fairly grat   wept
> For his forty-acre corn field was fairly fuckit flat.[7]

These songs, however, were not considered acceptable in polite society, and, as with the work of the Kailyard school, their scope tends to be limited to the description of a marginalized culture. At best, they evoke this culture lucidly and effectively, but they fail to recognise the political pressures upon it and the reasons for its evanescence.

At the time when *A Drunk Man* was written, then, the Scottish literary tradition was blocked by its own acceptance of marginality, and while *A Drunk Man* explicitly aligns itself against such a stance, it also recognises its dominance:

> (To prove my saul is Scots I maun begin   must
> Wi' what's still deemed Scots and the folk expect,
> And spire up syne by visible degrees   soar; then
> To heichts whereo' the fules ha'e never recked.
>
> . . .

(23)

It is in its opening verses, however, that *A Drunk Man* most clearly enacts its difficult and overdetermined relation to its immediate literary precursors:

> I amna' fou' sae muckle as tired--died dune.   drunk; much; exhausted
> It's gey and hard wark' coupin' gless for gless   very; upending
> Wi' Cruivie and Gilsanquhar and the like,
> And I'm no' juist as bauld as aince I wes.
>
> The elbuck fankles in the coorse o' time,   elbow gets clumsy
> The sheckle's no' sae souple, and the thrapple   wrist; gullet
> Grows deef and dour: nae langer up and down   unimpressionable
> Gleg as a squirrel speils the Adam's apple.   lively; climbs
>
> Forbye, the stuffie's no' the real Mackay,   Besides
> The sun's sel' aince, as sune as ye began it,
> Riz in your vera saul: but what keeks in   rose; peeks
> Noo is in truth the vilest 'saxpenny planet.'
>
> And as the worth's gane doun the cost has risen.
> Yin canna throw the cockles o' yin's hert   one
> Wi' oot ha'en' cauld feet noo, jalousin' what   suspecting
> The wife'll say (I dinna blame her fur't).
>
> It's robbin' Peter to pey Paul at least . . .

---

7. A bowdlerized version of this song is printed in *Kerr's 'Bothy Ballads'*, ed. G.S. Morris (Glasgow: James S. Kerr, 1957).

And a' that's Scotch aboot it is the name,
Like a' thing else ca'd Scottish nooadays
--A' destitute o' speerit juist the same.
(23)

It is easy to recognise here the elegaic tone characteristic of the Kailyard school; but the allegorising of a fading imaginative power as the watering down of the whisky in modern Scots pubs recalls rather the content of the Bothy Ballads, and the play between these two traditions allows MacDiarmid to situate his own work with respect to both. To recuperate the nostalgia of the Kailyarders into a framework of boozy humor is to ridicule the former--while recognising its necessity--at the same time as it brings the latter into the realm of official literature and allows MacDiarmid to use both traditions within a broader framework.

What is also in question here is *A Drunk Man's* relation to its pre-nineteenth-century precursors in Scottish literature. The cultural marginality of the Kailyard school had been in part a consequence of the influence of the abject patriotic tradition that Tom Nairn allegorizes as the "tartan monster,"[8] and while *A Drunk Man* inescapably recognises its debt to this tradition, and particularly to "Tam o' Shanter," it also claims to exceed the limits of the Burns poem and to evade the latter's return to "normality":

'Noo Cutty Sark's tint that ana,   lost; and all
And dances in her skin--Ha! Ha!

I canna ride awa' like Tam,
But e'en maun bide juist where I am.   must stay

I canna ride--and gin I could,   if
I'd sune be sorry I hedna stood,

For less than a' there is to see
'll never be owre muckle for me.   too much

Cutty, gin you've mair to strip,
Aff wi't, lass--and let it rip!' ...
(49)

At the same time, however, as he worked out his relation to Burns, MacDiarmid also suggested that modern

---

8. See Part II of Chapter Two, Tom Nairn, *The Break-Up of Britain: Crisis and Neo-Nationalism* (London: New Left Books, 1977).
    Anyone who has been inside a Scottish gift shop in one of the major tourist sites need be in no doubt as to the nature of the Tartan Monster. Its voice resonates across Scottish culture even when produced for natives of Scotland.

Scots poets look for inspiration not to Burns but to the mediaeval makars, chiefly Dunbar and Henryson, and *A Drunk Man*'s
irreal style has antecedents in vision poems such as Dunbar's
"The Dance of the Sevin Deidly Synnis." Thus the poem's relation to its literary-historical context is doubled both diachroni-
cally and synchronically: its refusal of any continuous "sober"
meaning is not only a rejection of the reductive tendencies of
contemporary Scots writing (Kailyard or Bothy Ballad), but it is
also a comment on the more distant literary past (mediaeval or
romantic).

     If the Scottish literary tradition was fragmented by
the early twentieth century, however, the Scottish language was
no less so, and it will be useful here to consider MacDiarmid's
use of Synthetic Scots, a language drawn partly from experiential
knowledge and partly from contemporary and historical dictionaries. As a glance at any Scottish dictionary will show, the Scots
language, from centuries of disrepute as incorrect and non-
bourgeois discourse, has not been homogenized in the way that
English dialects have, and thus there are many Scots words
which in different parts of the country--or even locally--have
diverse and even antithetical meanings. MacDiarmid's use of
terms from different geographical and historical places, then,
results not only in a language that looks unfamiliar and uneven
to Scots as well as to others; it also enables him to play across a
wide range of sometimes contradictory meanings. Thus
"Synthetic Scots" is not simply an attempt to valorize the Scottish language in spite of the necessary inauthenticity of such a
project, nor, on the other hand, is it a personal invention of
MacDiarmid's; it is rather a strategy by which Scots (of all
kinds) can be remobilized to produce a new kind of poetic language whose characteristics are an effect of, and effect, the
political and ideological structure in which MacDiarmid's work
is situated.[9]

     One of the moments where MacDiarmid most inter-
estingly uses the diversity of meaning in Scots is in the call for
"Silence" at the end of *A Drunk Man*. This "Silence" is often
seen as an acknowledgement of the ineffability of the poetic
enterprise or of the collective Scottish identity for which Mac-

---

9. In this context, we may be a little suspicious of the frequent scenes in twentieth-century Scottish literature that describe the self-recognition of the Scot through an awakened understanding of the vernacular. I am thinking here, particularly, of the speech at Chris's wedding in Gibbon's *Sunset Song* and
of the scene in William MacIlvaney's *Docherty* where a schoolboy learns to differentiate between Scots
and English words. Such scenes are powerful and effective, but, I think, seriously idealist in their
assumptions about the Scottish language.

Diarmid strives to speak. Nancy Gish, in *Hugh MacDiarmid: The Man and his Work*, usefully points out that "Silence" "does not resolve the contradictions left at the end," but does assume that it "claims for the poet an inner fullness" which "no negation or limitation can touch."[10] I would suggest, however, that what is at work here is the assumption that a definitive assertion about Scottishness cannot be constructed from within a non-hegemonic tradition; and that this assumption works, here, even at the level of MacDiarmid's language. The line opens up a play of possible meanings that leave the poem's message complex and contradictory. "Yet ha'e I Silence left, the croon o' a' " carries at least four possible meanings: "a' " represents "all" probably as "every*thing*" but also possibly as "every*one*," whereas "croon" is both a Scots rendering of "crown" and, in its sense (also available in English) as an enunciation, is glossed by *Chambers Scots Dictionary* as "the lowing of cattle; a low murmuring sound; the purr of a cat; a mournful song, wail, lament." (As a verb, "croon" may also mean "to roar in a menacing tone like an angry bull" or "to use many words in a wheedling way.") "Silence," then, might here be, as "the crown of everything," the particularly Scottish imagination as an idealized and impossible object of hermeneutic investigation: but it might also be a collective voicing irrecuperable to the official literary tradition, whether as low murmur, as wail, as vociferous pathos, or as angry roar. Like the symbol of the thistle throughout *A Drunk Man*, "Silence" here carries not only ambiguous but multiple and contradictory meanings.

A Drunk Man insists, then, on placing itself in the double bind by which a nationalist epic can only very problematically be produced out of a marginalized culture whose aesthetic, or political, enterprises will tend to re-adopt a hegemonic form (as the antithesis of thistle and rose suggests). But it is not simply a question of subjective or creative alienation: *A Drunk Man* develops its contradictions to the point where meaning seems to be irreducibly multiple, where what is at stake is not only the difficulty of expression within a marginal culture but the necessary *dispersal* of meaning, in a culture which has not yet been rationalized by its accession to the power of the nation-state in its modern form. Without the availability of a Standard Scots (which Synthetic Scots in its *bricolage* is not) Scottish cul-

---

10. Nancy K. Gish, *Hugh MacDiarmid: The Man and His Work* (London: Macmillan, 1984) 89-93. This is perhaps the most comprehensive reading of the end of the poem.

ture can hardly find a place from which to reject (or accede to) an identification with its hegemonic "center" in Englishness.

The contradictory nature of *A Drunk Man*, however, has also been described as itself an essentially Scots characteristic: G. Gregory Smith's notion of the "Caledonian antizysygy,"[11] which he describes as a sudden shift of tone from the eerily sublime to the humorously everyday, has been evoked many times as a feature of MacDiarmid's work and of *A Drunk Man* in particular. Such a switching-effect is clearly present throughout the poem, and nowhere more clearly than in the shift between the canny wife and the eerie figures such as the bride and the "silken leddy." A discussion of the role of the Caledonian antizysygy in *A Drunk Man*'s representation of women, then, may lead us centrally into the question of how MacDiarmid negotiates his position as writer of a late nationalist epic.

It may be of use here to refer to Freud's pairing, in the essay "The Uncanny," of the words *heimlich* and *unheimlich*.[12] Freud points out that the closeness of these words suggests that an uncanny effect may arise when something that was once canny, or familiar, and which has been forgotten, reappears; and we may evoke here the disturbing or revolting return of the lover's beauty in "Scunner," as well as the return to an apparently traditional womanliness--"But I can gi'e ye kindness, lad"--at the close of the "Wha's the Bride" passage. If the "canny" figure of Jean, as representative of an essential everyday Scottishness, is being reread here as the once-forgotten, and now debased or alienated, object of desire, we may say that the poem, at the same time as it posits or "brings back" a Scottish identity, also reminds us that such an identity *can* only *re*appear, and then only as uncanny. The restitution of a "lost" Scottish nationalism is no longer viable: the processes of centering, ideologically and politically, that have made knowledge fragmentary for non-hegemonic countries, no longer express themselves in terms of, for example, Englishness against Scottishness. In the system of worldwide monopoly capitalism overwhelmingly dominated by the United States, it is simply no longer the case for a left Scottish nationalism that "England is our enemy." (This is well expressed by Ishbel Cruikshank when she says in the title poem of *Not for the English* that English people "have gone (necessarily) / From not being able to imagine violence /

---

11. See Chapter 1 in G. Gregory Smith, *Scottish Literature* (London: Macmillan, 1919).
12. Sigmund Freud, *The Complete Psychological Works*, trans. James Strachey (London: Hogarth Press, 1955) 17: 217-52.

To being unable to imagine anything, including, thankfully, /
Themselves."[13] England, in fact, is no more our enemy in these
days--however repulsive an ally it might be--than that other
repulsive ally, social-democratic sentimental Scottish separatism.

Within this structure, then, first world nationalisms
which attempt to begin by positing, for example, a unified and
comprehensible "Scottish subject" can only have a figurative, not
a material, reality. Scottish identity, like the Scots language, was
not ideologically centered at the time when such centering--
along with the rise of the bourgeoisie to power--was taking place
in other First World countries, and to attempt to reinvent a
homogenous Scots or Scot can thus, in the twentieth century,
only be a *synthetic* project, whether in the form of MacDiarmid's
dictionary Scots or in the form of the disjunctive and contradictory construction of *A Drunk Man*'s speaker.

Perhaps the most interesting aspect of *A Drunk Man*,
then, is its foregrounding of this difficulty, its re-mobilizing of
the contradictory aspects of Scottish culture whether in MacDiarmid's use of different literary traditions to play them off one
against another, his re-use of the stereotypical figure of the
drunken Scots poet to refuse to give the poem a common-sense
closure, or his manipulation of the shifts of tone recognized as
the Caledonian antizysygy to mark the impossibility of a linear
and coherent description of the essentially Scots.

What is also at stake, however, is that the central
stanzas of the "Wha's the Bride" passage raise questions which
traditional logic cannot resolve: and it is in this passage that *A
Drunk Man* is at its most complex in its attempt to synthesize an
aesthetic and a political project, or, perhaps more particularly,
to synthesize an aesthetic *with* a political project.

Perhaps the strangest thing about the "Wha's the
Bride" passage is that it sets forward a synchronic and
diachronic impossibility: the lost maidenhead (a familiar trope
from Scots popular culture) is also *not* lost, and, even more con-
fusingly, it was already lost before it could have been physically
present--"*A man that deed or I was born / This evil thing has
din.*" The hymen, then, is both broken and intact, and was
broken before the bride was born; what is in question is a clash
between the figuratively and the materially real, an insoluble--no
longer a merely antithetical--disjunction that goes beyond the

---

13. Ishbel Cruikshank, "Not for the English," *Not for the English* (Etterie Press, Dundee, 1935) 27-28.

terms of the Caledonian antizysygy and that recalls rather Freud's closing definition of the uncanny:

> ... an uncanny effect is often and easily produced when the distinction between imagination and reality is effaced, as when something that we have hitherto regarded as imaginary appears before us in reality, or when a symbol takes over the full functions of the thing it symbolizes ... (244)

This recognition of incommensurability within what appears to be only an antithetical shifting between two terms is characteristic of *A Drunk Man*; it may be worthwhile to quote here its most famous verse--

> I'll ha'e nae hauf-way hoose, but aye be whaur
> Extremes meet--it's the only way I ken   know
> To dodge the curst conceit o' bein' richt
> That damns the vast majority o' men.
>   (27)

This has often been taken as an expression of MacDiarmid's extravagant personality, or, more seriously, as delineating the complex nature of his concerns, as for example in his simultaneous commitment to Marxism and to Scottish nationalism. But what is central here is that there *is* no place where extremes meet--it is worth recalling the famous story of MacDiarmid's expulsion both from the Communist Party and from the Scottish Nationalist Party for his allegiance to nationalism and communism respectively--and thence that such a position can *only* be worked out "synthetically" or figuratively, and not practically.

In terms of the "Wha's the Bride" passage, the literal impossibility of the bride both having and not having her hymen intact cannot be thought without considering the structure by which woman is produced as functional to male authority and to the construction of male desire. If the social places of man and of woman are incommensurate, and if the commonplace by which the figure of woman is used as the object of imaginative extravagance or of nationalistic fervour is problematic, it is at least in part because all women have fathers, and in patriarchal society authority is constructed according to the role of the father. And in reading the "Wha's the Bride" passage, it might be useful to bear in mind the Freudian assumption that a daughter may be under the sway of the father's desire whether or not a sexual act has taken place. The woman here, then, may represent not only the phantasmagoric notion of a coherent people, but also the social necessity by which such phantasmagoria are neither innocent nor independent, but are submitted to the historical operation of power; "a man that deed or I was born" may represent, in the verses' allegorical context, the figurative but no less powerful authority of the dead father (and we should bear in mind, again, that in Freudian theory, not the real father, but the father as symbol of authority, the dead Oedipal father, is the basis of social organization). The problem, then, is that even before the play of identities takes place--even *before* the positing of an essential Scottishness--another authority has intervened such that the coherent description of an imaginative identity is not a feasible enterprise. We are fighting, then, not only against a contemporary hegemony but against the traces that that hegemony has left across our present imaginative capabilities.

But there is still more at work here. Scots for centuries has been contaminated by English; and MacDiarmid plays on the multiple meanings available in the language not only across the different usages that Scots itself puts forward but also across the *faux amis* that it echoes in Received Pronunciation. It is hard, then, not to hear in the line "A man that deed or I was born" the suggestion that *both* events could not have happened.

Thus, if the Scots reading of this line suggests a long-dead authority which has nevertheless contaminated the possibility of coherent essence to the point where it can only be "synthetically" reconstructed, the English reading is even more devastating. If we translate it into either "he died and I was not born" or "he did not die and I was born," we can read it as a testament to the weight of English upon Scots culture, whether as (in the latter case) the necessity of dealing with the English literary tradition or (in the former case) the claim that English culture is moribund but still constrains the Scottish tradition.

These are not merely precious readings of an inter-linguistic pun. If what is at stake is a discursive authority figured as patriarchal, then the question of a confrontation with this authority as "dead" or "alive" is quite real: should our strategy be to reject a decayed English tradition whose effects are primarily "figurative," which remains powerful only through the operation of our own cultural memories, or do we need to recognize that the English tradition survives and affects modes of Scottish writing in ways that we can *practically* counter? and if we cannot necessarily tell which of these issues is at stake, how can there be a place from which we still can speak?

MacDiarmid introduces the closing section of *A Drunk Man* by raising this problem:

> Hauf his soul a Scot maun use
> Indulgin' in illusions,
> And hauf in gettin rid o' them
> And comin' to conclusions
> Wi' the demoralisin' dearth
> O' onything worth while on Earth . . .
>   (93-94)

"I'm weary o' the rose as o' my brain," the narrator continues, and it is clear that within this framework the question of subjectivity has either to be ditched or to be radically reformulated.

But this beginning of the gesture towards "Silence" is even more complicated--because, historically, English hegemony over Scotland was not simply a question of the subjugation of the Scottish subject but also of its inclusion into the ventures of British imperialism in the eighteenth and nineteenth centuries; thus, if after the '45, for example, the rights of Highlanders to bear arms and to assert their cultural identity were violently suppressed, their traditions were also rewritten in the Scottish regiments which have become and remain infamous for their exploits abroad (not least in contemporary Ireland).[14] It must, then, be said that it is not only the case that Scottish culture and the Scots identity have been contaminated by English hegemony, or even (insofar as we can now know them) preceded by it; they have also been privileged by and collaborated in it at the expense of other peoples, in a way that would seem to write off Scottish nationalism as opportunism.

Within this context, "Silence," however collectivized and however external to the literary canon, begins to look disturbingly like a gesture of complicity. We can hardly complain, it seems, that our Muse has lost her innocence; it is our own collaboration with literary and political authority that is at stake. The hymen may be there, but it is there under someone else's power, and it is *our* construction of its meaning that has allowed it to confront us in this way. We should be asking, then, not what links MacDiarmid's fragmented phantasmagoria to the "sobriety" of everyday life--whether the latter is to be read as reductive biologism or as social necessity--but rather how (if at all) his work questions the privilege that grounds its imaginative possibility.

---

14. The Jacobite Rebellion of 1745 was a futile attempt at the restoration of the Stuart monarchy, and was (mis)led by Charles Stuart, the "Young Pretender." Its failure served as a(nother) pretext for the repression of the Highlanders, who had made up a large part of the Jacobite army, and whose semi-tribal social structure was incompatible with the development of an Anglo-Scots bourgeoisie in the Lowlands.

In any explicit way, it does not. Despite MacDiarmid's vaunted internationalism, the passage near the beginning of *A Drunk Man* which deals with Burns nights abroad recognizes only the degeneration of the Immortal Memory:

> You canna gang to a Burns supper even
> Wi'oot some wizened scrunt o' a knock-knee
> Chinee turns roon to say, 'Him Haggis--velly goot!'
> And ten to wan the piper is a Cockney.

No' wan in fifty kens a wurd Burns wrote	knows
But misapplied is a'body's property,	
And gin there was his like alive the day	today
They'd be the last a kennin' haund to gie--	knowing; give

Croose London Scotties wi' their braw shirt fronts	conceited
And a' their fancy freen's, rejoicin'	
That similah gatherings in Timbuctoo,	
Bagdad--and Hell, nae doot--are voicin'	

> Burns' sentiments o' universal love,
> In pidgin' English or in wild-fowl Scots,
> And toastin' ane wha's nocht to them but an
> Excuse for faitherin' Genius wi' *their* thochts.
>
> (24)

The overt racism of this passage masks any recognition that the observance of Burns Night in Timbuktu or Baghdad implies a Scottish presence that might not be a welcome one; and the comparison of Burns to Christ a few stanzas later has disturbing resonances in the context of British missionary enterprises under imperialist expansionism.[15]

The assumption that a regenerate Scottish culture could save the world is legion in MacDiarmid's work as in that of other Renaissance writers, and its idealism is clearest in the closing section of *A Drunk Man*:

Oor universe is like an e'e	eye
Turned in, man's benmaist hert to see,	inmost heart

15. In the 1850s the British showed considerable interest in gaining control over Timbuktu, but were in fact beaten to it by the French, who established the French Sudan in 1896 (by which time the city, which had been the center of the Muslim religion in West Africa, was more or less completely in ruins). In 1958 the French Sudan (now Mali) became an autonomous republic, and in 1960 it gained independence. It need hardly be pointed out that (non-Celtic) nationalism was an issue here.

Bagdad, the capital of Iraq, was occupied by Britain in 1915. In 1920 British troops put down a nationalist revolution, and by the Treaty of Sevres, in the same year, Iraq became a mandate of the League of Nations under British administration. In 1924 the Iraqi parliament, reluctantly, agreed to a treaty with Britain by which British military bases would be maintained and Britain would have the right to veto Iraqi legislation.

MacDiarmid, who prided himself on being *au courant* with world events in great detail, and on his support of struggles for freedom, was writing *A Drunk Man* in 1925.

And swamped in subjectivity.

But whether it can use its sicht
To bring what lies withoot to licht
To answer's still ayont my micht.   beyond

But when that inturned look has brocht
To licht what still in vain it's socht
Ootward maun be the bent o' thocht.   outward must

And organs may develop syne   then
Responsive to the need divine
O' single-minded humankin'.

The function, as it seems to me,
O' Poetry is to bring to be
At lang, lang last that unity . . .
                    (99)

But MacDiarmid is not alone in these assumptions. Scottish nationalism has for most of the twentieth century been miserably culturalist, and it is probably the case that such a move could not be avoided in the twentieth-century attempt to reinvent bourgeois nationalism as a radical political strategy. The notion of an individual and national subject is of only very questionable use under advanced monopoly capitalism, where the redivision of an already territorialized world is at stake, except (in this case) as the attempt to assume ideological continuity between ourselves and the nineteenth-century ancestors from whom we have inherited our privilege.[16] It is this contradiction that *A Drunk Man* over and over again encounters. What is most of interest in MacDiarmid's poem is its recognition that it *does* encounter contradiction--though it does not always seem to recognize the logic of it--and its refusal at least to rewrite it into a nineteenth-century paradigm. It is difficult to ask a poem not to be culturalist; and *A Drunk Man* at least exposes the contradictions that force it into that corner. And, at certain moments where the possibility of a Scottish literature arises, and where its synthesis is questioned, as in the "Wha's the Bride" passage, the effect is eerie enough to disturb our recuperation of the poem as a solution to the "commonsense" problems of everyday life.

---

16. This is not of course to say that such a notion might not be of great *strategic* use in developing a viable Left movement: but to examine seriously the potential strategic uses of nationalism is far beyond the scope of this paper; and even in the particular Scottish context, the potential network of strategic alliances, and of strategic factionalism, is too complex to go into here except in the most rarefied way. Suffice it (for the time being) to say that these are complexities, as I have tried to demonstrate, which resonate (indirectly) in the rhetorical and logical difficulties of MacDiarmid's work.

NANCY GISH

MacDIARMID READING THE WASTE LAND: *THE POLITICS OF QUOTATION*

The relations between Hugh MacDiarmid and T. S. Eliot present a telling configuration of the politics of literature. While their personal interaction emblematically represents the dynamics of center and margin (both geographically--London vs. Edinburgh--and linguistically--London dialect ["standard English"] vs. Scots), their writings on politics and literary theory define opposing conceptions of nationality and culture. Though "opposition" describes their positions, the wholly unbalanced acknowledgement of literary scholars and the seemingly one-sided nature of what MacDiarmid chose to call their "friendship" played out their relative positions in the political heirarchies of literary reputation. More importantly, they helped define "Modern poetry" as what Eliot wrote, excluding or dismissing the radical challenge of MacDiarmid's work. *A Drunk Man Looks at the Thistle* is, at least in part, a direct response to *The Waste Land* and to its political and cultural agenda. But MacDiarmid's poetic rereading of Eliot reveals itself in the context of contrasting theoretical texts and in the representations of their slight personal connection. Though Eliot was to publish two poems and an article of MacDiarmid's in the *Criterion*, his response to their few lunches and letters was limited to private and cautiously phrased praise of the Scots poems and *In Memoriam James Joyce*. Their public relations remained those of a struggling marginal writer and a powerful publisher; certainly Eliot, although he knew MacDiarmid's work and published three pieces, did not himself review or discuss it nor did he strongly promote it.[1] Yet MacDiarmid frequently praised Eliot's early poetry. He felt the need, moreover, recurrently to invoke their "friendship" at the same time that he persistently repudiated Eliot's views.

---

1. The details of Eliot's and MacDiarmid's connection have been described in two recent articles. See Robert Crawford, "A Drunk Man Looks at *The Waste Land*," *Scottish Literary Journal* 14.2 (1987) and Alan Riach, "T. S. Eliot and Hugh MacDiarmid," *The Literary Half-Yearly* 29.2 (1988).

I. THEORETICAL CONTEXTS

A Drunk Man Looks at the Thistle inscribes MacDiarmid's comple(i)ment to and correction of *The Waste Land*. Specifically naming, alluding to, parodying, and appropriating from *The Waste Land*, MacDiarmid used Eliot as a counterpoint for his own representation of Scotland's claim to language, literature, and European culture. This textual challenge from the margin problematizes Eliot's position as *the* innovative modern poet and as *the* cultural critic speaking for the center. It also calls into question MacDiarmid's equivocal place in British literature and in the development of Modernist poetry.

My purpose here is twofold: to contextualize MacDiarmid's "quotation" of *The Waste Land* within a broad but suppressed debate on the status of diverse British literatures and cultures, and to demonstrate both the techniques by which MacDiarmid's use of Eliot structured his own method and the subversive political purpose to which he put them.

Although MacDiarmid published *A Drunk Man* in 1926, he commented on *The Waste Land* frequently in the early 20s, and a 1922 poem, "Spring, a Violin in the Void," already parodied Eliot's work.[2] But MacDiarmid's poetic confrontation with the text he immediately recognized as a major break-through in *English* literature represented the demonstration of ideas previously developed in response to G. Gregory Smith's *Scottish Literature: Character and Influence*, which Eliot had reviewed in the *Athenaeum*. Moreover, both MacDiarmid and Eliot later reiterated and amplified their positions: MacDiarmid in "English Ascendancy in British Literature" (1932), published, significantly, in the *Criterion*, and Eliot in "Notes towards the Definition of Culture" (1948).

G. Gregory Smith's book argues two major points about Scottish literature: that it demonstrates, throughout Scottish history, certain recurring characteristics, and that while it has frequently borrowed from English literature, it has influenced both English and continental literature in its turn. The recurring characteristics are defined as a consistent piling up of realistic detail and a contrasting delight in the fantastic and grotesque. Scottish literature he calls a "zigzag of contradictions," a combination of opposites he labels the "Caledonian antisyzygy," the emphasis being on a constant

---

2. Both Robert Crawford and Alan Riach have commented on this early use of Eliot, although they fail to note its parodic qualities.

intermingling or a "sudden jostling of contraries." From this history of a distinct set of characteristics, Scottish literature became the major source of the Romantic movement which influenced all of Europe.

Reviewing Smith's book in the *Athenaeum*, Eliot begins: "We suppose that there is an English literature, and Professor Gregory Smith supposes that there is a Scotch literature." The confidence of Eliot's undefined "we" establishes his stance at the outset. And yet its very lack of definition establishes his peculiar and suppressed politics. Are "we" the English, of whom Eliot is not one? The educated, of whom G. Gregory Smith is presumably a member? The Arnoldian arbiters of taste and seriousness? The royal "we"? Who is infallibly able to recognize "a literature"? Eliot, undaunted, draws the line: "When we assume that a literature exists we assume a great deal," he continues, and a Scottish literature, he concludes, does not exist. Eliot's unquestioned place at the center could hardly be more aptly framed than by the broad acceptance of that "we." MacDiarmid, included neither in the "we" who make such determinations nor in the "we" who assume their simple validity, both shared and affirmed Smith's claim for a distinctly Scottish literary tradition; more important, he found in Smith's concept of the "Caledonian antisyzygy" the justification of his own call for a Scottish literary renaissance.

The "debate" sparked by G. Gregory Smith's book begins in a peculiar fusion of agreement and disconnection. MacDiarmid and Eliot share the view that a "culture" and a "literature" are grounded in a single language; they disagree over the status of Scots as a language. Yet in response to Smith they address his main contention from contradictory positions. For Eliot, Smith's claim for a distinct Scottish literature fails because it cannot show what he calls an "organic formation," that is a "corpus of writers in one language...between whom there is a tradition," which are "in the light of eternity contemporaneous," and which are part of a mind "which is a greater, finer, more positive, more comprehensive mind than the mind of any period."[3] Smith, having focused on distinctive "characteristics" of "Scottish literature"--rather than a consistently distinct language and "mind"--has therefore, in Eliot's view, failed to show a literature at all: "To the extent to which writing becomes literature," Eliot asserts, "these

---

3. T. S. Eliot, "Was There a Scottish Literature?," rev. of *Scottish Literature: Character and Influence*, by G. Gregory Smith, *Athenaeum* 1 Aug. 1919: 680.

peculiarities are likely to be submerged."[4] For MacDiarmid, the "Caledonian antisyzygy" provided precisely the necessary key to difference, since he wished to delineate specifically Scottish experiences and ways of feeling. Yet, sharing Eliot's commitment to writing "in one language," he joined the "Caledonian antisyzygy" with a concept of Scots as a storehouse of uniquely Scottish experience available for recuperation in an identifiably Scottish literature. He acknowledged that Scots had fragmented into many dialects, all with limited range. His solution was to write "Synthetic Scots," that is, a language composed of Scots words from any period or region fused into a renewed literary language of far greater range and flexibility than any single spoken version. A deliberate cultural construction, Synthetic Scots was intended both to regain the lexical range possible in Middle Scots and to articulate what MacDiarmid claimed as distinctively Scottish experience and feeling. It would thus make available, in the twentieth century, a means by which Scottish writers could begin to create a modern literature.

By Eliot's chosen standard, however, Scots itself is at issue: "We are quite at liberty to treat the Scots language as a dialect, as one of the several English dialects which gradually and inevitably amalgamated into one language."[5] It is worth noting that a Scot might feel "quite at liberty" to say the same of English as spoken in England--or more particularly--southern England. If "English" has now become a worldwide language of commerce (and this was by no means so true in 1919), it has not done so by "amalgamating" into a universal use of the English of educated Londoners. Americans and Australians do not consider their speech a "dialect," and the Irish Field Day movement is claiming a distinctive Irish form of English. Yet unlike these versions of "English," Scots can be traced back as far as the "English" of England and had a literary tradition centuries before America and Australia were settled. My point is that Eliot's "we" once again assumes its own normative status within a vast range of possibilities.

To establish an alternative subject position within this heterogeneous field of discourse, however, is to confront an inherent dilemma: whatever MacDiarmid might say of a Scottish language or literature is always already addressed and excluded

---

4. Eliot, "Was There a Scottish Literature?" 681.
5. Eliot, "Was There a Scottish Literature?" 681.

by Eliot's totalizing metaphor of an "organic formation."[6] MacDiarmid, then, found himself in need of a counter narrative to undermine Eliot's "we" and to challenge in its turn the assumption, in the language of England, of an evolved superiority that established its claim to be "the" literature of Britain. Writing in *The Scottish Chapbook* in 1922, MacDiarmid initiated such a narrative by claiming for the Scots Vernacular the capacity to express moods, feelings, and experiences inexpressible in "English" and defined by Smith's Caledonian antisyzygy: referring to Smith's claim that Scottish literature is characterized by an "antithesis of real and fantastic," a "mingling of the most eccentric kind," MacDiarmid fuses this notion of unique and recurrent traits with a notion of linguistic expressibility:

> Professor Gregory Smith has in this words [sic] described the great vital characteristic of Scottish literature--a distinguishing faculty, which it can only shape forth poorly in English, but which is potentially expressible in the Vernacular to which it belongs.[7]

He then takes a further step to claim not simply a distinctive and authentic language but a superior vehicle for certain modernist techniques in literature:

> We base our belief in the possibility of a great Scottish Literary Renaissance, deriving its strength from the resources that lie latent and almost unsuspected in the Vernacular, upon the fact that the genius of our Vernacular enables us to secure with comparative ease the very effects and swift transitions which other literatures are for the most part unsuccessfully endeavoring to cultivate in languages that have a very different and inferior bias.[8]

MacDiarmid would go on to argue in all forums that the very fact of having lapsed from daily and widespread use could give Scots words a distinctiveness and ability to defamiliarize no longer possible in a conventionalized and overworked English, that the capacity to mean many conflicting things at once gave to Scots words a compression and complexity comparatively unavailable in English, and that Scottish people shared kinds of feeling and perceptions for which no English words even exist. An obvious example is "yow-trummle," which MacDiarmid glossed as "the cold weather in July after the sheep-shearing,"

---

6. I wish to thank Lorrayne Carroll, who discussed this problem with me and pointed me to Gayatry Spivak's essay, "Can the Subaltern Speak?," which has influenced my thinking on the issue. See *Marxism and the Interpretation of Culture*, ed. Cary Nelson and Lawrence Crossberg (Champaign: U of Illinois P, 1988) 271- 313.
7. Hugh MacDiarmid, "Causerie," *The Scottish Chapbook* 1.7 (1922): 182.
8. MacDiarmid, "Causerie" 182.

and which is literally translatable as "ewe-tremble." But readers of MacDiarmid keep coming up against poems which turn on the peculiar, often complex or contradictory meanings of words like "keethin' sicht," "scunner," or "byspale."[9]

But more significant for his opposition to Eliot's conceptualization of language and culture was his argument for the sources of these differences. If Eliot grounded his denial of a Scottish literature on a posited abstract "European mind" of which an "English mind" was a part, MacDiarmid grounded his claim for a separate Scottish literature in history and concrete experience. Writing of George Reston Malloch, he anticipates the very claims Eliot would make:

> These cannot be expected to regard Malloch as really a Scottish poet any more than they regard Ben Jonson as a Scottish poet. They will say "He may be a Scotsman, but for all practical purposes his poetry is English poetry." They cannot be expected to appreciate the subtle spiritual differences which distinguish all that is Scottish from all that is English even where (often most acutely where) superficial appearances convey impressions of absolute identity. They forget that what distinguishes Scottish literature from English literature is not the use of the Doric, nor any difference in the selection of themes--but just that elusive but unmistakable "family resemblance"...[10]

This argument, drawn directly from Smith, insists on specifically Scottish experience, not the "use of the Doric" itself, as the ground of Scottish literature, rather than language. But MacDiarmid concurrently and consistently argued that such experience was fully expressible only in Scots; in the the body of his theoretical writing, the two claims become inseparable. Moreover, having thus affirmed Smith's definition of characteristic traits or "family resemblance" as the basis of a literature, MacDiarmid attributes these to the fact of a separate history: "...although the differences can hardly be appreciated without a comprehensive apprehension of the psychological histories of the two peoples."[11]

---

9. A "keethin' sicht" is "the view of the motion of a salmon, by marks in the water." It comes from "kythe," which is "to be manifest," "to come in sight." "Scunner," both a noun and a verb, is "loathing," "abomination," "a surfeit," and "the object of loathing," though it is now often used only to mean irritation or annoyance. As a verb it includes the meaning of causing disgust or loathing. "Byspale," which MacDiarmid uses to describe the infant Christ, means "a person or thing of rare or wonderful qualities; frequently used ironically," "a byword, a proverb," and "an illegitimate child." (Definitions are from Jamieson's *Dictionary of the Scottish Language*.) For an illuminating discussion of MacDiarmid's use of specific Scots words and the problem of English equivalents, readers should see Kenneth Buthlay's "Adventuring in Dictionaries" in this volume.
10. Hugh MacDiarmid, "Modern Scottish Bibliographies," *The Scottish Chapbook* 1.5 (1922): 142.
11. MacDiarmid, "Modern Scottish Bibliograpies" 142.

In other words--and this is the focus of disagreement--MacDiarmid saw in "Synthetic Scots" precisely that potential "one language" within which "a corpus of writers" "shared a tradition," not because it was uniform and constituted a single mind but because it constituted a broad range of cultural possibility in feeling and experience available to Scottish speakers but not available in the "English" language. The language question and the definition of literature are thus linked for both Eliot and MacDiarmid, but in quite different ways. Moral, personal, and spiritual differences, MacDiarmid argues, derive from "separate traditions...diverse destinies." Granting that Scots had lapsed as a literary language because of the domination of England, he argued for its genuine past tradition and its future potential, contained in recuperable, because historically grounded, differences and the "vast storehouse" of words in Jamieson's *Etymological Dictionary of the Scottish Language*.

For Eliot, Scots was a "dialect"; lacking a continuous existence as a separate literary language, it could not constitute the ground of a "mind of Scotland," and Scottish writing could therefore exist only as a subspecies of English literature. For MacDiarmid, Scots was a language lapsed in use and having "leeway" to make up, but having a capacity to express what can only be partially and clumsily approached in English. To move from Scots to English is precisely to translate--as it is to move from German or French--with all the diminution and displacement that implies. To lose Scots would be, indeed, to lose "Scottishness," which is not mere incidental quaintness but an inherently valuable difference, a unique way of living and feeling. As such, it is in fact the vehicle of a separate and distinctive "literature."

The fundamental theoretical basis for Eliot and MacDiarmid's mature positions on British literature(s) were thus already present in their work by 1922 when *The Waste Land* and "The Watergaw," (MacDiarmid's first Scots lyric) were published. By the 1930s and 1940s they had fully and explicitly developed these positions. Eliot's persistent validation of "tradition," defined by the "mind of Europe" and originating in Greek and Latin literature, became identified with the upholding of Christianity as the single Western philosophy capable and worthy of sustaining "civilization." Given this increasing commitment to an overarching scheme in which all Western forms of culture participate, the function and value of "regional literature" becomes both more problematic and more necessary to incorporate for the common good. Indeed, a full chapter in "Notes towards the Definition of Culture" is devoted to placing (putting in its place) "the region." While this lengthy analysis appears late in his work (1948), his criticism of the 20s and 30s--in its focus on constructing a canon of "great" writers who are inheritors of the Greek and Roman legacy and contributors to "tradition" prepares the way. In 1932, for example, the year of "English Ascendancy in British Literature," Eliot argued in "Modern Education and the Classics" that "...the defence of the Classics should be...permanently associated where they belong, with something permanent: the historical Christian Faith."[12] "Regional literature" can then be seen, in one sense, as merely imitative or idiosyncratic, outside the realm of authentic literary value.

Yet Eliot recognized "the region" as a concept he wished to save from ridicule as inevitably an absurd lost cause or comic attachment to defunct languages. He wished, rather, to demonstrate its proper location within what he viewed as the universal and timeless Western tradition. He did so by seeking to demonstrate the region's "absolute" value in sustaining a "characteristic culture" in each area; such a "characteristic culture" allows each "region," on the one hand, to play a role in the world via its link with what Eliot calls one of the "greater peoples."

In "Notes towards the Definition of Culture" Eliot divided non-English literatures into other genuine "organic formations," French or German, for example, within the larger "mind" of Europe (whatever that was) and "satellite" literatures --such as Irish, Scottish, or Welsh--whose value lay in their contribution to the central and primary literature of England. The importance of Welsh poetry, say, lay in the "contribution" Welsh writers in English could make to poetry and to English poetry. The value of Welsh poetry in Welsh lay in sustaining a way of thinking and feeling that is distinctive *so that* it may bring fresh material and feeling to writers in English. Welsh literature in Welsh is, in itself, of no importance to the "world at large."[13] Eliot's definitions make clear that literary value is based in economic and political power, for "the unmistakable *satellite* culture is one which preserves its language, but which is so

---

12. T. S. Eliot, "Modern Education and the Classics," *Selected Essays* (New York: Harcourt, Brace & World, 1964) 459.
13. T. S. Eliot, "Notes Towards the Definition of Culture," *Christianity and Culture* (1949; New York: Harcourt, Brace & World, 1960) 130.

closely associated with, and dependent upon, another, that not only certain classes of the population, but all of them, have to be bi-lingual." Since the English have no need or reason to learn Welsh, literature in that language is not judged by any intrinsic aesthetic standard; rather it becomes part of an "ecology of cultures" whose benefits are not mutually equivalent but are necessary. Without such an "ecology," Eliot argues, "complete uniformity of culture throughout these islands would bring about a lower grade of culture altogether."[14] Eliot's concept of "satellite" cultures and an "ecology of cultures" defines the place of British literatures other than English as both subsidiary and subsidizing. That is, they are, on the one hand, auxiliary and subordinate, and on the other, useful, even commendable, sources of tribute, metaphoric hostages to provide ever fresh funds of cultural possibility.

At times the notion of the relations between regions in a larger group appears a mutual interaction, a "constellation of cultures, the constitution of which, benefiting each other, benefit the whole."[15] Yet the hierarchical structure of this "constellation" is explicit throughout. England, for example, is not itself a "region," or at any rate "the Englishman...does not ordinarily think of England as a 'region,'" and hence may imagine that [his] interests lie in homogenization of culture. But in asserting that the issue must therefore be generalized, Eliot consistently argues for the English appropriation of regional culture as sources of varied influence for England. Just as England is not perceived as a "region," Englishness is not a source of "racial character" existing to enrich the Scots, Irish, or Welsh, nor does it need defense:

> I am not concerned, in an essay which aims at least at the merit of brevity, to defend the thesis, that it is desirable that the English should continue to be English. I am obliged to take that for granted. . . .[16]

It is not at all clear why this obligation is self-evident. The persistent assymetry between England and the "regions" of Britain finds its most telling expression in a repeated analogy of regions with class: "I now suggest that both class and region, by dividing the inhabitants of a country into two different kinds of groups, lead to a conflict favourable to creativeness and

---

14. Eliot, "Notes" 131.
15. Eliot, "Notes" 132.
16. Eliot, "Notes" 131.

progress."[17] The mutuality of "benefit," between regions as between classes, is expressly based in dominant and subordinate groups and an inequality of value, in which lower groups offer services to higher ones.

Yet Eliot's analysis remains an issue of language, for his definition of a "satellite" culture is based in the preservation of its language (Gaelic in Ireland, Wales, and the Highlands of Scotland, and presumably "dialect" difference in the Lowlands of Scotland). It is the preservation of language which maintains a distinct "racial character" individual enough to subsidize or "contribute" to the ostensibly rich fusion which is "English" literature and which remains the literature of England.

Ironically, at this point Eliot and MacDiarmid coincide, for it is the "vast resources" latent in the Vernacular which constitute for MacDiarmid that Scottishness Eliot too would preserve. MacDiarmid's most vivid and combative articulation of this position is the now well known statement about Jamieson's *Dictionary*:

> We have been enormously struck by the resemblance--the moral resemblance--between Jamieson's Etymological Dictionary of the Scottish language and James Joyce's *Ulysses*. A *vis comica* that has not been liberated lies bound by desuetude and misappreciation in the recesses of the Doric: and its potential uprising would be no less prodigious, uncontrollable, and utterly at variance with conventional morality than was Joyce's tremendous outpouring. The Scottish instinct is irrevocably, continuously opposed to all who "are at ease in Zion." It lacks entirely the English sense of "the majesty of true corpulence."[18]

Allying the Scots and Irish, MacDiarmid sets them together against the English as the revolutionary and new in language and culture against the conventional and complacent. More important, like Eliot he locates "Scottishness" within language, but he sees Scots as a vast source of value *for Scotland* and for ways of being and thinking in the world which have intrinsic and opposing rather than contributory value.

The necessity of sustaining distinctive cultures in order to allow and nourish difference--and for the Celtic countries, therefore, the resistance to English linguistic hegemony--is a running argument throughout MacDiarmid's work, at times extreme and polemical, at times carefully argued, at times assumed, and at times contradictory. I am focusing on

---

17. Eliot, "Notes" 132.
18. Hugh MacDiarmid, "Causerie" 183.

"English Ascendancy in British Literature" because it seems to me the most focused and thorough argument against Eliot's concept of regions and regional literature. Though written in 1932, well before "Notes towards the Definition of Culture," it could have been a direct response; it may well have been a catalyst. Certainly it formed a part of the discussion to which Eliot intended to contribute, and it was the version of his position MacDiarmid chose to publish in England.

In "English Ascendancy in British Literature" MacDiarmid argues for a fundamentally opposite conception of cultural and literary relations within Britain, a conception based in "complementarity" and "correction" among equally genuine "literatures." MacDiarmid's conceptions of complementarity and correction are aimed specifically at countering the notion of subsidizing or tributary "contributions" of "lesser" to "greater" peoples, a point he establishes at the outset:

> Burns knew what he was doing when he reverted from eighteenth century English to a species of synthetic Scots and was abundantly justified in the result. He was not contributing to English literature, but to a clearly defined and quite independent tradition of Scottish poetry hailing from the days of Dunbar and the other great fifteenth century 'makars'. . . .[19]

He attacks, moreover, precisely the assumptions on which Eliot was later to take his stand--the status of Greek and Roman "classics," the hierarchical relations between British countries, the assymetry of "contributions" and values, and the superiority of English as a literary medium. Referring to the "classical" Gaelic tradition, he claims it has had for at least two thousand years "an alternative value of prime consequence when set against the Greek and Roman literatures." He then questions the meaning of its suppression:

> One may well speculate what the results to-day would have been if this great literature, instead of being virtually proscribed by the 'English Ascendancy' policy and practically forgotten, had been concurrently maintained with the development of 'English Literature.' Would such a synthesis or duality of creative output (each element of it so different that they could have complemented and 'corrected' each other in a unique and invaluable fashion) not have been infinitely better than the sorry imperialism which has thrust Gaelic and dialect literatures outwith

---

19. MacDiarmid, "English Ascendancy" 116.

the pale and concentrated on what has become, to use Sir William
Watson's phrase, 'scriptive English'. . . .[20]

The assertion of equality of values and mutuality of exchange is
repeated and reemphasized throughout the article. "English
literature," MacDiarmid argues, "is maintaining a narrow
ascendancy tradition instead of broad-basing itself on all the
diverse cultural elements and the splendid variety of languages
and dialects, in the British Isles." "Confinement to the English
central stream," he claimed, "is like refusing to hear all but one
side of a complicated case...."[21]

MacDiarmid's nationalism has been challenged on
many grounds, including a claim that it is ultimately racist in its
assumption of a distinguishable Scottish psychology and is
frequently based on reverse claims of superiority.[22] Although
some of his work is vulnerable to this critique, his argument
most often centered on an affirmation of difference and
variation. His nationalism was persistently posited on internationalism, a claim _for_ Scotland within a more balanced set of
relations. By way of definition, one might compare Christopher
Norris's discussion of Paul de Man's _Le Soir_ articles in which he
distinguishes between two ways of reading de Man's apparent
affirmation of nationalist claims: "Again there is a crucial
ambiguity here, depending on whether one takes it that de Man
is advocating a unified Belgium modeled on the German-
Flemish alliance, or that he rather envisages a genuine state of
reciprocal interdependence where the different communities
would exercise a degree of autonomy and self-determination."[23]
Despite MacDiarmid's frequent inconsistencies, the latter most
persistently defines MacDiarmid's conception of nationalism
and constitutes the central argument of his _Criterion_ article.
More important for my purposes here, this conception of
"reciprocal interdependence" informs the poetics of _A Drunk
Man Looks at the Thistle_ and its deliberate challenge to _The
Waste Land_.

Yet the status of any poem MacDiarmid might write,
particularly if written in Scots, was already constructed within an
ongoing debate about the possibility, nature, function, and value
of non-English British literature. More constricting still, the
structure of Eliot's argument is so totalizing that it locates

---

20. MacDiarmid, "English Ascendancy" 117.
21. MacDiarmid, "English Ascendancy" 122.
22. See, for example, Keith Dixon, "Hugh MacDiarmid and the Gaelic Idea," _Pays de Galles, Ecosse,
Irlande,_ ed. Bernard Sellin (Brest: Centre de Recherche Bretonne et Celtique, 1987).
23. Christopher Norris, _Paul de Man_ (Routledge: New York, 1988) 186.

MacDiarmid by definition in the margins, incorporated in advance into the comic mode of regionalist enthusiast for lost causes and lapsed languages. MacDiarmid's call for multicultural diversity and complementarity within Britain confronts the fact, not only of Eliot's excluding "we" but of the authority of the *Athenaeum* and *Criterion* against his own "regional" journal.

MacDiarmid's tactics, in both his prose reactions to the conceptualization of culture sustained throughout Eliot's career and his poetic response to their articulation in *The Waste Land*, were aimed not simply at engaging in an acknowledged disagreement within British letters but in restructuring the debate itself. He set out to subvert the discourse which excluded him by challenging the "we" who share the "English" language and culture, by enacting his own conception of language and culture. His poetry, and primarily *A Drunk Man Looks at the Thistle*, constituted this enactment of a distinctively Scottish modern literature, written in Scots, and explicitly "complementing" and "correcting" the cultural position of *The Waste Land*. His later theoretical validation of such poetry--the article on "English Ascendancy"--was itself a second tactic of subversion: by placing it in the *Criterion* he took his own discourse into what he called "the enemies' camp." Situated between the early definition of a national literature sparked by opposing reactions to G. Gregory Smith and the later theories of the function of diverse British literatures, MacDiarmid's long poetic "quotation" of Eliot can be read as a demonstration of his posited distinctive literature.

That such a literature, for both Eliot and MacDiarmid, is grounded in a distinct and continuous language makes the assertion of a Scottish literature particularly subversive. Having developed from Middle Scots, derived in turn from Northumbrian, modern Scots can claim, despite its uneven development, a continuous existence separate from the line of the modern English of England. Secondly, unlike Gaelic, it is less easily dismissed out of hand as incomprehensible to the "greater peoples" and hence dispensible. At its most difficult, it is as accessible to "English" speakers as Chaucer or the Pearl Poet, and in most cases it is far more so. If "English" and American readers, say, need a glossary to read *A Drunk Man*, it is no more necessary than the OED and several languages to read Eliot and Pound. MacDiarmid's insistence in the early work on writing in Scots assumes the validity of demanding mutual linguistic acquisition. That the success of this maneuver can be questioned on the grounds of his more limited audience does not alter the political implications of his choice.

II. REREADING ELIOT

Having grounded his long response to Eliot in the Scottish Vernacular and an opposing cultural agenda, MacDiarmid "rewrote" a response to modern life using at least three modes of "quotation": affiliation, appropriation, and translation. His use of Eliot's long poem reflected both genuine admiration for Eliot's technical achievement--an admiration voiced early and often--and intense resistance to Eliot's definitions of culture and literature. Hence the peculiar fusion of association and mockery, "affiliation" as half grudging kinship. In 1922 MacDiarmid published "The Watergaw," initiating the period of his "golden lyrics," deliberate experiments in language meant to show that the Scottish Vernacular could express the entire range of human experience and to make possible a modern literature for Scotland. By 1925 he had found the lyric inadequate for so ambitious a project, and in *The Waste Land* he found a mode of expansion he could turn to his own purposes.

He initiated this enterprise by allying his Scottish modernist innovation with Eliot's in English. To "affiliate" is to adopt "into the position of a child: but always *fig.* of a parent institution adopting or attaching others to itself as branches...," also "to attach a smaller institution *to*, or connect it with a larger one as a branch thereof."(OED) "Affiliation" is also to "receive into intimate connection" with. It thus has a dual direction, both taking in and attaching to. In 1928 MacDiarmid described Eliot as "a Scotsman by descent--but it's a damned long descent,"[24] thus both "affiliating" him into Scottishness and repudiating his views as a "descent," in both senses of the word. Twice he incorporated this image of Eliot directly into *A Drunk Man*, in both cases citing *The Waste Land*. At line 345 he calls Scotland a more genuine candidate for such a poem:

> T. S. Eliot--it's a Scottish name--
> Afore he wrote 'The Waste Land' s'ud ha'e come

---

24. Hugh MacDiarmid, Letter to Neil Gunn, 3 May 1928, in *The Letters of Hugh MacDiarmid*, ed. Alan Bold (Athens, GA: U of Georgia P, 1984) 222.

> To Scotland here. He wad ha'e written
> A better poem syne--...[25] (30)

And at line 1648 he suggests that Scotland's only options are to align itself with the Russia of Dostoevsky's vision or to become, indeed, a Waste Land, reduced to a hanger-on of England without a unique Scottish culture:

> Baith bairns and Gods'll be obsolete soon   both children
> (The twaesome gang thegither), and forsooth   twosome go
> Scotland turn Eliot's waste--the Land o' Drouth. (122)

This "adoption" of Eliot serves several purposes. It establishes Scotland and MacDiarmid in an international context and allied as "kin" with an already acknowledged modernist figure. Eliot is drawn in half seriously, half mockingly, as a Scot, perhaps a prodigal son but a representative nonetheless: technically brilliant to the wrong purposes. "Descent," moreover, with its double meaning as descendant from and fallen from, sustains this reading.

Wanting to share Eliot's authority but reject his cultural assumptions, MacDiarmid treats him as a fellow radical challenging the system, yet one who has, unfortunately, taken on a self-defined position at the center. MacDiarmid's claim of distant kinship to a "fallen" Scot thus reverses the location of margin and center, a reversal he will act out more fully through appropriating Eliot's techniques and using translation as a form of satire.

His opening salvo in this larger form of counter narrative came in the form of an advance blurb to promote his own long poem. On 17 December 1925, MacDiarmid placed an advance blurb in the *Glasgow Herald* for a new long poem:

> Mr Hugh M'Diarmid has now completed a gallimaufry in Braid Scots verse, entitled 'A Drunk Man Looks at the Thistle'. It is, in fact, a long poem of over a thousand lines split up into several sections, but the forms within the sections range from ballad measure to vers libre. the matter includes satire, amphigouri, lyrics, parodies of Mr T. S. Eliot and other poets, and translations from the Russian, French, and German. The whole poem is in braid Scots, except a few quatrains which are in the nature of a skit on Mr Eliot's 'Sweeney' poems, and it has been expressly

---

25. Hugh MacDiarmid, *A Drunk Man Looks at the Thistle*, ed. Kenneth Buthlay (Edinburgh: Scottish Academic Press, 1987) 30. All further references to *A Drunk Man Looks at the Thistle* are from this edition; page numbers will be included in the text.

designed to show that braid Scots can be effectively applied to all
manner of subjects and measures.[26]

Singling out Eliot as object of parody, MacDiarmid allies that
act directly with the design of revealing the copiousness of braid
Scots. The deliberate tension set up by this proclamation plays
itself out in the poem. MacDiarmid's practice in *A Drunk Man* is
a highly self-conscious and explicit challenge to Eliot and what
Eliot represents, carried out on at least two major levels. On one
level MacDiarmid appropriated Eliot's techniques and themes
but subverted, overturned, and redefined them. On a second
level, the more fundamental transformation MacDiamid makes
is the "translation"--in a broader sense--of Eliot's "Waste
Land."

I would like to describe briefly what I have called
MacDiarmid's first level of challenge, his use of Eliot's
individual techniques and themes as a counterpoint or
alternative to Eliot's own vision, and to look more specifically at
the notion of "translation" or re-inscription in Scottish form.

Though *A Drunk Man* ended up more than twice as
long as MacDiarmid's advance blurb promised, it retained the
heterogeneous display of form, style, and language; it retained
as well the parodies of Eliot's poems and the "few quatrains"--6
to be exact, or 24 lines out of 2,685--which parody Eliot in
English, the only totally English lines in the entire poem. More
significantly, the poem not only alludes to *The Waste Land*, it
resembles Eliot's poem in several ways, partly due to oddly
similar histories. Like Eliot, MacDiarmid began with a mass of
separate notes later cut, selected, and arranged with the help of
a friend but retaining varied and disparate material including
allusion, quotation, fragments of legend, myth, and popular
culture.[27] The description of the poem as a "gallimaufry" might
well apply to both poems. Moreover, MacDiarmid took over
from Eliot not only the formal method of joining many partially
separable poems into a composite but also the broad concept of
a land laid waste. The thistle is Scotland's national symbol, and
the Drunk Man's preoccupation is with its decline and its
potential for re-growth and blossoming. His themes, too, are
similar: sexuality as both desire and horror, the possibility of an
authentic language, the nature of speech and silence, and the
loss of value in a disintegrating society. Yet if MacDiarmid

---

26. Quoted in "Introduction," by Kenneth Buthlay, *A Drunk Man* x.
27. For a full account of the poem's composition and the vexed question of the part played by F. G.
Scott, see Kenneth Buthlay's "Introduction" to MacDiarmid, *A Drunk Man*.

deliberately appropriated many of Eliot's techniques and themes--and his statements and allusions suggest that he did--his purpose was not imitative but confrontational.

Like affiliation, appropriation can go both ways. In one sense it means to "annex, or attach a thing to another as an appendage"; in another sense it means "to take possession of for one's own, to take to oneself." (OED) For Eliot, all non-English British literature is annexed, attached as an appendage, to "English literature." Having been thus appropriated into "English literature," MacDiarmid re-appropriated it in another sense, taking Eliot's work for his own purposes. His act is particularly ironic in its oblique acknowledgement of the decline in Scottish literature cited as definitive by Eliot. Literature in Scots had been almost entirely reduced, in the nineteenth century, to portrayals of extremely limited, folksy, rural life, and MacDiarmid's "leeway" in the language was the absence of a lexicon for the modern world. He lacked, too, a recent poetic tradition on which he could draw for a modern Scottish poem. As Eliot looked to French models, MacDiarmid looked, in part, to Eliot's innovations for a formal model, becoming a "thief of language."[28] Eliot having dismissed Scottish literature as consistently indebted to English literature,[29] MacDiarmid deliberately foregrounded a new "debt" for the purpose of asserting Scottish difference.

MacDiarmid points to his own heavy use of allusion and quotation by basing it early and frequently on Eliot's own poetry. He refers to Eliot not only explicitly, in the lines I have cited, but implicitly by recurrent use of characteristic images from *The Waste Land*: longing for water, dripping water, bare white bones, London in heaps of rubble, lightning, wind. He alludes also to other early poems: "Burbank with a Baedeker, Bleistein with a Cigar," "Sweeney Among the Nightingales," and "Rhapsody on a Windy Night," each time to contrast a Scottish with an English vision.

But his specific revisions of theme do not depend only on direct allusion. Repeatedly MacDiarmid takes up such themes as sexuality, human and divine speech, or the relation of dark and light, and twists them out of Eliot's shapes, often mocking them in carnivalesque uprisings of laughter, as when God chooses "a village slut to mither me" or when Mary is

---

28. The term is drawn from Claudine Hermann's description of women, quoted in Alicia Ostriker, *Stealing the Language* (Boston: Beacon, 1986) 210-11.
29. Eliot, "Was There a Scottish Literature" 680.

canny in her handling of Joseph. It is worth noting that although
it would require far more space than I have here to
demonstrate, *A Drunk Man* fits almost totally into Bakhtin's
definition of Menippean satire. If, as Calvin Bedient claims, *The
Waste Land* begins in Menippean forms but closes them off,[30] it
is those radical forms that MacDiarmid took over but chose not
to close. According to Bedient--and I think he is correct--*The
Waste Land*, "Self-overcoming Menippia,...stills all that babble,
stops up the pollutingly overheard, and even all generic
strayings, except for what it carefully and homiletically selects
and combines in its now deliberate creation of an exemplary and
allegorical ficton." MacDiarmid refuses to force the multiple,
diverse, and discordant voices of his poem into an exemplary
fiction; his refusal, in fact, is a major recurring action of the
poem. There is, moreover, no Absolute speech even to seek.
MacDiarmid's divine voice, for example, is comically reduced:

> "Let there be Licht," said God, and there was
> A little: but He lacked the poo'er
> To licht up mair than pairt o' space at aince,
> And there is lots o' darkness that's the same
> As gin He'd never spoken   if
>
> (152)

MacDiarmid posits no separate, pure "heart of light." Light is
found within the dark, and only by humans who reach further
into the dark than God. In all these cases, MacDiarmid assumes
a notion of language and literature directly opposed to Eliot and
allied with his notion of Dostoevsky as one who included
multiple voices and perspectives on life and accepted all sides of
it--even misery, disease, and fear. MacDiarmid's explicit
rejection of Eliot's Modernist thematic appears in their
opposing responses to sexuality. For Eliot the desire for
innocence, embodied in the Hyacinth girl, is both poignant and
profoundly disturbing, a moment of failure evoking in the
unresponding narrator visions of the "heart of light, the silence."
The encounter of male and female as adults is repeatedly
portrayed as violation and silence--the narrator's "nothing" in
the face of a hysterical wife, Philomela's bleeding mouth, the
Rhine maiden's "no comment," the clerks "unreproved" assault.
And the poem moves toward a quest for purity, freed from the
burning of desire.

---

30. Calvin Bedient, *He Do the Police in Different Voices* (Chicago: U of Chicago P, 1986) 8.

In one of the most aesthetically satisfying and thematically elusive passages of *A Drunk Man*, MacDiarmid rewrites the intersection of innocence and revulsion. In the separable poem published as "O Wha's the Bride?" the encounter of bride and bridegroom takes the traditional Scottish ballad form of a dialogue without conclusion, distanced resolution, or judgment. Horrified at the discovery that his bride carries within her the seed of all the men of all her ancestors-- the non-innocence inherent in human, bodily existence--the groom demands to know who cuckolded him:

> O Wha's been here afore me, lass,
> And hoo did he get in?
>   *--A man that deed or I was born*
> *This evil thing has din.*
>
> And left, as it were on a corpse,
> Your maidenheid to me?
> *--Nae lass, gudeman, sin' Time began*
> *S'hed ony mair to gi'e.*   (52)

For the bride--and all the women's voices--there is no original innocence, no unviolated virgin. She offers kindness and willing hands instead and promises more:

> *And on my lips ye'll heed nae mair,*
> *And in my hair forget,*
> *The seed o' a' the men that in*
> *My virgin womb ha'e met. . . .*   (52)

Lest this affirmation of the female body and sexuality as revulsion, knowledge, *and* ecstacy seem simply unconnected to Eliot's more consistent disgust, the link is made explicit in another woman's voice, the moon/woman of "Rhapsody on a Windy Night," speaking for herself:

> *Wi' burnt-oot hert and poxy face*
> *I sall illumine a' the place,*
> *And there is ne'er a fount o' grace*
> *That isna in a similar case.*   (136)

Taken from Eliot and re-presented, MacDiarmid's moon/woman claims, like the bride, that there is no light, no grace, no source of knowledge or love not already implicated in human experience, even degradation--nor is that a loss. MacDiarmid's appropriation of Eliot's images, themes, and multiple voices thus functions directly to confront and redefine their meaning.

The function of this focused challenge, however, goes well beyond the articulation of an alternative world view, though asserting the distinctiveness of Scottish experience and psychology is inseparable from his overall aim. He set out also to bring the Scottish language into the contemporary world through translation: he wished to transmute, to alter, the material he found into a mode of Scots capable of expressing Scottish experience in a modern form. In the *Glasgow Herald* advance notice he defined that aim: "to show that braid Scots can be effectively applied to all manner of subjects and measures." He wished to re-generate, give a new birth, to a language--the Vernacular he called, in "A Theory of Scots Letters," "an inchoate Marcel Proust, a Dostoevskian debris of ideas--an inexhaustible quarry of subtle and significant sound,"[31] the unliberated Joycean "vis comica" he found in Jamieson's *Dictionary*. Although *The Waste Land* provided a formal model for a modern long poem, which MacDiarmid could take over and use to reveal the potentialities of Scots, Scots itself lacked modern expressions. MacDiarmid's second need, then, was to make Scots functional within the model provided. In an early prose piece, a quasi-fictional dialogue on Rebecca West's novel *The Judge*, an English speaking character speculates on the thick Scots monologue of the other:

> He was purposely using many obsolete words, ...he was deliberately inconsequent, allusive, and obscure. As keen students of the Vernacular will appreciate, he was making scores of little experiments in Doric composition and style even as he spoke-- subtle adaptations of ancient figures of speech to modern requirements, finding vernacular equivalents for Freudian terminology--all infinitely difficult work but infinitely necessary if the Doric is again to become a living literary medium. His perfect knowledge of Ross's "Helenore," Duff's Poems, the Maitland Poems, Douglas's Vergil, and the like, stood him in splendid stead, and the dexterity with which he drew upon them delighted me immensely.[32]

MacDiarmid's problem, in other words, was linguistic as well as formal and technical. He needed to find the words and sources for a poem equivalent to *The Waste Land* but in Scots and of Scotland. He thus created his "gallimaufry" of heterogeneous styles using methods described in this passage. One might think of these methods as "modes of translation." They include 1) the

---

31. Hugh MacDiarmid, "A Theory of Scots Letters," *The Scottish Chapbook* 1.8 (1922): 210.
32. Hugh MacDiarmid, "Following Rebecca West in Edinburgh," *The Scottish Chapbook* 1.3 (1922): 70.

use of obsolete and obscure words adapted to modern requirements, 2) experiments in Doric style for modern ideas, often for the "translation" of modern Russian and European poems into Scots (ironically via English translations), 3) the "translation" in a broader sense of tradition, that is, an Eliotic display of allusion and quotation drawn predominantly from Scots sources. And 4) the intensifying and foregrounding of this experiment with Scots by dropping back into English for just six quatrains parodying Eliot.

        Although with that six quatrain exception the entire poem is in Scots of varying difficulty, MacDiarmid includes, among his heterogeneous styles, occasional passages of what Kenneth Buthlay calls "Dictionary Scots," virtuoso displays like the following:

Maun I tae perish in the keel o' Heaven,	must; small
And is this fratt upon the air the ply	fretwork; fold
O' cross-brath'd cordage that in gloffs and gowls	dark patches; hollows
Brak's up the vision o' the warld's bricht gy?	bright scene

(168)

These, with translations of complete poems by Zinaida Hippius, Else Lasker-Schuler, George Raemakers, and Edmund Rocher, display the range and flexibility of Scots, while allusions to Burns, Dunbar, J. R. Selkirk, John Davidson, James Hogg, Carlyle, James Thomson, and so on mingle with Milton, Gray, Eliot, Dante, Dostoevsky, without comment or explanation. They are assumed within a larger concept of tradition. Like the prose Scots speaker, the Drunk Man shows his "perfect knowledge" of Ross, Duff, Douglas, and the like. And like Eliot, MacDiarmid draws on folk culture, legend, and myth, but again, he draws it from Scotland without explanation. We have no footnotes to the practice of couvade (sticking a fork in the wall to transfer labor pains to a husband), the Common Riding Festival (annual fair in Border towns which includes the ceremony of riding round the official boundaries of land held in common), the Burns Supper, or even the thistle itself. Fortunately, the recently published annotated edition now makes these references easily available. But MacDiarmid, like Eliot, initially assumed the reader's familiarity or willingness to work--more so in fact, not only because he refused to supply *any* notes despite suggestions that he do so but because he was demanding a move outside the canonized tradition. Moreover, he was demanding, as with language itself, a mutuality of effort,

reciprocal study for English readers to understand allusions to
works not included in Eliot's "mind of Europe."

He moves back to Eliot's "tradition" for satirical
purposes, again challenging Eliot--or rather his culture--and
making the point by translation--that is, dropping into English in
order to reject it. The quatrains open with allusions to Gray's
"Elegy" and "Sweeney Among the Nightingales," then shift to a
mocking re-phrase of comically bad Scottish blank verse, to an
invitation to dance. The last quatrain sums up the rest:

> This is the sort of thing they teach
> The Scottish children in the school.
> Poetry, patriotism, manners--
> No wonder I am such a fool. . . . (158)

"Poetry" here is Gray and Eliot, patriotism the acceptance of
mediocre sentimentality, and manners an Anglicized, shallow
social event. "Hoo can I graipple wi' the thistle syne...?" asks the
Drunk Man. How can I, in other words, understand my own soul
and the soul of Scotland when they are displaced by the poetry
of others and the trivialization of their heritage.

Kristeva's description of any text as "a mosaic of
quotations...the absorption and transformation of another,"[33]
and--in the practice of Lautréamont, for example--a "constant
dialogue with the preceeding corpus, a perpetual challenging of
past writing,"[34] takes on a particular significance in the work of
marginalized writers. The process she defines is foregrounded in
both Eliot and MacDiarmid, but in MacDiarmid it is overtly
presented as opposition, debate, and contradiction. It is, one
might say, an insistent attempt to transform Eliot's monologue
into genuine dialogue with the Scottish tradition.

MacDiarmid's point in quoting, alluding to,
parodying, appropriating and "translating" Eliot (most
particularly by parodying Eliot in the only six quatrains in
"English" in the poem) takes on a more clear and profound
political significance in the context of his writings on politics,
language, and culture and the contrast with Eliot's own directly
opposing arguments. It is precisely Eliot's conception of literary
power and place that MacDiarmid saw inscribed in *The Waste
Land* and chose to re-inscribe in *A Drunk Man Looks at the
Thistle*. By the overt, even advertised tactics of affiliation,
appropriation, and translation, MacDiarmid creates the com-

---

33. Julia Kristeva, "Word, Dialogue and Novel," *The Kristeva Reader*, ed. Toril Moi (New York: Columbia UP, 1986) 37.
34. Kristeva 40.

plement and correction he later called for. That is, his poem acknowledges the tradition established and affirmed in *The Waste Land* but asserts an *other* view and purpose. It thus "corrects," that is, balances and extends the limited notion of the poem he "quotes," presenting a counter narrative to the "mind of Europe" from which Eliot had so neatly excluded Scotland. While *The Waste Land* appears radical, it is in fact simultaneously deeply conservative in its careful damage control, its impulse to contain, to shape and exclude, to stay within a closed tradition. MacDiarmid sought to explode that tradition by the very lessons he learned from Eliot's potentially subversive technique.

RODERICK WATSON

LANDSCAPES OF MIND AND WORD: MacDIARMID'S JOURNEY TO THE RAISED BEACH AND BEYOND

Five months before he died, Hugh MacDiarmid acknowledged "On a Raised Beach" as "one of the very best things I've written,"[1] and most critics today would be happy to agree. Even so, only the last 29 lines of the poem were included in the 1962 *Collected Poems*, and early studies of MacDiarmid's work accorded it far less attention than they did to that other masterpiece, *A Drunk Man Looks at the Thistle*. These days its status is much clearer, and I believe that it ranks with T. S. Eliot's *Four Quartets* as one of the finest and most troubling philosophical poems of our century. Furthermore, (to sustain the parallel with Eliot), if we liken "The Waste Land" to *A Drunk Man*, on the grounds of the part it played in the poet's development and reputation, then "On a Raised Beach" marks a career and conceptual turning point every bit as significant for MacDiarmid as *Four Quartets* was for Eliot.

Needless to say, the two works confront each other from radically opposed points of view. MacDiarmid's profoundly atheistic stance is to wrestle with the absurdity of personal identity, human culture and idealism, in the face of the indifference, the mystery, and even the glory of brute matter. Eliot, on the other hand, seeks the willing surrender of personality along with spiritual and intellectual pride, in submission to an unapproachable but still caring personal God. The two poems confront each other from opposite shores, yet between the little hamlets of England and the wilder reaches of Whalsay, they can still be said to share some common ground. Atheist and Christian they may have been, but the poets were both haunted by the vision of something somehow to be sought outside the cycle of earthly

---

1. Letter to W. R. Aitken, 28 Apr. 1978, *The Letters of Hugh MacDiarmid*, ed. Alan Bold (London: Hamish Hamilton, 1984) 591.

change, and as writers they both had to confront the problem of its inexpressibility.

As part of his solution Eliot turned to the mystical paradoxes of St. John of the Cross--seeking some "still point of the turning world" where "the darkness shall be the light, and the stillness the dancing"; while MacDiarmid opened his poem with a notoriously "stony" invocation as if to conjure up the untranslatable and coldly disinterested world of Sartrean existents: "Hatched foraminous cavo-rilievo of the world, / Deictic, fiducial stones. . . ."[2] We should note, too, how he mixed his arcane terms with teasing references to established religions, such as ". . . where is the Christophanic rock that moved?"--for he recognised the iconoclastic implications of his vision if the undifferentiated rocks on a remote Shetland beach were truly fruit from "the forbidden tree"--no longer exclusive to Eden and ". . . blacker than any in the Caaba." "Eat this," he offered, "and we'll see what appetite you have left / For a world hereafter." Both poets, then, stood on their beach of stones, their dry salvages, and (from the years between 1933 and 1943) their different conclusions speak with arduous eloquence of a crisis in faith and even in language itself--a crisis to be made even more explicit for us in later years, by way of existential philosophy, modern linguistics, and the writings of Beckett.

We shall return to the existential aspects of "On a Raised Beach," but it can be said to mark a watershed of a different sort in the long course of MacDiarmid's art, and indeed, in terms of conventional literary technique at least, he would never write so well again. Apart from that, however, the poem represents an uncharacteristically single-minded pause for reflection in MacDiarmid's *oeuvre*, for by comparison much of the earlier poetry was given over to his mercurial delight in the flux and mobility of Cencrastus; while his later work returned to the fray once more, with an epic search for "the whole inheritance of human knowledge" pursued with "immense erudition" in a "fury of incontrovertible detail." With "On a Raised Beach," however, the poet seems to have wanted to escape from the whirl, at least for a moment, to seek instead the absolute stability of a "ground bass." This essay will try to explore the imaginative and personal reasons which lay behind this decision.

---

2. This can be glossed as "Cross-engraved, perforated, sunken-carved-relief of the world, / Directly expository, dependable stones."

3. See Hugh MacDiarmid, *Lucky Poet* (London: Jonathan Cape, 1972) xxxi-xxxiv.

I also want to argue that the insights, ambiguities, and wider implications of "On a Raised Beach" help to explain why the poet's earlier persona as a quintessentially Romantic maker and shaper of dynamic images was finally laid to rest in favour of the "poetry of fact," with the lists, borrowings, and *bricolage* to be found at such length in *The Kind of Poetry I Want* and *In Memoriam James Joyce.*[4]

WATER AND LIGHT

The key to this shift can be found in how MacDiarmid treats landscape on his raised beach, for in this poem he moves away from his habitually preferred images of natural flux and constant movement, to seek instead images of stone and utter stasis. In the earlier "North of the Tweed," for example, the poet had meditated on another Scottish landscape, and here, too, he found it difficult to put the ineffable and subtle essence of the real into words:

> Despair seems to touch bottom time and again
> But aye Earth opens and reveals fresh depths.   always
> The pale-wa'd warld is fu' o' licht and life   pale-walled
> Like a glass in which water faintly stirs.
> Gie owre a' this tomfoolery, and sing   give over
> The movin' spirit that nae metaphor drawn
> Frae water or frae licht can dim suggest.[5]

Such images of water and light are characteristic of MacDiarmid's muse, for they epitomise his vision of how both physical and mental worlds can be seen as an endless process of becoming--a Bergsonian flux of the most subtle and continual movement.[6]

In common with most intellectuals of the twenties, the Scots poet shared an interest in Bergson's ideas, and his "Beyond Meaning" series for *The New Age* of 1924 had early drawn attention to the concept that "the Universe is that same stream of continual change, or *becoming*, as Bergson calls it, that

---

4. It has to be acknowledged, of course, that MacDiarmid had a propensity for using a "mosaic" of other men's words from the very start--he confessed as much in *Annals of the Five Senses*, his first book.
5. From *To Circumjack Cencrastus*, published in 1930, in Hugh MacDiarmid, *Complete Poems of Hugh MacDiarmid*, eds. W. R. Aitken and M. Grieve (London: Martin Brian and O'Keeffe. 1978) 269-71. All subsequent references to the poems are from this edition.
6. For an extended discussion of this aspect of "Water Music," see Roderick Watson, " 'Water Music' and the Stream of Consciousness," *Scottish Literary Journal* 5.2 (Dec. 1978): 6-19.

we experience in ourselves."[7] The stream soon came to be personified in MacDiarmid's verse as the mysterious "sea serpent," whose loops he was content merely to glimpse in *A Drunk Man*, or as Cencrastus himself, from the poem of that name, whose elusive coils inform the universe with unendingly changeless change. By 1931 the poet was most often exploring these qualities in an imagery of water, not least because his interest in making a collection of poems about his home town had led him to remember how Langholm was filled by the spirit of water, for there the Rivers Wauchope, Ewes and Esk meet and flow together.[8] Poems from this period, such as "Water of Life," or "The Point of Honour" (from *Stony Limits*), show that MacDiarmid is primarily concerned with the physical *mobility* of water and that this attribute is what makes it a life-*demonstrating* substance for him, rather than its more traditional role as a life-*supporting* substance:

> Foul here, fair there, to sea and sky again
> The river keeps its course and ranges
>   Unchanged through a' its changes.[9]

Even when confined in a glass, the moving spirit of water will remain the same, as in the famous opening lines of "The Glass of Pure Water":

> Hold a glass of pure water to the eye of the sun!
> It is difficult to tell the one from the other
> Save by the tiny hardly visible trembling of the water.
> This is the nearest analogy to the essence of human life
> Which is even more difficult to see.
> Dismiss anything you can see more easily;
> It is not alive--it is not worth seeing.[10]

Difficulty and subtlety, we should note, are a necessary and indispensable part of the contract, its guarantee of authenticity, and indeed the poet had confronted this problem in his very earliest writing:

> No processes of thought could convey that sense of blood running
> blindly through a net of glimmering surmises; of thought that was

---

7. C. M. Grieve, "Beyond Meaning IV," *The New Age* 35.12 (1924).
8. The collection, to be called *The Muckle Toon*, was part of a never-to-be-realised larger scheme; but many of the poems earmarked for this first volume appeared in *First Hymn to Lenin and Other Poems* (1931) and *Scots Unbound and Other Poems* (1932).
9. "Water of Life," *Complete Poems* 316.
10. *Complete Poems* 1041.

but as a mesh of cheating gleams on the verge of the incalculable floods of life.[11]

Ten years after *Annals*, the poem "Water Music" was specifically designed to catch those "incalculable floods," and to meet the challenge, MacDiarmid created a Joycean "babble" of obscure and onomatopoeic Scots words: "Brade-up or sclafferin', rouchled, sleek, / Abstraklous or austerne." ("Bold and lively or slovenly, rough, sleek, / Obstreperous or austere.") In "North of the Tweed," however, (to return to that poem and its interest in water and light) he had used landscape images in a much more conventional fashion. Even so, the method worked, for although (in a paradox typical of Romantic poetics), he confesses an inability to convey the full beauty of the scene, he nonetheless manages to create a very beautiful passage of nature description:

Water nor licht nor yet the barley field	
That shak's in silken sheets at ilka braith,	each
Its lang nap thrawin' the quick licht aboot	
In sic a maze that tak's and gies at aince	such a
As fair oot-tops the coontless ripplin' sea.	
There's nae chameleon like the July fields;	
Their different colours change frae day to day	
While they shift instantly neath the shiftin' licht	
Yet they're owre dull for this, stagnant and dull;	too
And even your een, beloved, and your hair	eyes
Are like the barley and the sea and Heaven	
That flaw and fail and are defeated by	lie
The blind turns o' chance.[12]	

Far from being reduced to silence in the face of his impossible task, the poet adds three further fine stanzas, and then, in the closing lines, he turns to music as well--"I'll pipe instead." Even with a tune called "The Point of the Dead," the poem concludes on a note of elevated and rich accomplishment.

At other times, however, the "moving spirit that nae metaphor . . . can dim suggest" proved to be more elusive. One of the drunk man's chief preoccupations, after all, had been to try to express some ultimate identity between his own heart (those "fountains ootloupin' the starns") and the "Octopus Creation," one of whose many manifestations was the "licht nae man had ever seen" until he has "the stars themsels instead o'

11. C. M. Grieve, *Annals of the Five Senses* (Montrose, 1923) 177.
12. *Complete Poems* 270.

een."[13] By the end of the poem, however, such a relentlessly solipsistic drive to find experience beyond experience and expression beyond expression, had brought only exhaustion. Tired of "Aye yabblin' o' my soul," he had climbed off "the weary wheel" (at least for the moment), in favour of the final silence of repletion. A few years later the concept could seem even more problematical, and the poet's goal had become no less than an "Impossible Song":

> We are like somebody wha hears
> A wonderfu' language and mak's up his mind
> To write poetry in it--but ah!
> It's impossible to learn it, we find,
> Tho' we'll never ha'e ony use again
> For ither languages o' ony kind.[14]

Bergson could have predicted such difficulties, for his definition of the flow of *élan vital* explains that by its very nature it is what cannot be caught, described or analysed, for the moment we define it, we fix it, and when it's stopped it ceases to be.[15]

THE INEXPRESSIBLE

MacDiarmid was long familiar with such problems, for most of the studies in *Annals of the Five Senses* had been concerned with those "continual allurements to new intricacies of introspection," during which "not one of the countless impressions his brain was registering every instant, but immediately it was cleanly stamped, suffered a 'sea-change' into something entirely and most inconsequently different."[16] Nevertheless, the prose studies of *Annals* had set out to convey that sea change with considerable verve, just as his subsequent works were to show a similar fascination with flux in all its forms, from the sensibility of the drunk man, to the pursuit of Cencrastus and the protean imagery of water itself.

There are, however, obvious problems in any attempt to express the inexpressible, and for a number of reasons these began to impinge on MacDiarmid with particular force in the early thirties. First of all, his personal life was under consider-

---

13. *Complete Poems* 163.
14. From *Stony Limits, Complete Poems* 508.
15. "If a mental state ceased to vary, its duration would cease to flow," Henri Bergson, *Creative Evolution*, trans. A. Mitchell (London: Macmillan, 1911) 2.
16. *Annals* 14, 12-13.

able strain, for his marriage to Peggy had broken up and he had to endure a succession of financial and physical problems in London, Liverpool, and Surrey, all at the height of the Depression. *To Circumjack Cencrastus*, his last effort at a book length poem in the form of *monologue interiéur*, had not been very successful, and it seems likely that the effort of maintaining an expansively solipsistic and Whitmanesque persona had finally come to seem too great, even for MacDiarmid.[17] (It appeared only once more--in shorter form--as "Ode to All Rebels" in *Stony Limits*). We should remember, too, that a growing commitment to overtly political propaganda in his art would certainly demand a less solipsistic and volatile voice than that offered by the drunk man. Finally, and most crucially, an imaginative crisis was becoming apparent in the logic of the theme itself.

Bergson coped with the inexpressibility of *élan vital* by admitting that it could never be grasped by the rational mind, but only by intuition. To this end he used metaphors and analogies in his prose, taking care to point out that they could only *evoke* a subject which was itself beyond literal description. In this respect MacDiarmid's imagery of water and light had achieved the same purpose in the familiar manner of all post-Romantic literary symbolism. In the early thirties, however, he was beginning to move towards an overtly rational and materialist expression in his art, and the symbols of Whisky, Moonlight, Serpent, Light, and Water would no longer fit so well a "scientific" or a Marxist muse, not least because their pursuit seemed to have no end and hence no stable or attainable goal.

The problem of the inexpressible and the unattainable was familiar to MacDiarmid from yet another source, for it had featured in the "Inactual" philosophy of his old friend Denis Saurat as part of the debate in his book *The Three Conventions*. (This work had been serialised in *The New Age* before being published in New York in 1926, and then republished in London in 1932.) In the company of Edwin Muir and F. G. Scott, MacDiarmid had been very close to Saurat when the latter was working at Glasgow University in the Twenties; he specifically cited "Denis Saurat's great book" in a footnote to *Cencrastus*, and he was still recommending *The Three Conventions* as a "much too-little-known work" in that part of his autobiography

---

17. Dostoevsky's *Notes from Underground* is an eloquent testament to the psychological strain of maintaining the ego in a constant flux of creative contradiction.

which finally appeared as *The Company I've Kept*.[18] A brief account of one or two salient points will be enough to show why the "Inactual" is relevant to MacDiarmid's imaginative plight in the three years following *Cencrastus*.

Like Bergson, Saurat regards reality as a process of endless becoming, and he, too, extols intuition as a way of seizing an apprehension of that reality. But when we come to *express* that moment, he says that we will always and inevitably be frustrated by the nature of language itself, and by the way that language controls our thought processes. Here, for example, is the first proposition in Saurat's metaphysics, followed by his discussion of its implications:

> 1. Every existence is infinite; every expression is limited. The expression of any thought or being is necessarily incomplete.
>
> I say: "A man is going by in the street." It is impossible for me to express all I can see and feel about that man; it is impossible for me even to see or feel it. . . . For instance I do not take any notice of the color of his hat, the length of his coat, the expression on his face; the analysis of any feature would spread into the infinite. I choose to select the very general fact that he belongs to the human species and I go into no details. To get all the details, I should have to fix him at one particular unit of time; it is conceivable that then the total of the details would be finite. But the next instant most of the elements of the picture: his position, his expression, etc., would have changed; and no unit of time is short enough for me to catch him in a static position. He is in a perpetual transformation, and therefore infinite. To say anything about him, I have to choose what interests me in him, and leave out the rest: otherwise, I could say nothing.[19]

This is precisely the dilemma that faced MacDiarmid when he set out to "circumjack," that is to encompass or come to terms with, the curly snake of Being. (The poet chose to call this world snake "Cencrastus"--the central symbol of his vision of the infinite and changing variety of the cosmos.) For a while he had delighted in its elusive fluidity, especially when symbolised by water and "the quick changes o' the Esk that . . . 'Ud faur ootrin the divers thochts o' Man / Sin' Time began."[20] But MacDiarmid was conceiving a new commitment to the totality of things through "Organic, constructional work, / Practicality, and work by degrees,"[21] and his fascination with the

18. Hugh MacDiarmid, *The Company I've Kept* (London: Hutchinson, 1966) 269-71.
19. Denis Saurat, *The Three Conventions* (London, 1932) 79-80.
20. " 'Ud faur ootrin"--"Would greatly outrun." From "Water of Life," *Complete Poems* 318.
21. From "Second Hymn to Lenin," *Complete Poems* 325.

Landscapes of Mind and Word   239

making and remaking of poetic symbols was giving way to a
more "scientific" concern with the material world. Yet by
Saurat's definition the way of material analysis can only serve to
multiply its reference beyond number, for every "Actual" to be
expressed brings with it a new series of things which are unex-
pressed--the "Inactual"--and so on, *ad infinitum*.

This aspect of Saurat's theory bears a striking
resemblance to how Post-Structuralists have come to see language as a process of signification which need never stop, and in
our present context Terry Eagleton puts it very tellingly:

> ... meaning is not immediately *present* in a sign. Since the mean-
> ing of a sign is a matter of what the sign is *not*, its meaning is
> always in some sense absent from it too. Meaning, if you like, is
> scattered or dispersed along a whole chain of signifiers: it cannot
> be easily nailed down, it is never fully present in one sign alone,
> but it is rather a kind of constant flickering of presence and
> absence together. . . .[22]
>
> The implication of all this is that language is a much less sta-
> ble affair than the classical structuralists had considered. Instead
> of being a well-defined, clearly demarcated structure containing
> symmetrical units of signifiers and signifieds, it now begins to look
> much more like a sprawling limitless web where there is a constant
> interchange and circulation of elements, where none of the ele-
> ments is absolutely definable and where everything is caught up
> and traced through by everything else. If this is so, then it strikes a
> serious blow at certain traditional theories of meaning. For such
> theories, it was the function of signs to reflect inward experiences
> or objects in the real world, to "make present" one's thoughts and
> feelings or to describe how reality was ... [But] on the theory I
> have just outlined, nothing is ever fully present in signs: it is an
> illusion for me to believe that I can ever be fully present to you in
> what I say or write, because to use signs at all entails that my
> meaning is always somehow dispersed, divided and never quite at
> one with itself. Not only my meaning, indeed, but *me*: since
> language is something I am made out of, rather than merely a
> convenient tool I use, the whole idea that I am a stable, unified
> identity must also be a fiction. Not only can I never be fully pre-
> sent to you, but I can never be fully present to myself either.[23]

Eagleton's explication defines for us once again the
dilemma that faced MacDiarmid when he decided to give himself over so whole-heartedly to the experience and the expression of the flux of the universe as found within and without him-

---

22. Saurat would say that every expressed "Actual" draws into being an unexpressed "Inactual" from which new "Actuals" are in turn created once we begin answering questions about what is left unsaid--"Where was the man going? Why was he going there?" etc.
23. Terry Eagleton, *Literary Theory* (Oxford: Basil Blackwell, 1983) 128, 129-30.

self. In terms of both philosophical and linguistic theory, he was meeting barriers which seemed to require of him an increasingly massive expenditure of creative energy--". . . pridefu' still / That 'yont the sherp wings o' the eagles fleein' / Aboot the dowless pole o' Space, / Like leafs aboot a thistle-shank, my bluid / Could still thraw roses up / --And up!"[24] He had managed to keep the roses of imagination balanced on the fountains of his own blood in *A Drunk Man*, (although even then he had longed to let them drop "Like punctured ba's that at a Fair / Fa' frae the loupin' jet!"), but by the early thirties the strain was beginning to tell.

SHETLANDS OF THE MIND

These, then, are the theoretical factors which must surely have prepared MacDiarmid to meet that raised beach. Late in 1933, on the bare island of Whalsay, it must have seemed to him that a world of stone could offer some absolute and irreducible stability at last, and that here, too, what had come to seem like "the futile imaginings of men" might be "chilled to the core" in the effort to apprehend the infinite once and for all.

There were psychological and physical factors behind this desire too, of course, and these had to do with the hard times he had experienced in London and the South, the geographical remoteness of his new circumstances, and a renewed commitment to the severities of Leninism. Here, then, are the final steps in his path towards a "likeness of stone":

> . . . I have come back to my starting point all but physically. Physically I am at the extreme other end of my country. I came to Whalsay, this little north Isle of the Shetland Group, in 1933. I was absolutely down-and-out at the time--with no money behind me at all, broken down in health, unable to secure remunerative employment of any kind, and wholly concentrated on projects in poetry and other literary fields which could bring me no monetary return whatever, involved continuous intense effort ridiculously out of proportion to my strength . . . since isolation and a too complete self-centredness were definitely dangerous, not only to the qualities of the work to be produced but to my own mental stability or . . . at least to the generation and maintenance of the necessary, or at any rate the most helpful, moods.[25]

---

24. From *A Drunk Man, Complete Poems*, 147. "Dowless"--"imponderable," also "feeble."
25. *Lucky Poet* 41.

MacDiarmid was indeed becoming estranged from old friends and cultural contacts in Scotland, and, from the vantage point of a self-consciously extreme Marxism, he delighted in attacking his erstwhile fellow Nationalists as "nitwits" and "nonentities." Newly expelled from the National Party because of his allegiance to Communism, he promised to fight back in every way he could by " 'making things difficult' " as "an impossible person," and by "unscrupulously saying one thing to one person and the opposite to another, etc."[26] (MacDiarmid's Nationalism hoped to see Scotland as an independent socialist republic, and he was not alone in this ambition. His quarrel with the Scottish Nationalists, however, had to do with his determination to belong to their organisation and to the Communist Party as well.) In fact the tensions MacDiarmid was feeling ultimately came to a head in 1935 when he suffered a complete physical and mental breakdown which took him to a hospital in Perth for seven weeks. But in the early years, at least, the letters from Whalsay were full of confidence, with talk of "concentration," "rigorous disciplines," and "difficult" poems in "synthetic English"--too long for periodicals perhaps, but "up to my best level," and representing "valuable new departures."[27] Certainly there is no mistaking the imaginative impact which the Shetland landscape had on the poet, nor its relevance to the austere tones of "On a Raised Beach":

> ... the Shetlands call alike in the arts and in affairs for the true creative spirit. Anything pettier would be sadly out of place in these little-known and lonely regions, encompassed about with the strange beauty of the North, the fluctuation of unearthly colour at different levels of the sun, the luminous air, the gleam of distant ice, and the awful stillness of Northern fog. . . .
>
> It may take [visitors] a little time to realise that what is affecting them is the total absence of trees and of running water. . . . There is no less variety of form and colour; just as we find it difficult in other connections to imagine how we could get on without certain things we are accustomed to, so here it surprises one to discover how easily even the presence of trees and rivers can be dispensed with, and how, instead of a sense of loss, we soon realise that their absence throws into relief features we seldom see or underprize because of them--the infinite beauties of the bare land and the shapes and colours of the rocks. . . . It is, in fact, the treasures and rich lessons of a certain asceticism the Shetlands provide, and these offset in an invaluable way our normal indulgences in scenic

---

26. Letter to Neil Gunn, 22 June 1933, *Letters* 252.
27. See letters of 5 June 1933 and 17 Jan. 1934, *Letters* 148, 465.

display ... The lack of ostentatious appearances, the seeming
bareness and reserve, make the Shetlands insusceptible of being
readily or quickly understood; one must steep oneself in them, let
them grow upon one, to savour them properly. It is a splendid discipline.[28]

After the "chameleon" of the July fields, where the fluidity of
water and light had so long played out their "indulgences in
scenic display," MacDiarmid had at last found an appropriate
arena for a different and more bracing vision of reality as
"barren but beautiful." This was the realm of stones on a raised
beach, where he sought a sense of final stability only to come to
the hardest and most disturbing insights of his life.

A LIKENESS OF STONE

Feeling "out of touch with everybody else in Scotland" and
determined to remain "utterly irreconcilable,"[29] the poet had
come to identify himself with "Men capable of rejecting all that
all other men / Think," in pursuit of a "detachment that shocks
our instincts and ridicules our desires" (*Complete Poems* 426).
His mentor in this was Charles Doughty, and although the latter
was deeply conservative in his views, MacDiarmid felt him to be
a fellow spirit, sadly neglected and underestimated by the literary establishment. Author of an immense multi-volume verse
epic called *The Dawn in Britain*, Doughty is better known for the
austere prose of his *Travels in Arabia Deserta*, and it was this
work which offered the Scottish poet a vision of the desert and
desert culture as another landscape of the mind--stern, illiberal,
and exhilaratingly unforgiving. In fact the "seeing of a hungry
man" and the "burning crystal" in the following passage are
images which come from *Arabia Deserta*:

> I am enamoured of the desert at last,
> The abode of supreme serenity is necessarily a desert.
> My disposition is towards spiritual issues
> Made inhumanly clear; I will have nothing interposed
> Between my sensitiveness and the barren but beautiful reality;
> The deadly clarity of this 'seeing of a hungry man'
> Only traces of a fever passing over my vision
> Will vary, troubling it indeed, but troubling it only

---

28. Hugh MacDiarmid, *The Islands of Scotland* (London: B. T. Batsford, 1939) 55, 66-67. The latter
extract is also found in "Life in the Shetland Isles" from 1934, collected in K. Buthlay, ed., *The
Uncanny Scot* (London: MacGibbon and Kee, 1968) 90.
29. *Letters* 252.

> In such a way that it becomes for a moment
> Superhumanly, menacingly clear--the reflection
> Of a brightness through a burning crystal.
>   (CP 431)

Edinburgh University Library has a shorter manuscript version of "On a Raised Beach," and it is clear from this that the "inhuman clarity" of the desert gradually took over the poem. Dr. Ruth McQuillan has noted that this fair copy offers "a stratum of what one must call hope . . . which is more submerged in the published version,"[30] and certainly a comparison of the two texts will show that the additional passages all relate to those aspects of the stones which are "Cold, undistracted, eternal and sublime. / [stemming] all the torrents of vicissitude forever / With a more than Roman peace" (CP 427).

The accumulative force of such imagery is considerable, particularly when we see how MacDiarmid links the insensate world of matter with his own vision of the need for a ruthless dialectical materialism. To this end he lectured "detached intellectuals" on the need to come to terms with the "reality" of life--"But you must participate in it to proclaim it" (CP 432); and in response to establishment complacencies he paraphrased Dimitri Pisarev, the nineteenth-century Russian nihilist who held that "what can be smashed should be smashed. What withstands the blow is fit to survive":

> Let men find the faith that builds mountains
> Before they seek the faith that moves them. Men cannot hope
> To survive . . .
> Unless they are more concentrated and determined,
> Truer to themselves and with more to be true to,
> Than these stones, and as inerrable as they are.
> Their sole concern is that what can be shaken
> Shall be shaken and disappear
> And only the unshakable be left.
>   (CP 427)

The poet had long associated such "inerrable" purpose with Lenin, whose spirit he symbolised in the crystalline granite of his tomb, whose bones were like "eternal lightning" with the promise of Socialist victory--a promise not unambiguously summed up by the title of that little poem: "The Skeleton of the Future." From the raised beach, such a future will require "Spartan impassivity," and, even more, the exercise of an

---

30. Ruth McQuillan, "Hugh MacDiarmid's 'On a Raised Beach,' " *Akros* 12.34-35 (Aug. 1977): 91.

> . . . immense exercise of will,
> Inconceivable discipline, courage, and endurance,
> Self-purification and anti-humanity,
> Be ourselves without interruption,
> Adamantine and inexorable . . .
>   (CP 429)

   The end result of such stony discipline is to achieve "a constant centre, / With a single inspiration, foundations firm and invariable," and such a goal makes very clear the distance that MacDiarmid has travelled from the mobility of the Drunk Man, whose exhortation to "be yourself" used to be a plea to give oneself over to the character of the universe as a place of endless and dynamic change:

> Like staundin' water in a pocket o'
> Impervious clay I pray I'll never be,
> Cut aff and self-sufficient, but let reenge
> Heichts o' the lift and benmaist deeps o' sea.[31]   nethermost

On the raised beach, however, the dreaded "impervious clay" seems to have been willingly replaced by a "truth" which is "as free / From all yet thought as a stone from humanity," and now MacDiarmid glories in isolation:

> Here a man must shed the encumbrances that muffle
> Contact with elemental things, the subtleties
> That seem inseparable from a humane life, and go apart
> Into a simple and sterner, more beautiful and more oppressive
> world,
> Austerely intoxicating; the first draught is overpowering;
> Few survive it. It fills me with a sense of perfect form,
>   (CP 428)

It is not difficult to sense the poet's intoxication with his icy intellectual certainty: from the grim wit of "that larking dallier, the sun, [which] has only been able to play / With superficial by-products since"; to the sheer arrogance of "I have still to see any manifestation of the human spirit / That is worthy of a moment's longer exemption than it gets. . . ." And there is an unmistakable glee (typically Scottish in its Calvinist undertones) to the magisterial insistence of the following lines:

> Listen to me--Truth is not crushed;
> It crushes, gorgonises all else into itself.
> The trouble is to know it when you see it?
> You will have no trouble with it when you do.

---

31. From *A Drunk Man, Complete Poems* 88.

Do not argue with me. Argue with these stones.
Truth has no trouble in knowing itself.
This is it. The hard fact. The inoppugnable reality,
Here is something for you to digest.
Eat this and we'll see what appetite you have left
For a world hereafter.

(CP 430)

Such monolithic certainty (the adjective is more than appropriate) literally promises to crush us or turn us to stone, while "those who speak glibly" will be given "the whole earth / For a Demosthenean pebble to roll in their mouths." The brutally authoritarian and oppressive force of such statements depends on us realising that the stones will *not* be turned to bread, and that such an aid to oratory could only serve to choke the speaker.

In fact MacDiarmid's determination to embrace "anti-humanity" as a necessary route to the "reality of life" takes him far beyond any recognisable social or political issue, until he finds himself in a realm of the spirit so rarified that "Not so much of all literature survives / As any wisp of scriota that thrives / On a rock." Only here can he find "the road leading to certainty," for "an emotion chilled is an emotion controlled" on the journey to that final bedrock where "All else in the world cancels out, equal, capable / Of being replaced by other things," except for the stones, for "They alone are not redundant" (CP 426).

A MIND AS OPEN AS THE GRAVE

A considerable part of the power and purpose of "On a Raised Beach" is directed to the attempt to conceive what a kingdom of such ontological reductiveness might be like, and then with the problem of putting it into words. The opening lines offer one solution, for their invocation of the stones as "glaucous, hoar, enfouldered, cyathiform" etc., certainly conjures up an unfamiliar and alien world. (The line means, "with a green-grey bloom, frosted, black as a thundercloud, cup-shaped.") As an exercise in linguistic estrangement, vocabulary like this shakes our usual confidence in what *can* be known or described: "Deep conviction or preference can seldom / Find direct terms in which to express itself" (CP 423).

At other times the poet seeks to express the indivisible, irreducible nature of his vision by pointing out that "There are plenty of ruined buildings in the world but no ruined stones. / No visitor comes from the stars / But is the same as they are." Further analogies suggest themselves, from more traditional metaphysical systems:

> ... the kindred form I am conscious of here
> Is the beginning and end of the world,
> The unsearchable masterpiece, the music of the spheres,
> Alpha and Omega, the Omnific Word.
>   (CP 428-29)

By definition, of course, the all-creating "Omnific Word" can never be heard and will never be uttered by any human agent. Even so, he feels that "it is wrong to indulge in these illustrations / . . . to try to drag down / The arduus furor of the stones to the futile imaginings of men" (CP 425).

Paradoxically, it is the very *openness* of the stones' being that defies understanding ("The widest open door is the least liable to intrusion"), and until we ourselves manage to match their time-scale and their steadfastness of purpose, we will never be able to approach them. MacDiarmid's steadfastness has already been noted in his dedication to "anti-humanity"; but his longing to approach the stones with their "direct and undisturbed way of working" and the "silence of supreme creative power," takes him further still--to the very threshold of extinction. The poem is half in love with that "more the Roman peace," and at times it comes close to recognising that a longing for the ultimate stability of rock, (as opposed to the endless flux of water and light), is no less, really, than a longing for death itself:

> I am no more indifferent or ill-disposed to life than death is;
> I would fain accept it all completely as the soil does;
> Already I feel all that can perish perishing in me
> As so much has perished and all will yet perish in these stones.
>   (CP 424)

It is worth noting that this passage and the following one too do not appear in the early version of the poem, as if the fatalistic implications we have been tracing only developed for MacDiarmid--even as hints--as the theme matured in his imagination.

> Death is a physical horror to me no more.
> I am prepared with everything else to share
> Sunshine and darkness and wind and rain

And life and death bare as these rocks though it be
In whatever order nature may decree,
But, not indifferent to the struggle yet
Nor to the ataraxia I might get   stoical indifference
By fatalism, a deeper issue see
Than these, or suicide, here confronting me.
It is reality that is at take.
Being and non-being with equal weapons here
Confront each other for it. . .

(CP 428)

"Non-being" would seem to be the "arduus furor" of the stones, ". . . always on the point, it seems, of showing clear"; but then the poet wonders if the distinction between two such states is not in fact illusory, for if "being" and "non-being" *are* separate, we will only be able to experience their ultimate unity when we die; that is to say, the artificial sense of severance between us and the world of objects will only be brought to an end when we ourselves become inanimate things. Here, too, the gulf between signified and signifier--"object and image"--will finally be bridged. He recognised, however, that this is an invitation to suicide, and an "aesthetic vision," furthermore, to which he is particularly "susceptible." Thus the following complex lines acknowledge the attractiveness of death, even if they do remain inconclusive because the poet chooses to change the subject rather than to resolve it:

It is reality that is at stake.
Being and non-being with equal weapons here
Confront each other for it, non-being unseen
But always on the point, it seems, of showing clear,
Though its reserved contagion may breed
This fancy too in my still susceptible head
And then by its own hidden movement lead
Me as by aesthetic vision to the supposed
Point where by death's logic everything is recomposed,
Object and image one, from their severance freed,
As I sometimes, still wrongly, feel 'twixt this storm beach and me.
What happens to us
Is irrelevant to the world's geology
But what happens to the world's geology
Is not irrelevant to us.

(CP 428)

The possibility that we can "reconcile ourselves to the stones" only by dying, is raised again at the end of "On a Raised Beach," and this time the ambiguities remain closer to the surface. At one level, of course, it is MacDiarmid's intention in the closing lines, simply to offer a rhetorical figure which stresses how difficult it is to get a life worth having in our present society. In this vein, he concludes (with wry comfort) that at least we cannot lose any more of our birthright when we are dead:

> It is not more difficult in death than here
> . . . to get a life worth having;
> And in death--unlike life--we lose nothing that is truly ours.
> (CP 433)

Yet that imagery of death which has preceded these lines casts a darker and more ambiguously pessimistic shadow than mere wit can dispel:

> --I lift a stone; it is the meaning of life I clasp
> Which is death, for that is the meaning of death;
> How else does any man yet participate
>   In the life of a stone,
> How else can any man yet become
> Sufficiently at one with creation, sufficiently alone,
> Till as the stone that covers him he lies dumb
> And the stone at the mouth of his grave is not overthrown?
> (CP 432)

In the face of such insight, the poet's exhortation to "detached intellectuals" to "participate" in life comes to seem peculiarly ambivalent, for his example of participation is to lift the very stone which leads him to say--"it is the meaning of life I clasp / Which is death." In the same way, the political and material "reality" implied in the lines below seems rather ironically bleak if we re-examine their apparently pragmatic advice in the knowledge that the true meaning of the stone is to be "death":

> These bare stones bring me straight back to reality.
>   I grasp one of them and I have in my grip
> The beginning and the end of the world,
> My own self, and as before I never saw
> The empty hand of my brother man,
> The humanity no culture has reached, the mob.
> Intelligentsia, our impossible and imperative job!
> (CP 432)

Imperative or not, the task has got to be too much for any "intelligentsia" when "Every stone in the world covers infinite death, beyond the reach / Of the dead it hides; and cannot be hurled / Aside yet to let any of them come forth."

In the light of such grim finality, it is significant that the shorter manuscript of the poem ends with the poet standing up and walking away from the beach where he lay down "an eternity ago," as if he could move from its mortal implications:

> But I cannot sit here till I am
> Like one of these stones even if I want to.
> I have not the will-power
>> The best I can do
> Is to make my verses as bare, as rough.
> So now I rise. Yet I am strangely not strangely at peace[32]

In the published version, however, the poem concludes with a return to the paradoxically obscure "enchorial characters" of the opening invocation; and, as if to confirm its status as a sealed and self-referring system, the last lines recite the majestically arcane name for a rhetorical device they have just defined: "And, with the same word that began it, closes / Earth's vast epanidiplosis."

CONCLUSION AND BEYOND

What conclusions can be drawn from the poem's place in Mac-Diarmid's work as a whole? To summarise, I believe that he looked to the raised beach for stability, for a political, material and philosophical "ground bass" which would counterbalance the demanding whirl of the drunk man's subjectivity, and offer some respite from the pusuit of that "movin' spirit that nae metaphor drawn / Frae water or frae licht can dim suggest." "It is necessary," he wrote, "to make a stand and maintain it forever"; and he looked for his stance in the world of stone. Yet in such monolithic certitude he seems to have found only death; and it is as if the inner logic of the poem kept bringing his imagery back to the fixity of death, suggesting too, despite his intentions perhaps, and despite his intellectual bravado, that the true face of his "clear and searching gaze" was a face of stone.

In this respect it is particularly significant that so much of MacDiarmid's subsequent writing was to be a return to "man's incredible variation" and the inexhaustibly heterogeneous resources of the world. After the crushingly static, singular and inner analysis of "On a Raised Beach," the poet

---

32. From manuscript in Edinburgh University Library; also reproduced in Appendix A of Catherine Kerrigan, *Whaur Extremes Meet* (Edinburgh: James Thin, 1983) 216-30.

turned back to synthesis, "with that piling up of details the
completed effect of which 'is one of movement'...."[33]
Compared to the single-minded focus of the "Raised Beach,"
The Kind of Poetry I Want and *In Memoriam James Joyce* are
resolutely many-sided and outward looking, as if the poems were
determined to assemble all forms of human knowledge, like
some universal encyclopaedia which welcomes each new detail,
however esoteric, as yet another contribution to its selfless
vision of the whole and "the common identity of all things in
nature":

> ...what Wassermann told Pierre Loving in 1914 appealed to me
> greatly. 'I am interested primarily in life, in making a synthesis of
> life which is based firmly upon my own visible contacts', he said. 'I
> try not to ignore the inner vision; the inner vision is of over-
> whelming importance, but my objective observation is always at
> work correcting that inner grasp of reality. My aim is to pack the
> whole complex modern scene into my books...'[34]

Of course MacDiarmid continued to ponder the
problems of language, which "is just as much a determinant of
what is expressed in it as a medium of expression"[35]; and then of
what lies beyond language--for "total speech is impossible" and
how *can* one find "the word with which silence speaks its own
silence without breaking it"?[36] Yet it is the flow and the multiplicity of the world of words to which he turns, to find yet
another metaphor (albeit a more intellectual one) in the spirit of
his earlier use of water and light. The Omnific Word of "On a
Raised Beach" has given way to the less singular and less
oppressive concept of an Omnific Language. Poems such as *In
Memoriam James Joyce* and *The Kind of Poetry I Want* have
closed the threatening gulf between signifier and signified
(imaginatively at least), not by death, but by a fresh conception:
firstly of the world *of* language, and then of the world *as* language.

It happens, in fact, that Denis Saurat's *Three Conventions* had already proposed that "Matter is language," and his
thoughts will help to conclude this outline of the direction which
MacDiarmid was to take towards the last and most prolific stage
of his poetic career:

---

33. *Lucky Poet* (citing Gregory Smith) 111.
34. *Lucky Poet* 110.
35. Letter to *The Free Man*, 9 Dec. 1933, *Letters* 771.
36. From *In Memoriam James Joyce*, *Complete Poems* 742, 771.

> Now the language of matter is subject to laws, even as speech is; but the language of matter is used by the whole physical universe, spreading as far as we can perceive. Its laws are the result of collaboration, of the action in common, of the whole physical universe, and our part as men in that collaboration is small. We accept that language more than we create it.
>
> Matter is the language of the Universe.[37]

After the still and undistracted silence of the stones on his raised beach, MacDiarmid set out to speak that language.

---

37. Saurat 90-91.

CARL FREEDMAN

BEYOND THE DIALECT OF THE TRIBE:
JAMES JOYCE, HUGH MacDIARMID,
AND WORLD LANGUAGE

Few aspects of social life seem more irreducibly national than language. Several major languages are multinational, but none is genuinely international. There have been various attempts to construct an international tongue--whether by actual invention, as with Esperanto, or, as with Basic English, by the simplification of an existing national language--but no such project has enjoyed conspicuous success; and such interest as these efforts have aroused has been overwhelmingly of a utilitarian sort. Writers, concerned with the *literary* use of language, have been generally unimpressed. A few writers have moved from one language to another--Beckett from English to French, Vladimir Nabokov from Russian to English--but such moves are extremely rare and do not, in any case, disturb the general principle of the nation-centeredness of literary language (as the geographical resettlements of Beckett and Nabokov themselves help to illustrate). Probably the only authentic exception to this principle, at least in the Western tradition, has been postclassical Latin: and, even in this case, how many works in medieval or renaissance Latin, outside of the *Utopia*, really endure as literature? Dante's decision to compose his masterpiece in the despised national vernacular was, at the time, an act of courage and insight; but had he made the more obvious decision to write in Latin, the *Comedy* might today count as a comparatively minor work. International tongues, from the Esperanto of a few hobbyists to the Latin of the medieval schoolmen, are virtually never learned in early childhood or spoken by a cross section of any given society, and are seldom spoken consistently even by any given individual; and the empirical evidence seems to suggest that such languages do not possess the resources for literature of fundamental interest.

       But perhaps the problem can be approached in a quite different way. Such is the assumption which motivates two of the significant works of the twentieth century, James Joyce's *Finnegans Wake* (1939) and Hugh MacDiarmid's *In Memoriam James Joyce* (1955). These prose poems are profoundly rooted in their national traditions--the marginalized cultures of Ireland and Scotland, respectively, toward which the authors maintained intense and complicated relations--yet both also constitute extraordinarily ambitious attempts to transcend nationality and encompass a vision of world language; and MacDiarmid's project, as his title indicates, was undertaken with full awareness and appreciation of the Joycean precedent. In the following pages, I will first offer a relatively brief analysis of *Finnegans Wake*, far from exhaustive but I hope adequate for my purposes. Though Joyce's final work is not so widely read as its admirers believe it ought to be, it is at least placed in the established modern canon and, moreover, has in recent years received a certain amount of critical attention directly relevant to my own concerns. I will then extend my analysis to MacDiarmid's far more neglected text, and will attempt to suggest some new bearings for future discussion of it. I will conclude by considering to what degree these brilliant and outlandish works may be said to succeed or fail.

The enabling linguistic insight of *Finnegans Wake* is radically Freudian:[1] namely, that the conscious use of language--what we imagine to be our conscious manipulation of it--by no means exhausts the whole of the linguistic order. It is tempting to put the point in much stronger terms, and to claim that Joyce's text represents the language not of the conscious speaking subject but of the unconscious mind--a claim that might appear consonant with the conventional reading of *Finnegans Wake* as a book of the night, as an account, in large part, of H. C. Earwicker's dream. But, for Joyce as for Freud, the relation between language and the unconscious is actually a good deal more complex than such a formulation would allow. Psychoanalysis holds, on the one hand, that the unconscious is, in Jacques Lacan's well-known dictum, "structured as a language."[2] Insofar

---

1. Within the general context of Joyce's "root language," it does not seem irrelevant to point out that the name of Joyce, if translated into German, would become something like "Freud."
2. Jacques Lacan, "Of Structure as an Inmixing of an Otherness Prerequisite to Any Subject Whatever," in *The Structuralist Controversy: The Languages of Criticism and the Sciences of Man*, ed. Richard Macksey and Eugenio Donato (Baltimore: The John Hopkins UP, 1972) 188. It is of course to Lacan that most of us owe our understanding of the importance of language in psychoanalysis--though we should bear in mind his own insistence that his project is only to restate, with greater force and rigor, insights discoverable in Freud's own writing. The difficulty of Lacan's style is famous, and, though no paraphrase conveys a fully adequate understanding of his thought, the following secondary works are among the most useful: Anthony Wilden, "Lacan and the Discourse of the Other," in Jacques Lacan, *Speech and Language in Psychoanalysis*, trans. Anthony Wilden (Baltimore: The Johns Hopkins UP,

as it can be conceptualized at all, the unconscious must be understood not as a "place," nor even exactly as a "process," but as a *discourse*, a discourse which we do not speak but which speaks us; and we are thus constituted as the de-centered or eccentric effects of a transpersonal structure of signification which subjects us (in our essential lack of plenitude) to desire. The unconscious, as Lacan says, is the "discourse of the Other,"[3] and the latter term designates precisely the totality of language itself, or, in more general terms, the entire order of symbolic representation. But unconscious discourse is (like the true name of God in Christian theology) absolutely resistant to articulation in the language spoken or written by any human being; spoken *by* the whole of the symbolic order, it cannot be spoken *in* any actual text, for that which enables the category of textuality is therefore itself beyond textualization. Neither *Finnegans Wake* nor any other text we have ever read is genuinely written in the language of the unconscious. The latter can, however, be *translated* into texts readable by the conscious mind, with all the condensation, displacement, elaboration, censorship--in short, all the *alteration*--which the category of translation implies. The "texts" which psychoanalytic practice itself strives to interpret are just such translations, and a complex relation of textualizing labor exists between the unconscious and its manifest representation in a dream, parapraxis, or neurotic symptom.

All texts, of course, may be understood as translations of the strictly mute discourse of the unconscious; but the density of the work of translation varies considerably. In a text like the present one, composed at a high level of conscious resolution, the amount of translation involved is considerable, whereas the translation labor is comparatively (but only comparatively) slight when I "accidently" write of an acquaintance as a fiend rather than a friend (and the logical order which I attempt to impose is thus manifestly disrupted by the effects of unconscious desire). It is possible, then, to theorize a continuum along which any text could in principle be located; but the location of *Finnegans Wake* is especially complicated. Though Joyce seems to construct a language as nearly unconscious and so as sensitive to desire as possible, his self-conscious artistry is well

1981) 157-311; Fredric Jameson, "Imaginary and Symbolic in Lacan: Marxism, Psychoanalytic Criticism, and the Problem of the Subject," in *Literature and Psychoanalysis*, ed. Shoshana Felman (Baltimore: The Johns Hopkins UP, 1982) 338-95; Jacqueline Rose, "Introduction--II," in Jacques Lacan and the École Freudienne, *Feminine Sexuality*, ed. Juliet Mitchell and Jacqueline Rose, trans. Jacqueline Rose (London: Macmillan, 1983) 27-57.
3. Jacques Lacan, *Ecrits: A Selection*, trans. Alan Sheridan (New York: Norton, 1977) 312.

known, and no one could suppose that it is as easy to write *Finnegans Wake* as to make a slip of the pen or tongue. *Finnegans Wake* must, I think, be understood as a highly conscious text which attempts to mimic or represent language at a much lower level of conscious resolution, thus allowing the latter to be examined in more detail and at more length than is ordinarily possible. Earwicker's dream is important not so much for its significance in the residual narrative elements of the book as for the fact that the dream provides an analogue for the kind of textuality by which *Finnegans Wake* strives to operate. But the parapraxis--in which "accidental" phonetic relations can undermine the logic of conscious intentionality--is perhaps an even closer analogue. When Lacan states that Joyce's work constitutes both a refusal and an illustration of psychoanalysis,[4] he is partly referring, I believe, to the paradoxical attempt to manipulate--with remarkable architectonic elaboration--that which necessarily evades the full scrutiny of the conscious mind.

There is, then, a fundamental doubleness--or, better, a plurality--to the strategy of *Finnegans Wake*. On the one hand, there are, on the molar (i.e., "macro") level, the immensely intricate logical schemes which such dedicated exegetes as Campbell and Robinson, Clive Hart, and Adeline Glasheen have helped us to grasp.[5] On the other hand, there are, on the molecular (i.e., "micro") level, the incessant, multilingual, as-if-involuntary puns, whose quite different logic works to destabilize all such scheming. On the one hand, there is at least the shadow of a conventional narrative--the story of the Chapelizod pubkeeper H. C. Earwicker, his wife Anna Livia Plurabelle, their sons Shem and Shaun, and their daughter Issy. On the other hand, there is the break-up of narrative into dream-like shiftings, as the characters and settings vanish, return, multiply, divide, and turn into one another in an interminable series of permutations. On the one hand, there is the intensely *written* character of the text, each morpheme painstakingly constructed toward the (paradoxical) aim of achieving maximum polyvalency.[6] On the

4. Jacques Lacan, *The Four Fundamental Concepts of Psycho-Analysis*, ed. Jacques-Alain Miller, trans. Alan Sheridan (New York: Norton, 1981) ix.
5. Joseph Campbell and Henry Morton Robinson, *A Skeleton Key to "Finnegans Wake"* (New York: Viking, 1969); Clive Hart, *Structure and Motif in "Finnegans Wake"* (Evanston: Northwestern UP, 1962); Adeline Glasheen, *Third Census of "Finnegans Wake"* (Berkeley: U of California P, 1977).
6. Cf. Stephen Heath, "Ambiviolences: Notes for reading Joyce," trans. Isabelle Mahieu, in *Post-structuralist Joyce: Essays from the French*, ed. Derek Attridge and Daniel Ferrer (Cambridge: Cambridge UP, 1984) 58: "It is often said that *Finnegans Wake* is a book to be heard rather than read: nothing could be more false. Leaving aside the evident objection that no reading aloud could possibly reproduce the graphic distribution of the text . . . or the play of letters, there is no reading aloud that can

other hand, there is the almost unprecedented mimicry of sheer orality, directly based on the rhythms and flows of common Dublin speech. Perhaps no other modern work is, in one sense, so devoted to order, organization, and classical logic as is *Finnegans Wake*; Joyce, one may remember, was an ardent follower of Aristotle and Aquinas. But, in another sense, no other work gives such free play to the prelogical forces of desire that disrupt all imposed order and impel us intermittently to realize the extent to which we are constituted as de-centered beings, driven and mastered rather than driving and mastering. The utter Otherness of the unconscious itself finally lies beyond the grasp of the antithetical movements of *Finnegans Wake*; but the uniqueness of the work lies in its conjunction of translations from the unconscious in such radically different modes.

It is the plurality or heterogeneity of *Finnegans Wake* which accounts, I think, for the connections which several critics have drawn between Joyce's text and the psychoanalytic politics of gender.[7] Under a patriarchal regime, where the phallus functions as the primary signifier of the linguistic itself,[8] hegemonic logic is necessarily phallic in character, and full access to the classical Logos is normatively reserved for the dominant male gender. Contrariwise, that which evades and disrupts rationalistic order--puns, slips, as-if-unstructured flows of language, non-literate orality--may be assumed to enjoy a privileged relationship with the feminine, "for the end is with woman, flesh-without-word."[9] Even on the level of the overall schematic structure of *Finnegans Wake*, woman, while being foreclosed from full participation in articulate literacy, is shown to function more closely to the unconscious basis of all linguistic creativity. Anna Livia--who is geographically identified with the flowing Liffey, in contrast to the archetypically masculine Finnegan or Earwicker manifest in the phallic Hill of Howth--is reported to be the actual author of the letter (i.e., of the Joycean text itself), though her authorship is oral only; in order to achieve the fixity of print, the text must be transcribed by her son Shem the Penman, who is like Leopold Bloom a "womanly man" and hence capable of artistic mediation between masculine written meaning and

---

pass 'for inkstands' and 'for instance' together: the reading must choose; in other words, it creates a context."
7. Perhaps the most useful such work is Colin MacCabe, *James Joyce and the Revolution of the Word* (New York: Harper & Row, 1979) 133-57.
8. See Jacques Lacan, "The Signification of the Phallus," *Ecrits* 281-91.
9. James Joyce, *Finnegans Wake* (London: Faber and Faber, 1964) 468. Further references will be given parenthetically by page number.

feminine oral desire, between the "yarns" or structured narratives of the father and the "yearns" or wish flows of the mother
(620). The text further suggests that the daughter Issy (who, as
her name suggests, operates only by the logic of the purely cop-
ulative) has access to "gramma's grammar" (268), a near-abso-
lute linguistic horizon which eludes the scholarly studies of Shem
and Shaun alike.[10]

But it is on the molecular level of word play that the
text's most profound involvement with the feminine lies. It must
be understood that, psychoanalytically, the female child is not
completely denied access to the symbolic order, but, enjoying an
"inferior" relation to the phallus, she enters (or is constituted
by) the symbolic athwart its dominant mode of organization,
gaining access to a language inflected more heavily by the sameness, "arbitrariness," and materiality of the unconscious than by
the logical distinctions and ideal Logos of the hegemonic symbolic order--in sum, a language less extensively translated from
the unconscious.[11] Perhaps the paradigmatic instance of such
language is the pun, the chief mode of composition in *Finnegans
Wake*.[12] Even more radically than in any of its themes or narratives, it is in the pre-logical logic of its omnipresent punning--
with all the attendant stress on the substantial materiality of language and on polyvalent meaning-effects which elude hegemonic
notions of sense--that Joyce's text subverts its own thematization
and narrativity. In the pun, the word becomes flesh while relin-
quishing its status as word in the sense of Logos: "woman, flesh-
without-word."

Given this understanding of the pun, we may again
consider the matter of world language more directly. Just as
gender is both a linguistic and (sexual-)political category, so is
nationality also a term of language and of the political; and the
treatment of gender roles and relations in *Finnegans Wake* is
paralleled by and connected to an at least equally complex investigation of nationalism and internationalism. But this dimension
of the text has been largely ignored by Joyce's readers (excepting
MacDiarmid). In part, the neglect stems from a larger misun-
derstanding of Joyce's attitude toward Ireland. His cosmopolitan
erudition, his commitment to international socialism (until the
latter was betrayed by most of the European Socialist parties at

10. On this point, cf. Colin MacCabe 147ff.
11. I am here indebted to conversations with my colleague Michelle Masse, who has generously shared
with me her research in the psychoanalysis of gender and language.
12. Can it be a co-incidence that Shakespeare, whom Joyce and many others have considered the
greatest penman of all, is, with Joyce, the most notable author of puns?

the outbreak of the First World War), his low opinion of many Irish nationalist politicians, his contempt for Irish provincialism and for sentimental displays of vulgar Irishness, his general dislike of the writers of the Irish Renaissance (though he preserved a grudging respect for Yeats)--all these factors have combined with his voluntary geographical exile to encourage the misconception that Joyce was quite without nationalist feeling and that his internationalism was therefore but the lonely rootlessness of the expatriate.[13] Yet Joyce artistically consecrated his national capital to a degree unmatched in modern literature, and his work--most especially in *Finnegans Wake*, that "new Irish stew" (190)--is saturated in Irish history, culture, myth, and speech. In the earnest nationalism of Yeats and Synge, there is a degree of shallowness and artificiality, reflecting the somewhat borrowed enthusiasm of the Protestant outsider. The Catholic Joyce had no need of such affectations, nor--again unlike Yeats and Synge --did he frame his nationalism in a way that could give comfort to chauvinism; on the contrary, his feeling for Ireland is at one with his internationalism and the project of international language.

Indeed, one kind of Irish nationalism is throughout *Finnegans Wake* identified with the worst and most inartistic authoritarianism of phallocratic dominance. Shaun, the extreme of the manly man, is a figure of bigoted and mawkish Irishness, and at one point, in his avatar of Kev, he resorts to a violent, sentimental defense of the fatherland in order to avoid the knowledge of femininity which the Shemish Dolph, as he symbolically lifts up the skirts of Anna Livia, is trying to impart.[14] Dolph, by contrast, freely mocks the most canonical male heroes of Ireland.[15] Yet, in addition to this Ireland of official nationalism (from which Joyce himself fled), there is a different, more feminine Ireland, identified largely with Anna Livia and the River Liffey, the lifeblood of the nation. Marginalized and colonized nationality is, like woman, "incomplete" and inferior--one may recall MacDiarmid's identification of Scotland as feminine

---

13. For a good corrective to this widespread error, see Seamus Deane, "Joyce and Nationalism," in *James Joyce: New Perspectives*, ed. Colin MacCabe (Bloomington: Indiana UP, 1982) 168-83. One effect of this particular misreading of Joyce is that his standing in Ireland remained comparatively low long after his international reputation was secure; Deane, writing as an Irishman, evidently seeks *inter alia* to redress this injustice.
14. Cf. Colin MacCabe, *James Joyce and the Revolution of the Word* 144ff.
15. "This is brave Danny weeping his spache for the popers. This is cool Connolly wiping his hearth with brave Danny. And this, regard! how Chawleses Skewered parparaparnelligoes between Danny boy and the Connolly" (303). The reference, of course, is to Daniel O'Connell, Charles Stewart Parnell, and James Connolly; and the ridicule is directed less at them as historical figures than at their appropriation by a decadent official nationalism.

in *A Drunk Man Looks at the Thistle*. But Joyce, like MacDiarmid, finds in this very incompleteness--in the fact that, as
Stephen Dedalus says, the conscience of his race is as yet uncre-
ated--the possibility of a more profound artistic creation, a more
encompassing global vision, than powerful and fully
"independent" nations like England can attain. Whereas the
imperial nation--in all its illusions of mastery and centeredness,
in its fixity in the phallocratic Logos of secure national identity--
is necessarily blind and deaf to that which threatens such illusions, the marginalized nation may remain more sensitive to the
unconscious forces which subvert identity and order, and which
radically enable the potentiality of linguistic creativity.[16] There is
here a nationalism far more radical and genuine than the
aggressive Shaunish variety, which, after all, amounts to a desire
to emulate the English oppressor.

The wellspring of this Joycean nationalism is Anna
Livia, and it is in this connection that the orality of *Finnegans
Wake* is perhaps most crucial. The remarkable mimicry of colloquial oral discourse which informs the text--unmatched, probably, since *Huckleberry Finn*--reaches its appropriate high point
and culmination in Anna Livia's closing monologue (619-28).
Speaking as the voice of the life-giving Liffey as it flows out to
sea--dying, but only, like Finnegan, to be born again--she gives
perhaps the most eloquent expression in the entire text to the
fluent feminine language of nurture and desire. But, as with
Mark Twain's novel--which, as its title reminds us, was one of
Joyce's models--this free-flowing orality is also a deeply *national*
vernacular, uncannily reproducing the specific accents of Dublin.
It is an Irish voice far removed from the harsh, angular voice of
Shaun; in its fluidity, the voice of Anna Livia--the "eternal geo-
mater" (296-97) or mother of all the earth--opens up the possibility of a language as transcendent of the fixity of national fron-
tiers as the ocean into which the Liffey passes. It is in this connection that the feminine orality of the text is most importantly
connected to the schematic, logical, more "masculine" aspects of
Finnegans Wake. For the latter is not, as one might expect,
devoted to rigidly Shaunish official nationalism, but is bent to
the more "feminine" purpose of an inclusive internationalism
figured largely in the universalistic philosophical visions influ-

---

16. Cf. Seamus Deane 173: "The unfinished and the uncreated culture provided the opportunity for
the most comprehensible, the most finished, the most boundlessly possible art. . . . Only a minority
culture could seek an articulation of itself as a total culture."

enced by such thinkers as Vico, Bruno, and William Blake.[17] This conjunction of the feminine and the feminized masculine in the service of an internationalist nationalism is represented in microcosm in one of the key passages of the text. Shem, as the quintessential Irish artist, as the womanly man, and as Anna Livia's favorite son and the scribe of her oral discourse, writes in a way that prophetically anticipates the current French feminist category of "writing the body":[18]

> Then, pious Eneas, conformant to the fulminant firman which enjoins on the tremylose terrian that, when the call comes, he shall produce nichthemerically from his unheavenly body a no uncertain quantity of obscene matter not protected by copriright in the United Stars of Ourania or bedeed and bedood and bedang and bedung to him, with this double dye, brought to blood heat, gallic acid on iron ore, through the bowels of his misery, flashly, faithly, nastily, appropriately, this Esuan Menschavik and the first till last alshemist wrote over every square inch of the only foolscap available, his own body, till by its corrosive sublimation one continuous present tense integument slowly unfolded all marryvoising mood-moulded cyclewheeling history. . . . (185-86)

Shem extracts from his quite physical or "unheavenly" body a quantity of his own excrement; and, with this profoundly Irish material, this "Gaelic acid," he writes--in a way unsanctioned by such official institutions as the copyright laws, for he is, as Stephen Dedalus aspires to be, a forger--the universal integument of the world (the scheme according to Vico), using his own body instead of paper. Shem writes his own Irish body--the body of one who, like the Biblical Esau, does not enjoy paternal favor, and, who, like the Russian Mensheviks, is not only a revolutionary but a minority within the revolutionary party--but in the process it becomes the encompassing body of the world. Thus is a world language attained: not by denying nationality but by sublating it through the concrete resources of an oppressed, "feminine" nation whose very "incompleteness" enables an encompassing vision denied to those for whom nationalism is a matter of established phallocratic fixity. Less alienated from the

---

17. Similarly, the central male figure of *Finnegans Wake*, H. C. Earwicker, is not an entirely manly man like Shaun, but is himself somewhat feminized: "there's a great poet in you too" (619), says Anna Livia.

18. This concept, heavily influenced by Lacanian psychoanalysis and developed by such thinkers as Luce Irigaray and Helene Cixous, posits a specifically feminine writing more attuned to physicality and desire than is normative masculine discourse; the usual canon of authors who have achieved such writing is not, however, exclusively female, and Joyce is often mentioned among the male practitioners of writing the body. For a useful overview, see Ann Rosalind Jones, "Writing the Body: Toward an Understanding of *l' Ecriture feminine*," in *The New Feminist Criticism*, ed. Elaine Showalter (New York: Pantheon, 1985) 361-77.

unconscious, the womanly Irish scribe achieves a nearer realization of the radically international.

But, as in its investigations of gender, so it is also in its closely related investigations of nationalism and internationalism that the most decisive operations of *Finnegans Wake* occur on the most molecular level of the text, in the form of the pun. For among the distinctions of hegemonic order which the pun subverts are the distinctions between the various national languages themselves. It is easy, however, to misunderstand the function of Joyce's multilingual punning. Many readers have assumed that the punning exists for the sake of the multilingualism, as though the linguistically erudite Joyce were preposterously attempting to craft a utilitarian international language on the model of Esperanto or Interlingua. The preferable reading is the reverse: namely, that Joyce employs his immense knowledge of languages in order to attain the greatest polyvalency of meaning--the most radical punning--possible. For the point is that world language, inclusive language, is a comparatively feminine language as little alienated as feasible from the unconscious, and the basic working principle might have remained the same even if Joyce had been as poor a student of foreign languages as Yeats--though it is certainly true that the empirical presence of morphemes and linguistic relations drawn from literally dozens of languages does provide a powerful illustration of how the discourse least extensively translated from the unconscious crosses national and other boundaries most freely (the freedom limited, of course, by the ultimate and perfectly global horizon of the unconscious itself, which no human language can strictly articulate). The Joycean pun transcends nationality only secondarily through empirical multilingualism; primary is its function in undermining all ideal Shaunish fixity for the sake of materiality and desire.

There is, however, one further point to be considered here. Just as the language of the oppressed gender cannot function wholly without a certain amount of "masculine" meaning and organization, so the nationalist internationalism of oppressed Ireland cannot completely avoid the logic of imperial English. Unable and no doubt unwilling to compose a Gaelic-based *Finnegans Wake*, Joyce must write his Irish universalism in (or near) the tongue of the oppressor. Though it matters comparatively little whether a given pun draws on resources from Greek or French or Norwegian or what-not, English cannot be regarded as a national language like any other. Not only is it at once linguistic base and political enemy; it is the former only *because* it is also the latter. Accordingly, the multilingual punning serves not only an internationalism (and perhaps a residual commitment to international socialism) but also a specific war of national liberation. The Joycean pun subverts not only the general structures of classical phallocratic order, but also the particular logical purity of English vocabulary and syntax. If English is necessarily the linguistic base of *Finnegans Wake*, Joyce will contaminate it with the tongues of numerous "lesser" breeds in a manner repugnant to English chauvinism. If Joyce is forced to write the language of his oppressor, he will turn it into anything but the King's English.[19]

The King's English was, of course, also the great enemy for MacDiarmid, perhaps the most prominent literary Anglophobe in modern times.[20] But his problem was not precisely the same as Joyce's. For whereas the Irish writer (outside the relatively few who compose in Irish Gaelic) has no native language save English, the Scottish writer--though usually incapable of handling Scottish Gaelic, as MacDiarmid for the most part was--still has an alternative to English in Scots. The latter is not, as is often thought, a mere "dialect" of Standard English, but an independent language which enjoyed a major literature before Modern English even existed. In the nineteenth and early twentieth centuries, however, Scots decayed, for literary purposes, into the medium of decadent Kailyard sentimentalism; and it was from this condition that MacDiarmid himself, in the earlier part of his career, rescued it. Undertaking the task of a modern and Scottish Dante, he not only synthesized a new literary Scots but used it, perhaps most notably in *A Drunk Man Looks at the Thistle* and in many great lyrics, to produce the most important Scots poetry since Burns--or, as some would say, the most important Scots poetry ever written. However, in his

---

19. In an interesting essay (marred, however, by a predictable neglect of orality in *Finnegans Wake*), Jacques Derrida seems to come within sight of this point but decisively misses it: "Of course this hegemony [of a single language] remains indisputable, but its law only appears *as such* in the course of a *war* through which English tries to erase the other language [German, in the particular example which Derrida is considering] or languages, to colonize them, to domesticate them, to present them for reading from only one angle. But one must also read the resistance to this commonwealth, not only pronounce oneself but also write oneself against it. Against Him. And this is indeed what happens. Between islands of language, across each island. Ireland and England would only [!] be emblems of this. What matters is the contamination of the language of the master by the language he claims to subjugate, on which he has declared war" (Jacques Derrida, "Two words for Joyce," trans. Geoff Bennington, *Post-structuralist Joyce* 156).
20. See, e.g., Hugh MacDiarmid, *Lucky Poet: A Self-Study in Literature and Political Ideas* (Berkeley: U of California P, 1972) 23-24: "*Who's Who* has long given my hobby as 'Anglophobia.' But it is a great deal more than a mere hobby. It is my very life." The volume was first published in 1943; in an Author's Note to the 1972 edition, MacDiarmid adds in a less jocular vein: "The principal theme of *Lucky Poet*, and of all my other books, has been my unqualified opposition to the English ethos" (xii).

later "poetry of fact" (of which *In Memoriam James Joyce* is the most considerable example) he largely abandoned Scots in favor of a world language based on *and against* normative English. Though a (rather Joycean) nationalist internationalism remains his project early and late--MacDiarmid was consistently an ardent Scottish nationalist and international communist--his fundamental strategy for implementing this project does undergo an important shift. Despite his contempt for Ricardian Basic English as an expression of "The magnificent insularity/Which is the pride of the Anglo-Saxon mind,"[21] he came to adopt a version of English generally free of Scots diction and even Scots cadences in order to enforce his vision of Scottish internationalism. Despite his success in Scots, the overwhelming numerical superiority of English was finally a decisive factor; yet MacDiarmid's English is as unlike that ever written in England as his earlier Scots had been.

One of the main differences, then, between *Finnegans Wake* and *In Memoriam James Joyce* is that the latter is far less nationally textured: employing a "synthetic English," MacDiarmid not only abandons Scots but declines any distinctively Scottish English (such as his colleague Lewis Grassic Gibbon used) which would be the equivalent of the Irish English on which Joyce's work is based. MacDiarmid's work is less poetically textured--at least in all conventional senses--as well. The diction, rhythms, pace, and tone are deliberately prosaic; the stance is often elaborately didactic; and the poem as a whole is untotalized by either residual narrative or intricate philosophical schemes. Nor is the Joycean punmanship by which nearly unconscious discourse is so powerfully mimicked much in evidence. Some have questioned whether the poetry of fact is poetry at all, and it is true that *In Memoriam James Joyce* hardly displays the same degree of artistry as *Finnegans Wake*; though I think that MacDiarmid's later method is also due to his well-known love of antithetical extremes (e.g., intense lyricism *or* prosaic didacticism; a Scots not at all English *or* an English hardly even Scottish). But MacDiarmid's poem does contain resources of its own which make it not, indeed, an emulation of *Finnegans Wake*, but a worthy response to Joyce's masterpiece and one which maintains the same fundamental aims.

---

21. Hugh MacDiarmid, *In Memoriam James Joyce, Complete Poems 1920-1976*, ed. Michael Grieve and W.R. Aitken (London: Martin Brian and O'Keeffe, 1978) 2: 789. Further references will be given parenthetically by page number.

Like its Joycean precedent, *In Memoriam James Joyce* may be considered on both a molecular and a molar level. The latter is structured primarily by MacDiarmid's didactic plan, though this term may be misleading, since the poem is, as it says, constantly "Wandering from subject to subject/And roaming back and forth in time" (CP 797). It does, however, ultimately form a reasonably coherent manifesto, the content of which amounts in large part to a re-articulation of the concerns of *Finnegans Wake*--which, near the end of MacDiarmid's poem, is significantly praised as

> . . .vastly outrunning present needs
> With its immense complication, its erudition,
> (The intricacy of the connections defies description.
> Before it the mind halts, abased. *In tenuis labor*.)
> But providing for the developments to come. . . .[22]
>   (CP 887)

Among the "developments to come" is of course the current poem itself. Like Joyce, MacDiarmid makes a display of staggering erudition, in an explicit attempt to encompass all human knowledge in a universal vision. More than Joyce, he insists upon the importance of science as well as literary and historical culture, going so far as to demand that "the poetry of the age/Should be brought into conformity with its scientific spirit" (CP 766). The project of world language itself is discussed at length, and a large number of earlier attempts are cited-- including, but only dismissively, such pragmatic efforts as Basic English and Esperanto. Serious praise in this regard is reserved for those imaginative writers who have expanded the very limits of language. Of these, Joyce is of course foremost, but a great many other writers from extremely various times and places are included; one of the most interesting such discussions is an extended treatment of Karl Kraus and Hölderlin (CP 767-75), who are taken as masters of the antithetical linguistic poles of speech and silence respectively.

Within the general neo-Joycean context, several further themes have a special importance. As Joyce privileges marginalized Ireland, MacDiarmid (despite some characteristically acerbic criticism) grants a special importance to marginalized Scotland, but also, and perhaps more frequently, to the

---

22. Strictly speaking, this passage refers to "your work" (Joyce is consistently written about in the second person), and *Finnegans Wake* is not mentioned by title. But there can be little doubt that the description is of Joyce's last and most important work.

Celtic nations as a whole,[23] where "the poor man/Is seldom poor in spirit or address" (CP 820). Contrariwise, England--where "the men, and women too,/Are almost as interesting as the sheep" (CP 845) is repeatedly damned for philistine arrogance: an entire section of the poem is entitled "England is Our Enemy" (CP 858-70). In addition to this specific celebration of the wider cultural and intellectual horizons implicit in oppressed nationality, MacDiarmid expresses a more general praise of process and fluidity, and a concomitant opposition to identitarian notions of fixity and stable meaning, "arguments involving the 'is' of identity/And the older elementalistic 'logic' and 'psychology' " (CP 783). Since what is under attack here is nothing less than the classical Logos or the entire hegemonic structure of Western metaphysics, the illusion is traced back to its historical foundation in "Plato's undue emphasis upon static unity" and his "expulsion/Of the temporal and contingent/From the realm of the fully knowable" (CP 848). The alternative perspective can be put in terms of the unconscious--"A permeability of spirit/To those mouldings from the unconscious" (CP 877)-- but it can also of course be put in terms of language itself, and for MacDiarmid as for Joyce, the flow of language has important connotations of gender: "Speech. All men's whore. My beloved!" (CP 838). She is a beloved who, by the very nature of the case, cannot finally be held in fixed dominance--"She will never belong to any man./It is a freed slavery they [i.e., men] give her" (CP 839).

On at least two important matters MacDiarmid goes decisively beyond his Joycean model. Whereas the references of *Finnegans Wake* are overwhelmingly (though not entirely) Occidental, MacDiarmid insists upon the inclusion and even the primacy of the Orient within an authentically global vision. One section of the poem bears the anti-Kipling title, "The Meeting of the East and the West" (CP 852-57), and it is on this issue that MacDiarmid states one of his rare differences with his precursor: "For unlike you, Joyce, I am more concerned/With the East than the West" (CP 801). Though I will later discuss the outlandishness (in all senses) of the shows of erudition which MacDiarmid makes, it is worth noting here that one of the most extreme such instances is the reproduction of two (untransliterated) lines of Sanskrit poetry, gravely introduced as

---

23. This is not mere courtesy to Joyce, for MacDiarmid had a genuine devotion to pan-Celtic as well as to Scottish nationalism; one of his less realistic political proposals was for a Union of Soviet Socialist Celtic Republics, to include Scotland, Ireland, Wales, Cornwall, the Isle of Man, and Brittany.

being "of extreme beauty" (CP 856). An even more important difference between *Finnegans Wake* and *In Memoriam James Joyce*, however, is that the latter renders far more explicit the specifically political dimension of the internationalist project which both authors share. Though MacDiarmid does not here stress his revolutionary principles to the same degree as in *The Battle Continues* (another major work of the poetry of fact), they are nonetheless clearly in evidence. Even aside from an overt reference to historical materialism (CP 781), there are many passages--perhaps most notably in the opening lines of the section called "The Snares of Varuna" (CP 840ff.)--in which the current regime is violently denounced from a communist point of view. The poem certainly contains no political blueprint, for revolutionary solutions are not easy to formulate for one who writes as a politically isolated intellectual in a deeply unrevolutionary society.[24] But it must be remembered that MacDiarmid held Lenin, among politicians, in something of the same esteem that he held Joyce among imaginative writers, and, even in this poem specially dedicated to the Joycean vision, it is clear that an adequate internationalism must synthesize both perspectives.

The synthesis which is world language cannot, of course, be made only through manifest proclamation. As the Russian thinker Vladimir Solovyof (quoted in an epigraph) states, "The true unity of languages is not an Esperanto or Volapuk or everyone speaking French, not a single language, but an all-embracing language, an interpenetration of all languages" (CP 737), and to this insight must be joined MacDiarmid's equally Joycean demand for "a poetry not only stating or advocating these principles/But activated by them at every point" (CP 751).[25] In this regard, the molecular textual operations of *In Memoriam James Joyce* are crucial. Here we have to deal with an aspect of the poem even more controversial than its didacticism and prosaic cast, namely its high proportion of proper names (often quite obscure), foreign words (sometimes in non-Latin alphabets), and technical terms wholly unfamiliar to the general reader of poetry. Not infrequently the density of such estranging signifiers becomes so great as to render the text practically

---

24. For a discussion of this problem and a general consideration of aesthetics and politics in MacDiarmid's work, see Carl Freedman, "Possibilities of a Political Aesthetic: The Case of Hugh MacDiarmid," *The Minnesota Review* (Fall 1984): 41-57.
25. One may also recall Beckett's comment that Joyce's "writing is not *about* something; *it is that something itself*" (Samuel Beckett, "Dante ... Bruno. Vico ... Joyce," in Samuel Beckett *et alia, Our Examination Round His Factification For Incamination of Work in Progress* [Paris: Shakespeare & Co., 1929] 14).

unreadable in any conventional way. The effect is difficult to convey in brief quotations, but the following passage is reasonably typical:

> And Breton with its four dialects--Tregorois,
> Leonard, Cornouaillais, and Vannetais;
> Celtiberian *viriae* corresponding to Gaulish *virolae*
> Whence come the French *virole* and the Irish *ferenn*,
> Or Spanish *gurdus*, Gallo-Roman *gurdunicus*,
> Welsh *gwrrd*, French *gourd* (numb), or, again. . .
>   (CP 778)

It is easy to understand the objection that such work is rather dry by the standards even of expository prose, let alone poetry. Yet the charge of unreadability is, after all, also levelled against *Finnegans Wake*, and may say as much about our dominant habits of reading as about the text under consideration. What MacDiarmid is doing here is, I think, something closely analogous to the Joycean pun. He is breaking down the hegemonic order and organization of the classical Logos, and representing language in a more fluid, more nearly unconscious, more "feminine" state where sameness and the irreducible materiality of the signifier are liberated from the illusions of fixity and normative meaning, and where passages across such established boundaries as those of nation-states are enabled. As in *Finnegans Wake*, the actual presence of foreign languages is not so much the essential structure of the method as a particular means of achieving it (when are we more aware of the non-transparency of language than when confronted by a language which we have never learned, or, less drastically, when several different languages are thrown together with apparent indiscrimination?) though, again as in *Finnegans Wake*, the linguistic erudition does secondarily function to illustrate the internationalist aim. Like the Joycean pun, MacDiarmid's remorselessly "unreadable" lists are never without a kind of logic--for a strictly random series of letters would not be language at all--but it is a logic radically at odds with the unproblematized assumptions of our fully conscious selves.[26]

The word play of *In Memoriam James Joyce*, then, works to deconstruct the rather conventional logic of the poem's

---

26. Cf. Nancy K. Gish, *Hugh MacDiarmid: The Man and His Work* (London: Macmillan, 1984) 192: "If several lines of rare words challenge the reader to 'adventure in dictionaries,' several pages exhaust one's patience. Yet simply reading through them without looking them up creates a sense of the vast resources of available words and meanings that we never use. It is rather like making poetry of the dictionary itself." The analogy is suggestive, for though the words in the dictionary are not without order of a sort, it is an order that must seem quite "arbitrary" by the standards of hegemonic logic.

overall didactic plan (or plans), while also reconstructing the intent of the latter in a different way. It should be clear, therefore, that one of the complaints most often voiced about the poem (and about much of MacDiarmid's other work as well)--that the erudition is sometimes bogus--is beside the point. Confronted with Sanskrit characters that for us are little more than black marks, we may suspect that the poet himself is not much more qualified to judge the lines as "of extreme beauty." But the point is that the lines perform their function of estrangement regardless of MacDiarmid's credentials as a Sanskrit scholar, and that it is generically inappropriate to judge a poem by the standards applicable to an academic treatise. The dubiousness of the poem's scholarly soundness--and the authorial voice repeatedly insists upon such soundness with (mock) solemnity--is, I think, itself of literary and theoretical significance. The explicit and implicit claims of erudition are often so extreme that it is difficult not to regard the intent as in part parodic of academic scholarship which knows facts without even suspecting the "interpenetration of all languages" in (or near) the ur-linguistic unconscious; and perhaps parodic of such classical and academically oriented poets as T.S. Eliot also. But beyond such parody the hyperbolic show of learning serves a positive purpose as well: that is, to gesture towards the unthinkable inclusiveness of world language, the empirical resources of which must inevitably be beyond the scholarly grasp of any single individual.

A similar case may be made for MacDiarmid's notorious "plagiarism." The term is perhaps not technically proper--for MacDiarmid often gives references for his numerous borrowings, or places them between inverted commas, or both--but it is at any rate preposterous to judge *In Memoriam James Joyce* as though it were a sophomore term paper.[27] Yet it is worthwhile to raise the issue within the context of Joycean forging. Just as the latter term refers both to strong, difficult creation and to the illegal attribution of a text to someone other than its "real" author, so MacDiarmid's shameless liftings of words originally composed by others serves a double purpose, corresponding to the molar and molecular levels of the text. In the first place, the

---

27. The most celebrated instance of MacDiarmid's "plagiarism" in *In Memoriam James Joyce* concerns a large stretch of the discussion of Karl Kraus which was lifted (but with acknowledgement) from a review in *The Times Literary Supplement* by Erich Heller. Some accused the poet of plagiarism. He replied that "copyright is a legal matter and not a literary one," and compared his method in this regard to that of Ezra Pound. It is pleasant to report that Heller himself, though a little worried that *he* might be charged with the theft, was on the whole delighted. See *The Letters of Hugh MacDiarmid*, ed. Alan Bold (Athens: The U of Georgia P, 1984) 832-33.

actual content of the quotations generally serves some aspect of the poet's didactic purpose, and in appropriating them in order to make a new text of his own he is merely following the time-honored method of the commonplace book--as Joyce often is in *Finnegans Wake*, through Joyce satirically contextualizes his quotations more frequently than MacDiarmid. Still more important, however, is the fact of "plagiarism" itself. As with the claims of erudition, the practice is so extreme as to disable any supposed attempt at actual deception, but it works not only to suggest the vast resources of human knowledge which must be synthesized in a world vision, but also the necessarily *collective* nature of such an enterprise and the correlative undermining of such notions as private property and stable personal identity. By acknowledging the plurality of voices in his poem (while often declining to give proper academic footnotes), MacDiarmid attempts to subvert the normative assumption that a given (stable) text stands in a relation of middle-class ownership to a given (stable) subject. If MacDiarmid, like Joyce, is attuned to the material, fluid, and international pre-logical logic of the unconscious--though without Joyce's degree of specifically sexual interest--he is more concerned than Joyce with the communist politics inferable from the subversion of centered subjectivity and of the hegemonic Logos. The very word *plagiarism*, after all, was not invented until the seventeenth century--the beginning of the period of bourgeois rule in the British Isles--and *In Memoriam James Joyce* looks forward to a day when the term will once again be meaningless.

If one were to attempt to summarize *In Memoriam James Joyce* (and perhaps *Finnegans Wake* also) in a single term, the best choice, I think, would be that which constitutes the image probably most central to the poem--weaving, or, as Mac-Diarmid himself says, braidbinding:

> Have I failed in my braid-binding
> At this great crisis
>
> . . .
>
> At this moment when braidbinding as never before,
> The creation of the seamless garment,
> Is the poet's task?
>
> (CP 876)[28]

---

28. There is an allusion here to "The Seamless Garment," one of the finest, most autobiographical, and most intensely political poems of MacDiarmid's earlier career.

The image condenses a number of concerns crucial to the Joycean and MacDiarmidian projects. Braidbinding, like textual production, is an act of concrete material labor, but of a particularly fluent sort, and one often relegated to marginalized areas and to the marginalized gender. Its aim is synthesis, a synthesis in which the individual identity of the strands is transcended and problematized but not exactly obliterated. It is also an aesthetic activity, but, because of the practical physicality of the material involved, is little tempted toward aestheticism or the idealism of the Logos. Braidbinding achieves interpenetration and polyvalency, and, granting the transposition from the verbal to the visual, may stand as a figure of world language.

In conclusion, however, it may be appropriate to engage the question which MacDiarmid asks in the lines quoted above. Did he--did Joyce--fail at braidbinding? Are *In Memoriam James Joyce* and *Finnegans Wake* to be accounted successful works of literature or not? In one fairly obvious sense, both are certainly failures. *In Memoriam James Joyce* is comparatively little read even among the (growing) minority of readers who recognize MacDiarmid as one of the pre-eminent writers of the twentieth century. One doubts that it would even be in print were it not for the *Complete Poems*, the existence of which is made possible mainly by the Scots lyrics, by *A Drunk Man Looks at the Thistle*, and by the earlier work generally. *Finnegans Wake* is substantially better known, but largely, I think, because Joyce's earlier work is much more securely canonical than MacDiarmid's. If Joyce had not also been the author of *Dubliners, A Portrait of the Artist as a Young Man*, and *Ulysses*, his final book might well be a mere curiosity of modern literature; even as things are, many would insist that it is in fact little more than that. Against both of these outlandish works can be brought what is, in one way, the most decisive charge that can be brought against a work of literature: they are unreadable. Therefore, they are mostly unread.

But that is not the whole story. As I have maintained, the unreadability of these texts cannot be understood apart from their attempts to mimic a discourse which approaches the absolute unreadability of the unconscious, and which accordingly subverts our taken-for-granted notions of stable meaning, classical logic, and secure personal identity. In other words, unreadability is here not a simple function of dullness or difficulty, but involves the radical challenge to precisely those illusions most deeply constitutive of our mundane waking consciousness. Furthermore, such illusions of centered subjectivity are, as I have also suggested, not necessarily politically innocent. They have a privileged connection to the sanctity and "naturalness" of private property, and many would insist that they are fundamentally inseparable from hierarchy and domination in general: that our constitution as apparently stable, centered, unproblematic subjects amounts to a process of *subjection* in the most political sense.[29] It is possible, therefore, to conceptualize a genuinely international and radically collective mode of egalitarian social organization in which subjectivity as we currently know it would not, indeed, be wholly absent, but would be substantially transformed--a society in which language would not necessarily be tied to fixed tribal dialect in the way it always has been, and in which our waking lives would not be quite so alienated from unconscious discourse as is now the case. In such a situation, *Finnegans Wake* and *In Memoriam James Joyce* may well be much more readable texts. Under the current regime, they may retain a small, rather cultish following, but are unlikely ever to be much more widely appreciated than they are now. But it is not absurd to imagine the readers of some strictly utopian future examining these works with more than an antiquarian interest-- indeed, with a certain surprise of recognition.

Admittedly, such thoughts are extremely speculative. But the speculation is of the sort encouraged by *Finnegans Wake* and *In Memoriam James Joyce*. As he would certainly have wished, I will leave the last words to MacDiarmid himself. In a letter to a periodical in 1933, he wrote:

> As Dostoevski said, all human organizations tend to stabilise and perpetuate themselves--to become a "church" and to short-circuit human consciousness. This is most marked in our language-habit, our helpless submission to a fraction of our expressive possibilities--and in this connection it is vitally necessary to remember that language is just as much a determinant of what is expressed in it as a medium of expression. By the synthetic use of a language, then, I mean "the destruction of the toothless ratio"--"freedom of speech" in the real meaning of the term--something completely opposed to all our language habits and freely utilising not only all the vast vocabulary these automatically exclude, but illimitable powers of word formation in keeping with the free genius of any language. Theoretically--and to some extent practically--I go fur-

---

29. The relevant theoretical literature is already so vast that even a basic overview would require a full-length essay in itself. Suffice it to say here that nearly all such work is directly or indirectly derived from two essays by Louis Althusser, "Ideology and Ideological State Apparatuses," and "Freud and Lacan," both in Louis Althusser, *Lenin and Philosophy*, trans. Ben Brewster (New York: Monthly Review Press, 1971) 127-86 and 189-219 respectively.

ther and agree with Joyce in regard to the utilisation of a multi-linguistic medium--a synthetic use, not of any particular language, but of all languages. Personally, I write in English, or in dialect Scots, or in synthetic Scots--or in synthetic English--with bits of other languages. I recognise the values of any language or any dialect for certain purposes, but where I am concerned with the free consciousness I cannot employ these--I must then find an adequate synthetic medium.[30]

On a less formal occasion, but in a similar context, he also wrote: "Conservative critics hate it--it bewilders the general public--it is only a matter of time. . . .The old undifferentiated 'simple direct English' is as dead as a door-nail."[31]

---

30. *Letters* 771.
31. *Letters* 210-11.

STEPHEN P. SMITH

HUGH MacDIARMID'S LUCKY POET: AUTOBIOGRAPHY AND THE ART OF ATTACK

When Hugh MacDiarmid's ponderous autobiography, *Lucky Poet*, originally published in the paper-short war year of 1943, was republished in 1972, it met a generally hostile critical reception. One typical review, written by a fellow Scot, calls *Lucky Poet* "the most windy, shapeless or obscure of his productions," a book with a "preposterously prolix style." After savaging MacDiarmid's style, the reviewer questions the book's self-proclaimed status as an autobiography: "It is stated to be an autobiography, but apart from some scattered reminiscences of childhood it offers few facts of the expected kind." Why, asks the reviewer, should a writer of MacDiarmid's eminence pen a purported autobiography devoid of biographical information, offering instead a plethora of ideas, many stolen and often quoted from others, in a purple prose where "boasting, pomposity, half-baked paranoia and even a dismaying, arch kind of modesty, vie with each other for predominance."[1] In short, *Lucky Poet* may supply intellectual nourishment to a handful of MacDiarmid scholars and devotees intent on devouring every word of the Master, but provides a scanty meal--or too much--for readers seeking the aesthetic satisfaction provided by the autobiography which remains faithful to its function. As a result of this sort of reaction, *Lucky Poet*, like much of MacDiarmid's vast output of prose, has received scant critical attention from MacDiarmid's admirers and detractors alike, a state of affairs which has relegated the prose to the critical supporting role of commentary on or intellectual context for the poetry. In doing so, we have failed to recognize an intrinsically valuable body of work written by one of the great polemicists of the western world.

Lucky Poet in particular deserves re-evaluation. Written during MacDiarmid's self-imposed exile on Whalsay in

---

1. Angus Calder, "Anti-Laureate," *New Statesman* 84 (July-Dec. 1972): 133, 134.

the northeastern Shetland Islands, this strange book does indeed pose problems for the reader. As the review quoted above points out, MacDiarmid's polemic not only attacks a host of enemies, real and imagined, but often boasts of personal accomplishments beyond the ken of ordinary Scottish Nationalists, political internationalists, and bards expressing the souls of their nations. The few actual references to events in MacDiarmid's life lie scattered among vast stretches of material quoted from other sources, snatches of MacDiarmid's own poetry, discussions of theories and ideas from anthropology to zoology, and names-- sometimes interminable lists of names citing influences, enemies, teachers, bohemians, writers, philosophers, and eccentrics of every stripe. And always in the foreground the usually strident, occasionally quiet voice of the lonely genius in exile, exhorting the Scottish people to think, to see, to rebel. Many readers, intimidated or confused by the sheer weight of references and allusions, refuse to play MacDiarmid's game; others disparage the pomposity and arrogance of MacDiarmid's boastings, on the one hand, and the frequent viciousness of his attacks on the other. Both types of reader misunderstand the nature of *Lucky Poet*, an autobiography that attempts to perform a specific function; in MacDiarmid's words, "This book is accordingly an account of the development of my mind, 'absorbed in its own forked speculation', or, more precisely, of what Jung would call my *persona*, defined as 'the private conception a man has of himself, his idea of what he wants to be and of how he wants other people to take him.' "[2] *Lucky Poet* is what William Howarth might call an oratorical autobiography[3] which, in order to sustain the *persona* of the isolated but superior genius, often resorts to a technique which we might call prose flyting.[4]

Recent scholarship in the study of autobiography as a genre tends to make suspect remarks such as those quoted at the outset of this study: *Lucky Poet* does not offer autobiographical facts "of the expected kind." The great diversity of form and approach throughout the history of autobiography has led a foremost scholar of the genre to declare that a "definition

2. Hugh MacDiarmid, *Lucky Poet: A Self-Study in Literature and Political Ideas, being the Autobiography of Hugh MacDiarmid* (Berkeley: U of California P, 1972) XXVI.
3. William A. Howarth, "Some Principles of Autobiography," *Autobiography: Essays Theoretical and Critical*, ed. James Olney (Princeton UP, 1980) 88-95.
4. Flyting is a Scottish type of verse satire in which a literary protagonist attempts to diminish an opponent rhetorically in verses characterized by invective, exaggeration, and highly abusive language. It often takes the form of a debate or dialogue in which each opponent attempts to demonstrate verbal virtuosity at the expense of the other.

of autobiography as a literary genre seems . . . virtually impossible, because the definition must either include so much as to be no definition, or exclude so much as to deprive us of the most relevant texts."[5] If we "expect" certain kinds of information from *Lucky Poet*, we will indeed be disappointed; if we accept MacDiarmid's concentration on ideas rather than historical and biographical events as one possible type of autobiography, then we can perhaps appreciate MacDiarmid's achievement. To do so is to agree with Francis R. Hart's observation: "The nature of an extended autobiographical act makes it self-defeating for the interpreter to expect some predictable integrity or unity."[6] The autobiographer freely appropriates the form best suited to the dynamic process of recovering, selecting, and re-shaping those events from the past which form the present, or best explain that version of the self which the autobiographer seeks, consciously or unconsciously, to present to the world. The telling of a life can adopt many forms, only one of which is the careful recall and narrative shaping of lived historical events.

To warn us that his is not a conventional autobiography, MacDiarmid notes early in *Lucky Poet* that his work fulfills the prophecy of Lord David Cecil for the rise of the "semi-imaginative autobiography," a curious phrase to describe a genre which promises at least some degree of adherence to fact. Furthermore, MacDiarmid describes his method for securing his desired ends as "a fury of incontrovertible detail," an impressive array of learned allusions, appeals to authorities, and references to obscure books meant to achieve "a grand breadth and splendour of style with a Faberge-like jeweller's precision and delicacy,"[7] a phrase MacDiarmid quotes from his friend Kaikhosru Sorabji, composer of "epic" symphonies and incredibly difficult piano pieces. The result is a book whose style alternates between extensive quotation and MacDiarmid's own long, cumulative, syntactically convoluted sentences. In one of the few critical attempts to analyze MacDiarmid's prose, Owen Edwards rightfully emphasizes MacDiarmid's journalism background and penchant for uncovering the odd source to serve as foil to or support for his own ideas as explanations for his peculiar style[8]; Edwards summarizes MacDiarmid's "documentary approach"

5. James Olney, *Metaphors of Self: The Meaning of Autobiography* (Princeton: Princeton UP, 1972) 39.
6. Francis R. Hart, "Notes for an Anatomy of Modern Autobiography," *New Literary History* 1 (1970): 502.
7. *Lucky Poet* XVII, XVIII.
8. Owen Dudley Edwards, "Prose and Polemic," *The Age of MacDiarmid*, eds. P. H. Scott and A.C. Davis (Edinburgh: Mainstream Publishing, 1980) 243.

by saying that "much of his prose writing . . . is a matter of the artist being his own evangelist."[9] Every skilled evangelist is a skilled orator, for conversion to either faith or ideas demands a certain weight of persuasion.

In a recent effort to define the elementary principles of autobiography, William Howarth uses the elements of character, technique, and theme to delineate three types of autobiography analogous to types of portraiture in painting. Although one might question the inclusiveness of Howarth's approach, his analysis of autobiography as oratory sheds light on the themes and style of *Lucky Poet*.

First, Howarth defines "character" as the "image or self-portrait his [the autobiographer's] book presents . . . [determined by] his sense of self, of place, of history, of his motives for writing."[10] The typical character of the oratorical autobiographer arises from an acute sense of self-importance leading to the impulse to teach, to preach, to convert to a strongly held belief or principle of living. Such autobiographers usually possess a "positive sense of character" based on a "common motive: to carve public monuments out of their private lives."[11] Examples of this mode--Augustine, John Bunyan, Edward Gibbon, Henry Adams, and Malcolm X--respond, albeit to varying degrees, to the call of a vocation, religious or secular. In any case, each creates a *persona* who, whether "true" or not to historical facts, represents a sympathetic protagonist with whom the creative "I," the controlling ego of the present autobiographical act, can forge an instructional bond. Such was I; such I have become as a result.

MacDiarmid's *persona* in *Lucky Poet* accords well with Howarth's oratorical character, despite the complexity of MacDiarmid's sense of self. MacDiarmid's unwavering sense of self-importance, the source of much of *Lucky Poet's* seeming pomposity and exaggeration, stems from the highly selective nature of MacDiarmid's autobiographical memory in creating of his own life a public monument, both Scottish and universal. At one point he boasts of "speaking for Scotland in a way which few men, if any, have ever been qualified to speak"[12]; at another he equates his personal character traits with "the great historical directives of my people,"[13] comparing himself and Scotland to

---

9. Edwards 242, 241.
10. Howarth 87.
11. Howarth 92.
12. *Lucky Poet* 29.
13. *Lucky Poet* 36.

St. Paul and the spirit of universal history speaking through him. His primary task is to teach, a vocation prepared for by a life-time's work of finding, assimilating, and storing like a monolithic collective consciousness the accumulated knowledge of centuries. Thus MacDiarmid boasts of his "comprehensive and thorough knowledge of world-literature"[14] and of a superhuman grasp of information garnered from every corner of science, no matter how arcane:

> So for twenty years I have read everything about Scotland I could lay my hands on, developing as a consequence a faculty which seems to attract to me instantaneously all the available information on points no matter how obscure or technical from sources no matter how far scattered, and at the same time 'grangerizes' any such issue that is in my mind with a simultaneous recollection of all manner of connected . . . matters drawn from the whole field of my tremendous reading, and at once establishes a compenetrant complexity of relationships and ideas for their literary and political utilization.[15]

This statement reminds us of MacDiarmid's claim earlier in the book to have read all 12,000 volumes contained in the Langholm library during his childhood, a "fact" preparatory to future circumstances in which MacDiarmid finds his reading superior to that of any professor in his or her specialized field.[16]

To ask if such claims are true is to ask the wrong question. MacDiarmid, as autobiographer, does not lie to us any more than the writer of fiction does; MacDiarmid creates an appropriate version of his younger self by allowing memory to select only those details, perhaps embellished with fictive elements, which correspond to his present conception of self. In other words, memory is no more to be trusted in literature than in life, although, as defined by James Olney, memory can provide insight into states of present consciousness: "We should understand memory as a faculty of the present and an exact reflection of present being that also recapitulates and reverses the entire process by which present being has come to be what it is."[17] The past may or may not have existed as MacDiarmid remembers it, but his memory reconstitutes the past in conformity with his present, making that present the inexorable goal of

---

14. *Lucky Poet* 100.
15. *Lucky Poet* 254.
16. *Lucky Poet* 13.
17. James Olney, "Some Versions of Memory/ Some Versions of Bios: The Ontology of Autobiography," *Autobiography: Essays Theoretical and Critical*, ed. James Olney (Princeton: Princeton UP, 1980) 241.

the past: all events lead to the *persona* MacDiarmid creates in *Lucky Poet*. This private conception of self, bolstered by the selective manipulation of the past, manifests itself through two complementary self-images to which all others are subordinate. Both are introduced early in *Lucky Poet*.

First, MacDiarmid establishes the role of the isolated intellectual. Exiled and cut off from the main currents of European thought, MacDiarmid constantly juxtaposes his poverty and sickness with the literary isolation imposed upon him by the official London publishing scene. For instance, Chapter II follows up a discussion of his juvenile years as the intellectual son in a working class family by describing his condition on Whalsay, a full circle movement that, by 1933, had left MacDiarmid "with no money behind me at all, broken down in health, unable to secure remunerative employment of any kind, and wholly concentrated on projects in poetry and other literary fields which could bring me no monetary return whatever."[18] As the autobiography continues, MacDiarmid repeats this constant refrain, making it clear that his sufferings do not result from chance but from the deliberate schemes of enemies or well-intentioned but fumbling acquaintances. Despite his unquestioned popularity, MacDiarmid claims to have been excluded from group publications of Communist poetry because of the conspiratorial actions of an anti-Scottish, anti-working class, pro-Auden circle English Ascendancy press[19]; MacDiarmid's mastery of world literature and profundity of thought, in addition to differentiating him from "everybody else in the British literary world," have aroused the animosity of critics and writers alike[20]; even a testimonial presented to MacDiarmid in 1936, signed by a host of purported friends and admirers (including R. B. Cunninghame-Graham, Compton Mackenzie, and Sean O'Casey), becomes a betrayal designed to harm, not help, the outcast genius: "In so far from crowning my work . . . this Testimonial largely represented a disposal of me--the signatories (or some of them) felt that they had done the gallant and generous thing and so for the future I could be safely ignored."[21]

No one can deny that MacDiarmid's creation of the *persona* of the exiled genius is based on the actual circumstances of his life leading up to 1943. Nevertheless, as autobiographer,

---

18. *Lucky Poet* 41.
19. *Lucky Poet* 169-73.
20. *Lucky Poet* 100.
21. *Lucky Poet* 44.

MacDiarmid carefully nurtures this self-image by selecting only those details from his earlier life that prepare for and, as it were, shape his present destiny. Scant as they are, references to MacDiarmid's childhood stress his differentness from others, his inability to compete with others in a society bounded by bourgeois codes of behavior, and even his striking physical appearance that led teachers to predict both his intellectual superiority and his ultimate isolation from society.[22] In particular, MacDiarmid cites his working class background as an ideal preparation for his Communist affiliations, declaring that it had "made me a man naturally fitted for Communism,"[23] allowing MacDiarmid to grow into Communism without undergoing the physically and spiritually wrenching experience of the converted bourgeois. In this fashion, MacDiarmid creates the literary illusion that no actual transformation process had ever occurred, as though his present suffering, at one with the mass suffering of the working classes, had been ordained at birth, thereby condemning MacDiarmid to a life of paradox: physical and intellectual isolation combined with spiritual union with the proletariat. MacDiarmid clearly relishes his role as suffering genius when he compares his poverty on Whalsay to that of welfare recipients:

> And I am one of a very few perhaps among contemporary authors in this country, in that, at a time when huge numbers of men were unemployed and in receipt of the 'dole', and a very big section of our population were under the subsistence level, I would have scorned to be otherwise than equally naked in the 'economic blizzard' and indeed, not being eligible for the 'dole', was even worse off.[24]

MacDiarmid, like Joyce, displays a psychological need to play the role of the outcast, the exile by choice whose very life-work demands that he eschew the company of others. A biographically revealing section of verse from "Lament for the Great Music," written before *Lucky Poet*, unites this need for isolation to the poet's calling:

> I am as lonely and unfrequented as your music is.
> I have had to get rid of all my friends,
> All those to whom I had to accommodate myself.
> If one's capital consists in a calling
> And a mission in life one cannot afford to keep friends.
> I could not stand undivided and true amongst them.

22. *Lucky Poet* 17-20, 39-41, 64, 228, 231-33.
23. *Lucky Poet* 231.
24. *Lucky Poet* 176.

Only in the solitude of my thought can I be myself
Or remember you clearly.[25]

The second major role developed in *Lucky Poet* is
that of the bardic teacher who quite literally assumes the voice
of Scotland. Armed with inside knowledge of every aspect of
Scottish life and thought, MacDiarmid presumes with the arrogance of the prophet to speak for his race. We have already seen
his claim to be the only man truly qualified to speak for Scotland; in other sections of *Lucky Poet*, MacDiarmid exalts the
role of the national spokesman to the status of vatic Bard. At
one point, after discoursing at length upon the Grade System of
Education promulgated by C.T. Smith's *Apsa*, MacDiarmid
claims, "I am a modern Druid, and my conception of poetry is
one that allows at once for the functions of education, historical
guardianship, discussion of all manner of issues with all manner
of people at all manner of levels, reportage of all sorts, exercises
in the art of conversation, sheer entertainment, the fitting commemoration of great occasions, due summoning to high tasks,
and, in short, all the forms of appeal and commentary compati-
ble with intercourse with people who are, in Apsa's sense, 'fully
developed personalities possessing high-grade critical intelli-
gences.' "[26] The educative function of the Bard invests vast
stretches of *Lucky Poet*, between whose covers appear treatises
on linguistics, philosophy, education theory, psychology, anthropology, botany, economics, and political science, to name only
the most frequently discussed subjects. By quoting so many
authors on so many subjects, MacDiarmid does more than but-
tress his own ideas with conventional appeals to authority; the
cumulative effect of MacDiarmid's avalanches of facts and ideas
is to impress the reader with the Bard's assimilative powers, with
the ability not just to remember but to make the wisdom of
whole civilizations his own. This feat is made to seem all the
more remarkable by MacDiarmid's insistence that he has managed to stay current on all matters of importance, local and
international, during his Whalsay sojourn, and without ready
access to either books or men and women of letters.[27] By reciting
a host of details concerning every aspect of life, MacDiarmid
would, through a litany of ideas, make the thought flesh: "My
ambition was to be the creator of a new people, a real bard who

---

25. Hugh MacDiarmid, *The Complete Poems of Hugh MacDiarmid*, eds. W. R. Aitken and Michael
Grieve (New York: Penguin Books, 1985) 475-76.
26. *Lucky Poet* 141-42.
27. *Lucky Poet* 46.

'sang' things till they 'became', yet, as an individual, the incarnation of an immemorial culture."[28]

In this role of bardic teacher, MacDiarmid deliberately places himself in the lineage of legendary heroes of Celtic lore who, in their boasting and daring, embody the same hopes for an eventual Celtic resurgence espoused by MacDiarmid. After quoting appropriate lines from David Jones's *In Parenthesis*, MacDiarmid catalogues the sleeping heroes of Celtic myth--the *fer sidhe*[29] of the sleeping mounds, Arthur awaiting his resurrection in Avalon, Owen of the Red Hand--and then ratifies his own latter-day embodiment of Celtic values:

> My aims and achievements, my boasts, are simply repetitions, in the circumstances of the world of to-day, of those of Taliessin, Glewlwyd, and Widsith again. The essence of my luck as a poet is simply that I 'chance' to re-embody all these master ideas in a dynamic--an existential--way to-day. If I advance a claim to any personal credit it is simply because I have succeeded, by long-sustained and desperately hard work, in becoming completely conscious of these matters and all their inter-relationships and ramifications--receiving them into my very blood and bone and reliving them--and applying them anew to the crucial issues of the present and the future.[30]

Again, MacDiarmid's early recollections prepare for his role. In Chapter V, the catalogues of remembered rivers, flowers, birds, colors, and berries--skillfully intertwined with memories of his parents, especially his mother--emphasize the poet's prophetic association with the land of Scotland itself. The importance of place also emerges in MacDiarmid's attribution of his own absolutist views to the inherent republican radicalism of his native Borders, a region which led MacDiarmid to loathe the gentry and embrace the workers. At this time, he declares, only two occupations lured the young voice of Scotland: the laborer and the tramp. Here, tramp equals poet. Later in this same chapter, MacDiarmid recounts his early desire to be "an itinerant bard," wandering the by-ways of Scotland, selling his poems, and teaching his people.[31] Writing on Whalsay in lonely exile, MacDiarmid still sends forth the voice of the Bard who

---

28. *Lucky Poet* 81.
29. The *fer sidhe*, or "men of the hills," are the descendants of the legendary Tuatha Da Danaan (Children of Dana), ancient inhabitants of Ireland who established an underground empire after their military defeat at the hands of the Milesians (Gauls). They survive in modern Irish folklore as the fairy inhabitants of fairy mounds.
30. *Lucky Poet* 187.
31. *Lucky Poet* 218-28, 226.

would follow those roads if chance and the malignancy of a corrupt system had not dictated otherwise.

If MacDiarmid's *persona* in *Lucky Poet* conforms in many respects with Howarth's oratorical character, we might expect MacDiarmid's style to conform to Howarth's oratorical techniques. Up to a point, it does. Howarth stresses, for example, the rhetorical techniques often employed by the gifted orator: parallelism, amplification, and the use of refrain.[32]

Much of *Lucky Poet* could easily be dissected to reveal just these rhetorical tricks--especially the latter two--but MacDiarmid differs from Howarth's prototype in one important respect. Howarth's exemplars, such as Augustine and Henry Adams, "dismember their protagonists,"[33] separating the autobiographical narrator from an earlier version of self who existed before a conversion experience. As we have seen, MacDiarmid's bardic *persona* exhibits no sense of conversion or essential transformation; everything he cites in his formative years inexorably led to his present role, not by providing the negative example of failed alternatives--Augustine's early hedonism or Malcolm X's street life--but by investing MacDiarmid from the beginning with those qualities essential to the exiled poet and Bard of his race. Instead of turning inward to examine the defects of an earlier self, MacDiarmid's narrator vents his fury outwards, attacking enemies of Scotland, true poetry, and himself. These attacks, frequent and sometimes vicious, appear throughout *Lucky Poet*, often in conjunction with passages of immodest boasting and self-advertisement. Taken out of context, such passages leave the distasteful impression of an egotistical misanthrope striking out at all those who fail to see the rightness of MacDiarmid's ideas or the justice of his cause. Taken as a whole, however, the cumulative exaggeration of MacDiarmid's boasts and the sheer weight of his broadsword attacks signal a different motive from either literal self-conceit or free flying hatred. A useful precedent for this sort of boasting invective exists in the convention of Scottish flyting.

In Chapter I of *Lucky Poet*, MacDiarmid straightforwardly admits that his motives for writing his autobiography are mixed. In addition to explaining his life's work, MacDiarmid honestly states that "I have certain accounts to settle while . . . there is yet time."[34] This revenge motive leads MacDiarmid to

---

32. Howarth 93.
33. Howarth 94.
34. *Lucky Poet* 34.

an even closer identification with ancient Celtic poets, who wrote both "a very intricate and scholarly poetry" and "savage satire and invective."[35] MacDiarmid's fondness for direct frontal assault when on the offensive stems from his aversion to the tactics of over-civilized men who halt progress for fear of offending the bourgeois tastes of the middle class. The true revolutionaries cut through polite social graces to reveal corruption and initiate new orders. Thus MacDiarmid, in "Second Hymn to Lenin," hails the founder of the Soviet Union as "Barbarian saviour o' civilization"[36]; in *Lucky Poet*, he substitutes his own name for Lenin's while quoting lines from the same poem.[37] As Scotland's "barbarian saviour," MacDiarmid traces the meaning of his actual surname, Grieve, through an elaborate, and probably questionable, etymology that relates "Grieve" to, among other roots, the Irish *garv* (= rough, coarse), the Scottish *garvacht* (= roughness), and the French *chavirer* (= to turn inside out, to upset, to rough and tumble); he concludes: "My very name is therefore a living reminder of the danger of over-refinement . . . of the hope in poetry through becoming violent again."[38] MacDiarmid needs, then, a vehicle for attack which combines the style of primitive satire with the elevated status of the narrator as Celtic Bard. He finds it in the flyting of Dunbar.

MacDiarmid's championing of Dunbar, most visible in his declared motto, "Not Burns--Dunbar!,"[39] is well known. Throughout his career, MacDiarmid touted the great poet of James IV's court as the proper corrective to the more pernicious influence of Robert Burns, stating that "if Burns is the heart, Dunbar is the head, of Scottish poetry."[40] As Alexander Scott points out, MacDiarmid and the other writers of the Scottish Renaissance were doubtless attracted to Dunbar because of his broad range of matter and manner.[41] Beyond that, Dunbar's own self-portrait in his poetry provides a role model for MacDiarmid as autobiographer in *Lucky Poet*. Poems like "Quhy will ye, merchantis of renoun" and "Sic tydings hard I at the sessioun" strike a modern chord with their attacks on emerging capitalism and

---

35. *Lucky Poet* 166.
36. *Complete Poems* 324.
37. *Lucky Poet* 29.
38. *Lucky Poet* 379-80, 380.
39. Hugh MacDiarmid, *Albyn or Scotland and the Future* (London: Kegan Paul, French, Trubner and Co., 1927) 35.
40. *Albyn or Scotland and the Future* 39.
41. Alexander Scott, "Hugh MacDiarmid and the Scots Tradition," *Hugh MacDiarmid: A Critical Survey*, ed. Duncan Glen (Edinburgh: Scottish Academic Press, 1972) 3.

cosmopolitan Edinburgh, establishing Dunbar as a social critic.[42] Dunbar's incessant complaints to the king of royal slights and ingratitude in return for loyal service have led one literary historian to characterize Dunbar as "the solitary underdog, seeking in vain for a fair deal for himself and commenting wryly when others are accorded the recognition which he himself thinks ought to be his own,"[43] a view easily culled from poems like "Schir, ye have mony servitours," "Schir, yit remembir as of befoir," and "Schir, lett it nevir to toun be tald." Whether true to the historical figure of Dunbar or not, the character who emerges from the poetry accords nicely with MacDiarmid's perception of self as the unrecognized master of modern Scottish poetry, forced to watch the likes of Edwin Muir receive the critical recognition which MacDiarmid deserves but does not get. Like Dunbar, MacDiarmid sees himself as the victim of intellectually inferior but politically powerful flatterers and knaves. Like Dunbar, MacDiarmid strikes back, not in verse for now, but in prose flyting.

As a literary form, flyting has received very little critical attention, being virtually ignored in standard studies of satire. One bright exception is Douglas Gray's study of invective and flyting, in which he defines flyting as an essentially rhetorical art form that involves elements of play and "acting."[44] In its most famous extant example, Dunbar's flyting of Kennedy, flyting is clearly a sustained satirical attack characterized by exaggeration and extraordinarily abusive language. In the form of a dialogue, Dunbar and Kennedy engage in a contest of vituperative one-upmanship, heaping epithets on one another's head in a torrent of abuse that pits the skill of one poet against that of the other. The dialogue and contestant atmosphere of the flyting suggest a number of literary antecedents: the mediaeval *debat*, the French *tenson*,[45] and a number of popular forms of satire, including the French *charivari*[46]--one of the foreign roots to which MacDiarmid traces the name "Grieve." Although usually viewed as a purely literary exercise in which the poetic antagonists flex their verbal muscles without doing real damage, flyting

42. Cf. Tom Scott, *Dunbar: A Critical Exposition of the Poems* (Edinburgh: Oliver and Boyd, 1966) 79-91. All Dunbar titles and citations are from *The Poems of William Dunbar*, ed. James Kinsley (London: Oxford UP, 1979).
43. A.M. Kinghorn, *The Chorus of History: Literary-Historical Relations in Renaissance Britain* (New York: Barnes and Noble, 1971) 223.
44. Douglas Gray, "Rough Music: Some Early Invectives and Flytings," *English Satire and the English Tradition*, ed. Claude Rawson (Oxford: Basil Blackwell, 1984) 22.
45. Cf. James Kinsley, "The Mediaeval Makars," *Scottish Poetry*, ed. James Kinsley (London: Oxford UP, 1955) 28.
46. Cf. Gray 24-33.

has provoked extreme critical reactions among even Dunbar's admirers. Tom Scott calls "The Flyting of Dunbar and Kennedie" the "most repellent poem known to me in any language" and accuses the form itself of perverting the essential values of poetry.[47] The combination of conceited boasting and virulent attack evokes much the same reaction as that caused by similar passages in *Lucky Poet*; in both flyting and MacDiarmid's autobiography, the attacker deliberately exaggerates both his own attributes and the defects of his enemy, thereby elevating the protagonist in the reader's estimation. Throughout *Lucky Poet*, MacDiarmid uses this type of hyperbole to rhetorically diminish his opponents while simultaneously strengthening the solitary superiority of his chosen *persona*.

Dunbar's flyting of Kennedy begins with an accusation against Kennedy and his compatriot, "Quinting," that implies the existence of a previously written attack against Dunbar's character at court. In response, Dunbar challenges Kennedy to a flyting duel, warning first of the cataclysmic effects his words will have:

> The erd sould trymbill, the firmament sould schaik,
>   And all the air in vennaum suddane stink,
> And all the divillis of hell for redour quaik,
>   To heir quhat I suld wryt with pen and ynk:
>   For and I flyt, sum sege for schame sould sink,
> The se sould birn, the mone sould thoill ecclippis,
> Rochis sould ryfe, the warld sould hald no grippis,
>   Sa loud of cair the commoun bell sould clynk.
>   (ll.9-16)

After this boast of his powers, Dunbar coyly denigrates flyting as a literary form, claiming that "Flyting to use for gritly I eschame" (l. 18); only the violence of Kennedy's prior attack could move Dunbar to engage in a rhetorical contest whose reward is "Bot tinsale baith of honour and of fame" (l. 20). The sheer verbal delight of the ensuing attack belies Dunbar's professed reluctance, highlighting instead the virtuosity of Dunbar's verbal pyrotechnics. Interspersing bragging among the insults-- Dunbar will defeat Kennedy wherever he appears (ll. 65-72), Kennedy dares not insult Dunbar to his face (ll. 89-96), Dunbar's Lowland eloquence puts Kennedy's Highland gibberish to shame (ll. 105-112), Dunbar's words will exorcise the lean and ghostly Kennedy (ll. 161-184)--Dunbar's attack culminates in a cata-

---

47. *Dunbar: A Critical Exposition of the Poems* 175, 178.

logue of vile epithets that provides an example of the tenor of
the whole exercise:

> Mauch muttoun, byt buttoun, peilit gluttoun, air to Hilhous,
>   Rank beggar, ostir dregar, foule fleggar in the flet,
> Chittirlilling, ruch rilling, lik schilling in the milhous,
>   Baird rehator, theif of nator, fals tratour, feyindis gett,
>   Filling of tauch, rak sauch- cry crauch, thow art oursett;
> Muttoun dryver, girnall ryver, yadswyver- fowll fell the;
>   Herretyk, lunatyk, purspyk, carlingis pet,
>   Rottin crok, dirtin dok- cry cok, or I sall quell the.
>   (ll. 241-248)

The internal rhymes, balance of lines, and alliteration almost
work counter to the meanings of the words, creating an aura of
literary respectability that softens the hammer blows of the epithets. This blend of technical ingenuity and exaggerated invective gives the flyting its sense of playful gamesmanship; as Douglas Gray points out, such hyperbole in flyting creates a deliberate ambiguity of intention and establishes a kind of "joking relationship" between poet and victim.[48]

        Despite the seeming innocence of flyting as a literary
device, this form of satire assumes a darker aspect as well.
Gray's major contribution to a new understanding of flyting--
and, for our purposes, of MacDiarmid--is his explanation that
flyting served the purpose of directing real anger against its victim, a function which raises flyting above--or below--the mere
game-playing usually associated with it. After citing motives like
genuine envy and a desire to destroy opponents, parts of an
"often . . . destructive and negative element,"[49] Gray sums up the
two roles of Dunbar as satirist in words that sound very much
like a description of MacDiarmid's created *persona* in *Lucky
Poet*: "the outraged man of virtue, forced to defend his honor,
and that of the wild bard with his magical powers."[50] MacDiarmid, isolated genius and Bard of Scotland, equally outraged by
his neglect and the mediocrity of his countrymen, compelled to
defend his own intellectual and aesthetic positions while speaking for the soul of his race, uses the same boast and attack pattern of the flyting in many passages of *Lucky Poet*.

        Two representative passages illustrate MacDiarmid's
prose flyting. The first occurs in Chapter III, "The Kind of
Poetry I Want," during one of MacDiarmid's depictions of the

---

48. Gray 30.
49. Gray 29.
50. Gray 35.

Scottish literary scene. MacDiarmid sets up the attack in typical fashion by quoting at great length from three sources: himself, an unidentified friend, and Gorky. The first quotation from a self-penned statement of 1936 constitutes MacDiarmid's fare-well to those members of the Scottish Renaissance Movement unable or unwilling to espouse the radical politics of John Maclean and the Red Scotland line. With quotes within this quo-tation from Maclean and Lenin to support his argument, Mac-Diarmid here maintains the necessity for Scottish poets to oppose fascism by supporting an autonomous, Scots Gaelic, and Scots Vernacular republic.[51] The second quotation, from an unnamed friend's letter, moves from politics to the state of edu-cation in Scotland. The friend, with whom MacDiarmid agrees wholeheartedly, describes a deteriorating Edinburgh University whose function has shifted from imparting impartial knowledge to grooming civil servants for the empire.[52] After a brief descrip-tion of a weary meeting of "inane symposiasts" on Scottish liter-ature, the third quotation from a 1905 Russian publication pro-vides Gorky's extended definition of a philistine.[53] Far from merely filling space, MacDiarmid's quotations, here and else-where, form an important part of his polemical attack. These three quotations establish a context for the full fury of the final offensive, implying, through a dialectic of quoted material, an inter-related complex of misguided politics, retrogressive educa-tion, and cultural philistinism as the root cause of a new and dangerous breed of Scottish writer. MacDiarmid weaves together the major themes of the quoted material in a sarcastic description of contemporary Scottish writers, comparing them to the so-called French Contadours. MacDiarmid belittles their emphasis on Nature at the expense of working class existence, criticizes their poetic foundation as one built upon an absurd adherence to empirical rules, and dismisses them at last as shallow philistines.[54]

The effect of this summary repudiation, hard on the heels of three supporting quotations, is to soften the opposition for a full frontal assault. Irony rapidly turns to flyting invective in two stages. First, MacDiarmid espouses a poetry which "turns its back contemptuously on all the cowardly and brainless staples of Anglo-Scottish literature," as opposed to that written by writers

51. *Lucky Poet* 143-45.
52. *Lucky Poet* 145-46.
53. *Lucky Poet* 146-47.
54. *Lucky Poet* 147-48.

"half glow-worms and half newts."[55] Then, in a spectacular catalogue of dunces that must be read in full to be appreciated,
MacDiarmid, in true flyting form, launches the final volley of
words:

> My aim all along has been ... the most drastic *desuetization* of
> Scottish life and letters, and, in particular, the de-Tibetanization of
> the Highlands and Islands, and getting rid of the whole gang of
> high mucky-mucks, famous fatheads, old wives of both sexes,
> stuffed shirts, hollow men with headpieces stuffed with straw,
> birdwits, lookers-under-beds, trained seals, creeping Jesuses, Scots
> Wha Ha'evers, village idiots, policemen, leaders of white-mouse
> factions and noted connoisseurs of bread and butter, glorified
> gangsters, and what 'Billy' Phelps calls Medlar novelists (the
> medlar being a fruit that becomes rotten before it is ripe), Com-
> mercial Calvinists, makers of 'noises like a turnip', and all the
> touts and toadies and lickspittles of the English Ascendancy, and
> their infernal women-folk, and all their skunkoil skulduggery.[56]

MacDiarmid's alliterative catalogue of abuse, which includes
everything from popular catch-phrases to highly original epithets
to allusions to T. S. Eliot and Robert Burns, shares with Dunbar's flyting of Kennedy that same balance of fierce invective
and gleeful exaggeration that makes the attack's seriousness so
difficult to gauge. We are never quite sure what demands our
greater attention, the hatred and scorn behind the abuse or the
rhetorical fun of its vehicle.

       Immediately after this satirical climax, MacDiarmid,
again true to the flyting tradition, adds one of his many boasts.
In addition to his undeniable greatness as a poet, he writes, the
world should recognize that MacDiarmid is a twentieth-century
Orestes Bronson--a thinker, a practical organizer, a prolific
writer of political tracts. As for his contribution to Scotland in
helping to combat the forces of philistinism just skewered in the
preceding paragraph, MacDiarmid asserts that "I know no contemporary in Scotland to-day who has done, or seems likely to,
any better--or, indeed, half as well."[57] This bit of self-puffery
brings this particular attack full circle, reminding us of the
implied message of the three opening quotations; by reducing
his opponents so well, MacDiarmid strikes a triple blow for radical politics, education of the masses, and cultural elitism.

       A second example of prose flyting occurs in Chapter
V, "On Seeing Scotland Whole." In this section of the autobiog-

---

55. *Lucky Poet* 148, 149.
56. *Lucky Poet* 149.
57. *Lucky Poet* 149.

raphy, MacDiarmid relates his Langholm Academy days during which, despite his innate opposition to bourgeois careers, he had decided to become a teacher to please his parents. These plans were abandoned immediately after his father's death, a decision never regretted by MacDiarmid even in the midst of poverty. In fact, MacDiarmid's recollection of that important decision leads him to single out the Scottish teaching profession as satirical victim. After excluding George Ogilvie (not actually named in the text) of Edinburgh University's Junior Student Centre and two instructors at Langholm Academy, MacDiarmid excoriates the rest of the profession:

> ... the vast majority of them are hopeless Safety-Firsters, continually bending the knee to Baal in this connexion or that, or grovelling altogether, obliged, in order to secure their jobs, to tout and belly-crawl, and pull all manner of dirty little strings in the most ignominious fashion, the conscienceless agents of the Powers-that-Be, destitute of any vocation for teaching, and themselves most indifferently educated and utterly destitute of culture, while, as a body, they deserve the contempt with which they are generally treated in the community--as a kind of half-men, destitute of guts or principle, unconscionable toadies and time-servers.[58]

Harsher in tone than the previous example, this flyting of a specific target reminds us of the darker side of flyting. Dunbar achieves the same accusatory tone in verse through compression, relying primarily on the weight of nouns to subdue Kennedy:

> Thow crop and rute of tratouris tressonable,
>   The fathir and moder of morthour and mischeif,
> Dissaitfull tyrand with serpentis tung unstable,
>   Cukcald cradoun, cowart, and commoun theif.
>   (ll. 73-76)

Or, again, in "Schir, ye have mony servitours," a complaint poem that uses flyting devices, Dunbar characterizes court parasites:

> Fenyeouris, fleichors, and flatteraris,
> Cryars, craikars, and clatteraris
> Soukars, groukaris, gledars, gunnaris,
> Monsouris of France, gud clarat cunnaris.
>   (ll. 39-42)

MacDiarmid loses compression in his prose attack, expanding Dunbar's lists of insulting names into modifying phrases and

---

58. *Lucky Poet* 229.

subordinate clauses, but the tenor of his assault is much the same despite the vehicle of prose.

MacDiarmid next describes himself as a young boy, comparing himself unfavorably to his brother, the seemingly more confident and physically intimidating of the two. But the photograph to which he refers in the comparison reveals a physique that is no more reliable as an indicator of strength than MacDiarmid's present unassuming appearance, an appearance that disguises the real power of Scotland's greatest son. Now that MacDiarmid has fully exposed the incompetence of the nation's teachers, he can boast of his own superhuman abilities to meet the challenge of any occasion:

> And even to-day I look timid and modest--who have never known what it was to meet a situation I could not handle, who would be entirely equal to the occasion if I were summoned at a moment's notice to address the House of Commons or the House of Lords, or to lead a Scottish Sinn Fein rising; or, indeed, to deal with any other situation I can imagine. If there was ever a man who was ready, intellectually or physically, to start from any point to any other at a moment's notice, that man am I.[59]

MacDiarmid's boast equals in hyperbole the ferocity of the attack which precipitates it. The entire passage separates the condition of modern Scottish education from the lofty intellectual eminence of MacDiarmid in a pattern of invective and boasting that clearly proclaims itself to be a literary convention.

Numerous other attacks against a number of other foes in *Lucky Poet* could be cited. MacDiarmid's list of targets includes Scottish Nationalists, London critics, Anglicised Scots, Lord Lothian, Laurie Magnus, Edwin Muir, businessmen, lawyers, W. H. Auden, and every facet of the English Ascendancy. In one way or another, all these verbal sallies can be seen as methods not only of settling accounts, but of furthering MacDiarmid's stated purpose in writing *Lucky Poet*: to oppose the English ethos by embodying Celtic ideas in a new way.[60] And here we see the third and final element of Howarth's concept of oratorical autobiography fall into place: "The theme is *vocation*, the special summons that guided an entire life's work and now its story."[61] MacDiarmid's vocation, clearly set forth in *Lucky Poet*, was to become the voice of his race and nation, embodying the spirit of Scotland in exiled grandeur and flaying Scotland's

---

59. *Lucky Poet* 230.
60. *Lucky Poet* XII, 186-87.
61. Howarth 94.

enemies within and without her borders. MacDiarmid understood the perils of such a role, writing to R. E. Muirhead in a letter of 5 November 1928, that his "task is to be unpopular--a fighter--an enemy of accepted things."[62]

As one weapon in MacDiarmid's arsenal of ideas, *Lucky Poet* creates a larger than life *persona* because it undertakes a larger than life task. As autobiography, the book both explains and justifies MacDiarmid's view of himself as the protagonist in a universal conflict of ideas involving poetry, politics, and the very consciousness of his Celtic race. In keeping with MacDiarmid's belief that we know a man by his ideas, *Lucky Poet* does offer scant biographical "facts" as such, but by establishing the *persona* of the exiled Bard as a base of operations from which to launch his flytings, MacDiarmid's oratorical autobiography fulfills more important functions of this slippery genre. George Gusdorf best describes the final goal of autobiography when he says that "in autobiography the truth of facts is subordinate to the truth of the man who is in question," a view of autobiography which sees it as a symbol or parable of "consciousness in quest of its own truth."[63] *Lucky Poet* is MacDiarmid's own truth. To ask it to be simpler is to misunderstand MacDiarmid's purpose and to deny the complexity of MacDiarmid's character.

GLOSSARY

air = heir

baird rehator = vile (?) bard; knave (?) minstrel
byt buttoun = button biter

carlingis pet = old woman's spoiled child
chittirlilling = pig's guts (?)
clarat cunnaris = claret tasters
craikars = noisy fellows
crauch = beaten; defeated
crok = old ewe

62. *The Letters of Hugh MacDiarmid*, ed. Alan Bold (Athens, Georgia: U of Georgia P, 1984) 298.
63. George Gusdorf, "Conditions and Limits of Autobiography," trans. James Olney, *Autobiography: Essays Theoretical and Critical*, ed. James Olney (Princeton: Princeton UP, 1980) 43, 44.

crop and rute = head and roots of a plant; top and bottom
cry cok = admit defeat

dirtin dok = filthy arse

erd = earth

fenyeouris = pretenders
fleggar in the flet = flatterer (?) in the inner court of a building
fleichours = coaxers; cajolers

girnall ryver = granary robber
groukarirs = obscure word

hald no grippis = fall apart; lose cohesion

mauch = maggoty

ostir dregar = oyster digger

peilit = destitute

rak sauch = gallowsbird with rope of sallow (?- very obscure)
redour = dread; terror
ruch rilling = rough shoes made of unfinished hide
ryfe = split

schilling = husks of oats
sege = man
soukars = suckers; parasites

tauch = tallow; animal fat
thoill = endure; suffer

vennaum = venom; poison

yadswyver = mare buggerer

BIBLIOGRAPHY

Photo used courtesy of Michael Grieve.

W. R. AITKEN

A BIBLIOGRAPHY OF HUGH MacDIARMID

The bibliography that follows is in two sections. The first is a checklist of (a) books by MacDiarmid, (b) books he edited or translated, (c) periodicals he edited, and (d) collections and selections of his writings, whether made by MacDiarmid himself or by another. It is perhaps worth mentioning that C. M. Grieve's pseudonymous surname was spelt successively in different ways. He first used the pseudonym in 1922, and on the title-pages of his early books published by Blackwood the spelling used is M'Diarmid with a turned comma, not an apostrophe. Later we find McDiarmid, Macdiarmid, and finally MacDiarmid. All are recognized variants of the same name. Here the spelling MacDiarmid, which the poet used consistently from about 1932, is adopted throughout.

In listing MacDiarmid's books here I have omitted the limited printings of a single poem or two or a short essay, and I have done so for two reasons: these "pamphlets and small editions," as Duncan Glen called them, are rare and not always to be found in even the largest libraries, and their contents, at least as far as any poetry they contain, are included in subsequent collections that are listed.

The second section lists books and articles about MacDiarmid and his work, and is intended to supplement the bibliography of MacDiarmid criticism, 1924-1978, compiled by Michael K. Glenday and published in 1979 in the *Bulletin of Bibliography*.[1]

Critical appreciation of his work came late in MacDiarmid's career. He himself said, "It was in 1962, however, that the real breakthrough came."[2] It was in that year that a *Festschrift* of critical essays, tributes and personal reminiscences was published to celebrate his seventieth birthday. It was the first book devoted to MacDiarmid's life and work. Since then

---

1. *Bulletin of Bibliography*, 36 (1979), 91-98.
2. *The Company I've Kept* (1966), p. 189.

MacDiarmid criticism has proliferated: more than two-thirds of the entries in Michael Glenday's bibliography are from the seventeen years from 1962 to 1978.

C. M. Grieve died on 9 September 1978 and obituaries were published in many newspapers at the time: these are not listed here (apart from the notice in *The Times*, which was reprinted in the *Massachusetts Review*); but the tributes, memories and assessments published in the literary journals in commemoration of the poet are recorded. Certain other categories of material have been omitted, such as unpublished dissertations, ephemeral journalism, and articles in encyclopaedias, and reviews have been included only when they are in the form of an extended essay. Reviews of secondary works are not included.

In both sections and subsections the entries are in chronological order by the year of publication, and within any one year alphabetically by author. Two indexes are added: one of the titles of MacDiarmid's books, the other of the names of authors, critics and editors.

The indispensable current bibliography in this field is the *Annual Bibliography of Scottish Literature*, issued as a supplement to *The Bibliotheck*. There is also an annual critical survey, "The Year's Work in Scottish Literary and Linguistic Studies," issued in the *Scottish Literary Journal* (or its supplements) published by the Association for Scottish Literary Studies. Like all bibliographies and surveys of the kind, both are running behind schedule. The latest issue of the *Annual Bibliography* is the one for 1982. However, James Kidd of St. Andrews University Library, one of the bibliography's joint editors, has made available to me the MacDiarmid entries for the years 1983-88, as far as they have accumulated. For this invaluable assistance I am most grateful. I would also thank the librarians and staff of the libraries in which I have worked in preparing this bibliography: the National Library of Scotland and the libraries of the universities of Stirling and Edinburgh.

Dunblane
January 1989

1. BY MacDIARMID

BOOKS BY MacDIARMID

1. *Annals of the Five Senses*. [CMG] Montrose: C. M. Grieve, 1923.

    _____. Edinburgh: Porpoise Press, 1930.

    _____. Introd. Alan Bold. Edinburgh: Polygon Books, 1983.

    Poetry and prose.

2. *Sangschaw*. Edinburgh: Blackwood, 1925.

3. *Penny Wheep*. Edinburgh: Blackwood, 1926.

4. *A Drunk Man Looks at the Thistle*, Edinburgh: Blackwood, 1926.

    _____. Introd. David Daiches. Glasgow: Caledonian Press, 1953.

    _____. Edinburgh: Castle Wynd Printers, 1956.

    _____. Edinburgh: The 200 Burns Club, 1962.

    _____. Illus. Frans Masereel. Falkland: Duval & Hamilton, 1969.

    _____. Ed. John C. Weston. Amherst: U of Massachusetts P, 1971.

    An annotated edition with the spelling standardized by the editor.

    _____. Ed. Kenneth Buthlay. Edinburgh: Scottish Academic Press, 1987.

    A definitive edition, comprehensively annotated and glossed, with a scholarly introduction.

5. *Contemporary Scottish Studies: First Series*. [CMG] London: Leonard Parsons, 1926.

    Articles reprinted from the *Scottish Educational Journal*, June 1925-July 1926, with an introductory chapter, conclusion, and bibliography.

    Contemporary Scottish Studies. Edinburgh: Scottish Educational Journal, 1976.

    A new edition published to mark both the centenary of the *Journal* as a weekly paper and the jubilee of the first publication of these articles in book form. It reprints the complete series of articles, June 1925-February 1927, with the "furious and fascinating" correspondence they evoked. The introductory chapter, conclusion, and bibliography of the 1926 edition are not reprinted.

6. *Albyn, or Scotland and the Future*. [CMG] London: Kegan Paul, 1927.

7. *The Lucky Bag*. Edinburgh: Porpoise Press, 1927.

8. *To Circumjack Cencrastus, or The Curly Snake*. Edinburgh: Blackwood, 1930.

    A long poem reprinted only in part in *Collected Poems* (1962, 1967) and comparatively neglected.

9. *First Hymn to Lenin, and Other Poems*. London: Unicorn Press, 1931.

    The "First Hymn" was originally published in *New English Poems*, ed. Lascelles Abercrombie (London: Gollancz, 1931).

10. *Scots Unbound, and Other Poems*. Stirling: Eneas Mackay, 1932.

11. *Scottish Scene, or The Intelligent Man's Guide to Albyn*. With Lewis Grassic Gibbon. London: Jarrolds, 1934.

    _____. London: Hutchinson, for the National Book Association, n.d.

    _____. Bath: Cedric Chivers, 1974.

    A remarkable miscellany.

12. *Stony Limits, and Other Poems*. London: Gollancz, 1934.

    Poems in Scots and in English.

13. *At the Sign of the Thistle: a Collection of Essays*. London: Stanley Nott, 1934.

14. *Second Hymn to Lenin, and Other Poems*. London: Stanley Nott, 1935.

    The "Second Hymn" was first published in *The Criterion* 11 (1932): 593-98.

15. *Scottish Eccentrics*. London: Routledge, 1936.

    _____. New York: Johnson Reprint Corporation, 1972. Includes "A Note on the Author" by Norman MacCaig.

    A series of biographical essays.

16. *The Islands of Scotland: Hebrides, Orkneys, and Shetlands*. London: Batsford, 1939; New York: Scribners, 1939.

17. *Lucky Poet: A Self-Study in Literature and Political Ideas, Being the Autobiography of Hugh MacDiarmid (Christopher Murray Grieve)*. London: Methuen, 1943.

    _____. With a new "Author's Note" (xi-xvi). London: Cape, 1972.

    The autobiography includes a great deal of important poetry.

18. *A Kist of Whistles: New Poems*. Glasgow: Maclellan, 1947.

    Despite the subtitle, some of the poems had been written and published twenty-five years before.

19. *Cunninghame Graham: a Centenary Study*. Glasgow: Caledonian Press, 1952.

    R. B. Cunninghame Graham, traveller, short story writer, historian of South America and Scottish Nationalist, was born in 1852.

20. *Francis George Scott: an Essay on the Occasion of his Seventy-fifth Birthday*. Edinburgh: Macdonald, 1955.

    Scott set many of MacDiarmid's lyrics to music. He had been one of the poet's teachers and became a formative influence and valued friend.

21. *In Memoriam James Joyce: From A Vision of World Language*. Glasgow: Maclellan, 1955; rpt. with corrections, 1956.

    A long sequence of poems in English. Some five months before he died MacDiarmid wrote (in a letter to the present compiler): "Recently for the first time in several years I re-read the *In Memoriam James Joyce* and am more than ever convinced that it is a poem running right through from start to finish."

22. *Stony Limits and Scots Unbound, and Other Poems*. Edinburgh: Castle Wynd Printers, 1956.

    Reprints *Stony Limits and other poems* (1934) with the addition of certain poems excluded from the earlier edition, and the title-poem from *Scots Unbound, and other poems* (1932).

23. *Three Hymns to Lenin*. Edinburgh: Castle Wynd Printers, 1957.

    The "First Hymn" originally appeared in *New English Poems*, ed. Lascelles Abercrombie (London: Gollancz, 1931) and the "Second Hymn" in *The Criterion* 11 (1932). The "Third Hymn" was first published in its entirety in *The Voice of Scotland* 6 (April 1955): 12-20, although part had been printed in 1943 in the poet's autobiography, *Lucky Poet*.

24. *The Battle Continues.* Edinburgh: Castle Wynd Printers, 1957.

    A long poem relating to the Spanish Civil War and written at that time.

25. *Burns Today and Tomorrow.* Edinburgh: Castle Wynd Printers, 1959.

    An essay for the bicentenary of Burns's birth.

26. *The Kind of Poetry I Want.* Edinburgh: Duval, 1961.

    Parts of this long poem had been published in *Lucky Poet* (1943) and *A Kist of Whistles* (1947).

27. *The Company I've Kept.* London: Hutchinson, 1966; Berkeley, Calif.: U of California P, 1967.

    Further essays in autobiography.

28. *Celtic Nationalism.* With Owen Dudley Edwards, Gwynfor Evans, and Ioan Rhys. London: Routledge & Kegan Paul, 1968.

    MacDiarmid writes on Scotland (301-58).

29. *Dìreadh I, II, and III.* Frenich, Foss: Duval & Hamilton, 1974.

    The definitive edition of a sequence of three poems of which the first was published in *The Voice of Scotland* 1 (Dec. 1938): 13-21, and the second and third in *Lucky Poet* (1943).

30. *Scotch Whisky.* As tasted by Bill Simpson and others. London: Macmillan, 1974.

    MacDiarmid, as Governor of the Malt Whisky Institute, contributes chapter 5, "Great Malt Whiskies" (65-71).

31. *John Knox.* With Campbell Maclean and Anthony Ross. Edinburgh: Ramsay Head Press, 1976.

    MacDiarmid's essay is entitled "Knox, Calvinism and the Arts" (75-96).

32. *Aesthetics in Scotland.* Ed. & introd. Alan Bold. Edinburgh: Mainstream, 1984.

    The first publication of an essay written in 1950, with a coda from 1965.

33. *On a Raised Beach.* With drawings by Reinhard Behrens. Biggar: Valda Grieve, 1985. Limited ed. of 100 copies.

    This edition includes two versions of the poem: the one published in *Stony Limits* and the fair-copy MS reproduced in facsimile in Catherine Kerrigan's *Whaur Extremes Meet* (1983) (see 122 below).

BOOKS EDITED OR TRANSLATED BY HUGH MacDIARMID

34. *Northern Numbers, Being Representative Selections from Certain Living Scottish Poets*. [CMG] Edinburgh: T. N. Foulis, 1920.

_____. Second series. Edinburgh: T. N. Foulis, 1921.

_____. Third series. Montrose: C. M. Grieve, 1922.

35. *Robert Burns, 1759-1796*. London: Benn, 1926. *The Augustan Books of Poetry*.

36. *The Handmaid of the Lord*. By Ramon Maria Tenreiro. London: Secker, 1930.

> This anonymous translation is first listed among MacDiarmid's works in *Second Hymn to Lenin* (1935).

37. *Living Scottish Poets*. London: Benn, 1931. *The Augustan Books of Poetry*.

38. *The Golden Treasury of Scottish Poetry*. London: Macmillan, 1940.

> This representative anthology of Scottish poetry in Scots and English, and in Gaelic and Latin in English translation, includes MacDiarmid's translations from the Gaelic of "The Birlinn of Clanranald" by Alexander MacDonald (Alasdair MacMhaighstir Alasdair) and "The Praise of Ben Dorain" by Duncan Ban MacIntyre.
>
> There is a long introduction (vii-xxxvii) in which MacDiarmid argues the case for Scots against the views expressed by the poet and critic Edwin Muir in his book *Scott and Scotland* (1936).

39. *William Soutar: Collected Poems*. Ed. with an introductory essay (9-21). London: Andrew Dakers, 1948.

> Soutar (1898-1943) is second in importance only to MacDiarmid among the poets of the Scottish Renaissance movement.

40. *Robert Burns: Poems*. London: Grey Walls Press, 1949.

41. *Selections from the Poems of William Dunbar*. Edinburgh: Oliver & Boyd, for the Saltire Society, 1952.

42. *Selected Poems of William Dunbar*. Glasgow: Maclellan, 1955.

43. *Robert Burns: Love Songs*. London: Vista Books, 1962.

44. *Aniara: A Review of Man in Time and Space*. By Harry Martinson. Adapted from the Swedish by Hugh MacDiarmid and Elspeth Harley Schubert. London:

Hutchinson, 1963; New York: Knopf, 1963; Stockholm: Bonnier, 1963.

45. *Henryson*. Poet to Poet. Harmondsworth: Penguin Books, 1973.

46. *The Threepenny Opera*. By Bertolt Brecht. Trans. Hugh MacDiarmid. London: Eyre Methuen, 1973.

PERIODICALS EDITED BY HUGH MacDIARMID

47. *The Scottish Chapbook*. 1.1 (Aug. 1922) - 2.3 (Nov./Dec. 1923) Montrose. Monthly.

48. *The Scottish Nation*. 1.1 (8 May 1923) - 2.8 (25 Dec. 1923) Montrose. Weekly.

49. *The Northern Review*. 1.1 (May 1924) - 4 (Sept. 1924) Edinburgh. Monthly.

50. *The Voice of Scotland*. 1.1 (June/Aug. 1938) - 9.2 (Aug. 1958) Dunfermline (1938-39); Glasgow (1945-49); Edinburgh (1955-58). Quarterly (irregular).

51. *Poetry Scotland*. 4. Guest editor. Edinburgh: Serif Books, 1949.

52. *Scottish Art and Letters*. Fifth miscellany. PEN Congress Number, Edinburgh Festival, 1950. Literary editor. Glasgow: Maclellan, 1950.

COLLECTIONS AND SELECTIONS

53. *Selected Poems*. Macmillan's Contemporary Poets. London: Macmillan, 1934.

    A selection by the poet himself from *Sangschaw*, *Penny Wheep*, *A Drunk Man Looks at the Thistle*, *Scots Unbound*, and *Stony Limits*.

54. *Selected Poems*. Ed. R. Crombie Saunders. Glasgow: Maclellan, 1944.

    With the poet's approval the editor made "certain orthographical changes" in the poems in Scots.

55. *Speaking for Scotland: Selected Poems*. *Distinguished Poets Series* 3. Baltimore: Contemporary Poetry, 1946.

    This first American edition, a selection by the poet himself, is almost the same as the *Selected Poems* published by Macmillan in 1934, with the addition of three poems "not previously published in book form." There is a glossary followed by notes on the pronunciation of Scottish words, a few general notes, and "literal renderings into English" of five of the poems.

56. *Selected Poems.* Ed. Oliver Brown. Glasgow: Maclellan, 1954.

_____. Reissued as *Poems.* Glasgow: Scottish Secretariat, 1955.

57. *Collected Poems.* New York: The Macmillan Company, 1962; Edinburgh: Oliver & Boyd, 1962.

_____. Rev. ed. with enlarged glossary prepared by John C. Weston. New York: The Macmillan Company, 1967; London: Collier-Macmillan, 1967.

An Author's Note states: "This volume does not contain all the poems I have written, but all I think worth including in a definitive collection," but MacDiarmid subsequently pointed out that this Note was written for the MS he originally sent to his publishers, which they found to be "much too large for their purpose and only a portion of it was used." Unfortunately, the Note written for the larger collection was not altered when only a part of the MS was published. The *Collected Poems*, then, is "only a big selection" of MacDiarmid's poetry. It was supplemented by three later collections:

A Lap of Honour. London: MacGibbon & Kee, 1967; Chicago: Swallow Press, 1969.

A Clyack-Sheaf. London: MacGibbon & Kee, 1969.

More Collected Poems. London: MacGibbon & Kee, 1970; Chicago: Swallow Press, 1970.

These collections are now superseded by the *Complete Poems* (1978; 1985).

58. *The Uncanny Scot: a Selection of Prose.* Ed. Kenneth Buthlay. London: MacGibbon & Kee, 1968.

59. *Selected Essays.* Ed. Duncan Glen. London: Cape, 1969; Berkeley: U of California P, 1970.

60. *Selected Poems.* Ed. David Craig and John Manson. Harmondsworth: Penguin Books, 1970.

61. *The Hugh MacDiarmid Anthology: Poems in Scots and English.* Ed. Michael Grieve and Alexander Scott. London: Routledge & Kegan Paul, 1972.

A generous and well chosen selection. Michael Grieve, the poet's son, writes on "Hugh MacDiarmid: The Man" and Alexander Scott on "MacDiarmid: The Poet."

62. *The Socialist Poems of Hugh MacDiarmid.* Ed. T. S. Law and Thurso Berwick. London: Routledge & Kegan Paul, 1978.

A selection designed to illuminate the poet's commitment to Socialism. The editors contribute a long foreword (ix-xl).

63. *Complete Poems, 1920-1976.* Ed. Michael Grieve and W. R. Aitken. 2 vols. London: Martin Brian & O'Keeffe, 1978.

_____. With corrections and an appendix. 2 vols. Harmondsworth: Penguin Books, 1985.

The definitive edition. At the poet's insistence there are no scholarly notes or explanatory notes or elucidations, and the glossary is only a conflation of those the poet himself provided in his separate books. (See the note by W. R. Aitken, "On editing *The Complete Poems of Hugh MacDiarmid," Aquarius* 11 [1979]: 11-13.)

These volumes were extensively reviewed, both in 1978 and in 1985. (See in particular the long review-article by Ruth McQuillan, "The Complete MacDiarmid," *Studies in Scottish Literature* 18 [1983]: 177-209.)

Despite the inclusive title the publishers chose for MacDiarmid's *Complete Poems* and the 250 pages of "Hitherto Uncollected Poems" in the second volume, it is scarcely surprising, given the poet's "astonishing prodigality," that a number of published poems not included in these volumes have been found (or rediscovered) since 1978, in addition to the 10 printed in the appendix to the 1985 edition. Some of these poems have now been reprinted:

"Some Uncollected Poems." *Scottish Literary Journal* 12 (May 1985): 70-76.

Eleven poems, with a note by Kenneth Buthlay.

"MacDiarmid and the Beatniks." *Scottish Literary Journal* 13 (Nov. 1986): 87-90.

A note by Hamish Whyte on a quatrain printed in the *New Saltire* 4 (1962) and in MacDiarmid's *Letters* (810), with a facsimile of the manuscript draft.

"Yae MacDiarmid fuitnote." *Chapman* 45 (1986): 70-73.

A note by T. S. Law on MacDiarmid's "Flytin agains W. D. Cocker," with the text of the poem.

"Two Poems and a Fragment." *Scottish Literary Journal* 15 (Nov. 1988): 58-61.

Uncollected items found in the National Library of Scotland by Patrick Crotty, who introduces them.

64. *The Thistle Rises: an Anthology of Poetry and Prose.* Ed. Alan Bold. London: Hamish Hamilton, 1984.

A selection intended to demonstrate the scope and status of MacDiarmid's work.

65. *The Letters of Hugh MacDiarmid.* Ed. with an introd. Alan Bold. London: Hamish Hamilton, 1984.

"Grieve the man and MacDiarmid the poet are equally visible, if not indivisible, in the letters."

66. *Hugh MacDiarmid.* Arranged from the words of Hugh MacDiarmid by Henry Stamper. *Saltire Self-Portraits* 1. Edinburgh: Saltire Society, 1986.

The text of Henry Stamper's highly acclaimed portrait of MacDiarmid in his one-man show, *Between the Wars*, which the poet regarded as a great compliment.

67. *The Hugh MacDiarmid - George Ogilvie Letters.* Ed. Catherine Kerrigan. Aberdeen: Aberdeen UP, 1988.

MacDiarmid's correspondence with his former teacher, which began in 1911 and continued until 1932, is reproduced in its entirety, along with the small number of letters from Ogilvie to the poet that have survived. The extensive detailed notes are invaluable.

2. ABOUT MacDIARMID

68. Wright, Gordon. *MacDiarmid: an Illustrated Biography of Christopher Murray Grieve (Hugh MacDiarmid).* Edinburgh: Gordon Wright, 1977.

A patiently researched and carefully annotated scrapbook of information and illustrative material, with an introductory essay by Kenneth Buthlay, "Hugh MacDiarmid: Where Extremes Meet."

69. Bold, Alan. "MacDiarmid: The Man Himself." *Chapman* 22 (1978): 22-25.

Discusses MacDiarmid's interest in the linguistic experiments of Pound, Eliot, and Joyce, and his own use of Scots as an element in the development of the Scottish imagination.

70. Burgess, Anthony. "Hugh MacDiarmid: a Tribute." *Scottish Review* 12 (1978): 4-9.

An appreciation.

71. Buthlay, Kenneth. "Some Hints for Source-hunters." *Scottish Literary Journal* 5 (Dec. 1978): 50-66.

    Notes and reflections on some of MacDiarmid's "borrowings."

72. Caird, James B. "Hugh MacDiarmid." *Chapman* 22 (1978): 18-21.

    A valedictory tribute. "For people of my generation, MacDiarmid *was* Scottish literature."

73. Campbell, Ian. "Hugh MacDiarmid, 1892-1978." *Books in Scotland* 3 (1978): 11-12.

    An obituary assessment.

74. Craig, David. "Hugh MacDiarmid's Peak." *Scottish Literary Journal* 5 (Dec. 1978): 36-49.

    For the writer, the poems written between 1930 and 1936.

75. Daiches, David. "Vision and Reality." *Lines Review* 67 (1978): 7-8.

    Suggests that MacDiarmid was very much a poet of sensation, yet for him sensation existed in order to be transcended.

76. Graham, Cuthbert. "MacDiarmid and the North." *Leopard* 43 (Oct. 1978): 31-33.

    One approach to the later MacDiarmid is to remember that professionally he was a journalist.

77. Law, T. S. "A Brawlik Makar." *Chapman* 22 (1978): 14-17.

    One of the editors of *The Socialist Poems of Hugh MacDiarmid* points out that many socialists discount MacDiarmid's nationalism.

78. Mackie, Albert D. "Christopher Murray Grieve, 11th August 1892-9th September 1978." *Lallans* 11 (1978): 5-7.

    A tribute in Scots.

79. McQuillan, Ruth. "In Memoriam Alister K. Laidlaw." *Lines Review* 67 (1978): 5-6.

    An obituary note on one of Hugh MacDiarmid's pseudonyms.

80. Morgan, Edwin. "MacDiarmid's Later Poetry Against an International Background." *Scottish Literary Journal* 5 (Dec. 1978): 20-35.

    Includes a discussion, with examples, of MacDiarmid's use of some of his source material.

81. Murison, David. "Some Thoughts on the Man and his Work." *Lines Review* 67 (1978): 12-15.

Mainly on MacDiarmid's use of Scots and English. The writer edited the *Scottish National Dictionary*.

82. Scott, Tom. "Vive MacDiarmid." *Chapman* 22 (1978): 6-13.

A fellow-poet's appreciation. "Though Chris Grieve was dead, Hugh MacDiarmid was still alive."

83. Tait, Bob. "Poet and Prophet." *Leopard* 43 (Oct. 1978): 30.

MacDiarmid was great partly because he brought out double-edged traits in Scottish attitudes and hopes. There was a streak of "sheer theatrical perversity in his activities." In part a review of the *Socialist Poems*.

84. Torri, G. "An Interview with Hugh MacDiarmid." *Pacific Quarterly* (Moana) 3 (1978): 261-73.

85. Watson, Roderick. " 'Water Music' and the Stream of Consciousness." *Scottish Literary Journal* 5 (Dec. 1978): 6-19.

Directs attention to one important aspect of MacDiarmid's inspiration.

86. Bunting, Basil. "Hugh MacDiarmid Lost." *Agenda* 16.3-4 (1978-9): 81-82.

An anecdote of MacDiarmid "recognized and spontaneously honoured by men of no education and no pretension whatever." His death was "a rare loss."

87. Crawford, Thomas. "Autobiographical Anatomist: Notes on the Collected MacDiarmid." *Chapman* 23/24 (1979): 5-11.

The *Complete Poems* in the context of the reassessment after MacDiarmid's death.

88. Dunn, Douglas. "Editorial." *Aquarius* 11 (1979): 1-2.

Some thoughts, after MacDiarmid's death, on his "inconvenient vision" and the nature of his influence.

89. Fraser, G. S. "In Memory of MacDiarmid." *Aquarius* 11 (1979): 3-10.

Personal memories of the man and poet whom Fraser sees as "a Covenanter, not a Jacobite"; he comments on the transcendentalism of the later poetry and notes that "few atheists make such frequent use of the word 'God.' "

90. Gish, Nancy. "An Interview with Hugh MacDiarmid." *Contemporary Literature* 20 (1979): 135-54.

The interviewer found the poet "warm, sincere, honest, and direct about his own work and that of others, and always unabashedly certain of how to evaluate both." MacDiarmid comments on a number of American contemporaries.

91.   McCulloch, Margery. "Modernism and the Scottish Tradition: the Duality of *A Drunk Man Looks at the Thistle.*" *Chapman* 25 (1979): 50-56.

An attempt to rectify an over-concentration on aspects of the poem's Scottish context.

92.   "Mr. Hugh MacDiarmid: Creator of Scottish Renascence." *Massachusetts Review* 20 (1979): 3-6.

The anonymous obituary from *The Times* (London), 11 Sept. 1978, reprinted, and preceded by a reproduction of the Gehenna Press broadside (1967) of MacDiarmid's poem, "The Eemis Stane," with the portrait of the poet by Leonard Baskin.

93.   Murphy, Hayden. "An Irish View of MacDiarmid." *Books in Scotland* 4 (1979): 9-10.

An appreciation of the poet and review of the *Complete Poems* ("Overstatement is the only form of speech that can do these books credit") and the *Socialist Poems*.

94.   Ross, Raymond J. "Professor Daiches & Doctor Grieve." *New Edinburgh Review* 47 (1979): 33-34.

A reply to Daiches's review of the *Complete Poems* in the *New Edinburgh Review* 45 (1979): 25-27.

95.   Scott, Alexander. "An Interview with Hugh MacDiarmid." *Studies in Scottish Literature* 14 (1979): 1-22.

A wide-ranging conversation between the poet and one of the editors of *The Hugh MacDiarmid Anthology*.

96.   Campbell, Ian. "Gibbon and MacDiarmid in the German Democratic Republic." *Books in Scotland* 6 (1979-80): 6-7.

Comments on the publication in 1968 of a selection of MacDiarmid's poetry in German translation with an introduction which places the poet firmly in a European context.

97.   Bruce, George. "The Phenomenon of Hugh MacDiarmid." *Akros* 44 (1980): 16-34.

Challenges the view that MacDiarmid's poems in Scots are to be taken as wholly apart from his poems in English.

98.   Dunn, Douglas. "Hugh MacDiarmid: Inhuman Splendours." *New Edinburgh Review* 52 (1980): 17-21.

A perceptive review of *The Age of MacDiarmid*. (104)

99. Johnstone, William. *Points in Time: an Autobiography.* London: Barrie & Jenkins, 1980.

Johnstone (1897-1982), who was a cousin of Francis George Scott and perhaps MacDiarmid's closest friend among visual artists, has various reminiscences of the poet who provided poems for two of his projects.

100. Lindsay, Maurice. *Francis George Scott and the Scottish Renaissance.* Edinburgh: Paul Harris, 1980.

This centenary study of the composer Francis George Scott (1880-1958), MacDiarmid's teacher and friend, includes in an appendix (184-213) a survey of Scott's letters to MacDiarmid. A number of the poet's letters to Scott are in Alan Bold's edition of MacDiarmid's letters.

101. McQuillan, Ruth, and Agnes Shearer. *In Line with the Ramna Stacks: a Study of the Fishing Poems of Hugh MacDiarmid.* Edinburgh: Challister Press, 1980.

Examines MacDiarmid's use of language and experience from his Shetland years.

102. Perrie, Walter. "Nietzsche and the Drunk Man." *Cencrastus* 2 (1980): 9-12.

The writer concludes that "it is difficult for me not to see the consequences of Nietzsche's influence on MacDiarmid as unfortunate."

103. Roy, G. Ross. "Hugh MacDiarmid (1892-1978)." *Studies in Scottish Literature* 15 (1980): 1-2.

A memorial tribute.

104. Scott, Paul H., and Albert C. Davis, eds. *The Age of MacDiarmid: Essays on Hugh MacDiarmid and his Influence on Contemporary Scotland.* Edinburgh: Mainstream, 1980.

The essays fall into three groups: personal reminiscences, critical assessments, and the man and his politics. As in all volumes of the kind there is some unevenness in the quality: among the best are George Bruce on the MacDiarmid/Muir controversy, Kenneth Buthlay on the links between *A Drunk Man* and *Cencrastus*, and Owen Dudley Edwards on MacDiarmid's polemical prose.

105. Ackerman, Diane. "Hugh MacDiarmid's Wide-angle Poetry." *Parnassus* 9 (1981): 129-39.

Explores MacDiarmid's "naturally metaphysical mind."

106. Boutelle, Ann Edwards. *Thistle and Rose: a Study of Hugh MacDiarmid's Poetry.* Loanhead: Macdonald, 1981.

There is a good discussion of *A Drunk Man*, but unfortunately the survey as a whole relies too much on inaccurate texts.

107. Dooley, Anne. "Hugh MacDiarmid and the Gaelic Muse." *The Celtic Consciousness*. Ed. Robert O'Driscoll. Toronto: McClelland & Stewart, 1981; Port Laoise: Dolmen Press, 1982; Edinburgh: Canongate, 1982. 459-66.

> The place of the Gaelic tradition in MacDiarmid's work.

108. Gish, Nancy. "Reality at Stake: MacDiarmid's Early Long Poems." *Chapman* 30 (1981): 56-62.

> The writer concludes that MacDiarmid is primarily a philosophic poet and that *A Drunk Man Looks at the Thistle* and the "more complex and difficult philosophically" "On a Raised Beach" are his two most successful long poems.

109. Harvie, Christopher. "MacDiarmid the Socialist." *Scottish Labour History Soc. Journal* 16 (1981): 4-11.

> Discusses MacDiarmid's politics and his Socialist poetry.

110. Montague, John. "Hugh MacDiarmid: a Parting Gloss." *The Celtic Consciousness*. Ed. Robert O'Driscoll. Toronto: McClelland & Stewart, 1981; Port Laoise: Dolmen Press, 1982; Edinburgh: Canongate, 1982. 467-68.

> A memory of a visit to MacDiarmid a month before he died.

111. Morgan, Edwin. "On Hugh MacDiarmid's *Complete Poems 1920-1976*." *Comparative Criticism* 3 (1981): 303-09.

> A review-article of the "enormously impressive" collection which enables readers "to begin to understand, for the first time now that all the poems are gathered together, the unity of his work. . . . The overall effect seems to me to be clear, that he is one of the great modern poets."

112. Buthlay, Kenneth. *Hugh MacDiarmid*. Edinburgh: Scottish Academic Press, 1982.

> With a thorough revision and updating of the original 1964 text the best and fullest introduction to MacDiarmid becomes even more useful for the student of Scottish literature or the interested general reader.

113. McCulloch, Margery. "The Undeservedly Broukit Bairn: Hugh MacDiarmid's *To Circumjack Cencrastus*." *Studies in Scottish Literature* 17 (1982): 165-85.

> A reconsideration of a long poem that is all too often dismissed as a failure.

114. Morgan, Edwin. "James Joyce and Hugh MacDiarmid." *James Joyce and Modern Literature*. Ed. W. J. McCormack and Alistair Stead. London: Routledge, 1982. 202-17.

An essay more about MacDiarmid than Joyce suggests that the *Drunk Man* might have had a measure of influence on *Finnegans Wake*.

115. Perrie, Walter. *Out of Conflict*. Dunfermline: Borderline Press, 1982.

Includes three essays on MacDiarmid. The first, "Nietzsche and *A Drunk Man Looks at the Thistle*" (5-27), is a revision of the article published in *Cencrastus* in 1980; the second (31-52) deals with "Prosody and Politics in *In Memoriam James Joyce*"; and the third (55-60) comments on MacDiarmid's poem, "Servant Girl's Bed," from *Penny Wheep*.

116. Roy, G. Ross. "The Thorn on Scotland's Rose: Hugh MacDiarmid." *World Literature Today* 56 (1982): 58-61.

Informed reviews of Ann Edwards Boutelle's book and the collection of essays edited by Scott and Davis.

117. White, Kenneth. "En parlant avec Hugh MacDiarmid: poésie et metaphysique." *Poètes anglais contemporains*. Ed. Jacqueline Genet and R. Gallet. Caen: Centre de recherches de littérature & linguistique, 1982. 1-2.

White, a Scottish poet born in Glasgow in 1936, lives in France.

118. Bold, Alan. *MacDiarmid: The Terrible Crystal*. London: Routledge & Kegan Paul, 1983.

A chronological picture of MacDiarmid's poetry, written with insight and perception, and illuminated by apt and generous quotation.

119. Bold, Alan. *Modern Scottish Literature*. London: Longman, 1983.

In this comprehensive survey there is a chapter on MacDiarmid (26-40) and references to him throughout.

120. Buthlay, Kenneth. "An Awkward Squad: Some Scots Poets from Stevenson to Spence." *Scotland and the Lowland Tongue*. Ed. J. Derrick McClure. Aberdeen: Aberdeen UP, 1983. 149-69.

The poets in Scots who might be thought to have led up to the modern revival and the familiarity with their work which MacDiarmid at times showed.

121. Gish, Nancy. "Hugh MacDiarmid: The Early Work." *The New Pelican Guide to English Literature*. Ed. Boris Ford. Vol. 7: From James to Eliot. Harmondsworth: Penguin Books, 1983. 298-311.

A good introduction, admirably fitted for its purpose and surroundings.

122. Kerrigan, Catherine. *Whaur Extremes Meet: the Poetry of Hugh MacDiarmid, 1920-1934*. Edinburgh: The Mercat Press, 1983.

> The dates set sadly limit this book's value--for more than half of MacDiarmid's work was published after 1934, and his work, it can be argued, is very much of a piece--but the survey of the poet's early intellectual development is well done.

123. Kjellgren, Thomas. "Nu star vi i tur; budet har gatt till kelten." *Lyrikvännen* Nr.1/2 (1983): 62-67.

> A survey, in Swedish, of modern Gaelic poetry, with references throughout to MacDiarmid.

124. McQuillan, Ruth. "The Complete MacDiarmid." *Studies in Scottish Literature* 18 (1983): 177-209.

> A long review-article on the *Complete Poems* informed by the writer's particular knowledge of MacDiarmid's letters and manuscripts.

125. Montgomerie, William. "Hugh MacDiarmid's 'Empty Vessel.' "*Akros* 51 (1983): 17-18.

> Traces the ancestry of one of MacDiarmid's most effective poems.

126. Östergren, Jan. "Bangstyrigt snille--skrivande rebell . . ." *Lyrikvännen* Nr.1/2 (1983): 39-47.

> These notes, in Swedish, on the contradictory genius and restless pen of the poet include translations of parts of *A Drunk Man*.

127. Perrie, Walter. "Calling (Out) MacDiarmid." *Chapman* 35/36 (1983): 61-67.

> A philosophical investigation of the relationship between Hugh MacDiarmid and C. M. Grieve.

128. Rosenthal, M. L. "Hugh MacDiarmid's *A Drunk Man Looks at the Thistle*." *The Modern Poetic Sequence*, by M. L. Rosenthal and Sally M. Gall. New York: Oxford UP, 1983.

> This section of a larger work on what Rosenthal and Gall call the " 'new' genre, the modern poetic sequence," defines *A Drunk Man Looks at the Thistle* as a sequence of 59 separable poems. They argue that the poem is best understood with separately titled sections (the version published in *Collected Poems*) and that its power depends on "centers of affective power"--an analysis which tends to reduce the value of the longer discursive sections. The authors also comment on MacDiarmid's fusion of nationalism and cosmopolitanism.

129. Ross, Raymond J. "Hugh MacDiarmid and John Maclean." *Cencrastus* 11 (1983): 33-36.

The writer argues that for MacDiarmid the nature of the Scottish Socialist movement was embodied, above all, in the Republican Socialism of John Maclean (1879-1923).

130. Daiches, David. "Types of Vision: Edwin Muir and Hugh MacDiarmid." *God and the Poets*. Oxford: Clarendon Press, 1984. 176-204.

There is no orthodox representation of the Divine in MacDiarmid, but God is not absent as this rather terrifying kind of mystic searches for an expression of reality. MacDiarmid is with those poets who seek truth through cosmic vision.

131. Freedman, Carl. "Possibilities of a Political Aesthetic: the Case of Hugh MacDiarmid." *Minnesota Review* 7.23 (1984): 41-57.

An important early discussion of MacDiarmid from a postmodern perspective that is capable of addressing late prosaic works usually dismissed by more traditional approaches. Focusing on the generally neglected *The Battle Continues*, Freedman argues that in his later "poetry of fact" MacDiarmid "virtually invents a new articulation of politics and form."

132. Gish, Nancy K. *Hugh MacDiarmid: The Man and his Work*. London: Macmillan, 1984.

A thoughtful study which emphasizes the thematic unity of the entire body of MacDiarmid's poetry and avoids the facile traditional opposition of the two MacDiarmids.

133. Oxenhorn, Harvey. *Elemental Things: The Poetry of Hugh MacDiarmid*. Edinburgh: Edinburgh UP, 1984.

A survey with much to commend it, but written (as one would expect) perhaps more for an American readership; balanced and discerning in the analysis of *A Drunk Man*.

134. _____. "Water Music: Wordsworth, MacDiarmid, and Frost." *Southern Review* 20 (1984): 265-78.

A comparison of MacDiarmid's, Wordsworth's, and Frost's nature poetry. Seeing Wordsworth rather than Burns as MacDiarmid's most similar predecessor, Oxenhorn argues for MacDiarmid's use of comparable poetic subject matter and experiments in technique and "plain speech" toward the contrasting end of celebrating change. He contrasts MacDiarmid also to Frost as more fresh, less meditative, yet committed to the natural world as "larger than human sorrow and folly."

135. Wang Zuoliang. "Reflections on Hugh MacDiarmid." *Studies in Scottish Literature* 19 (1984): 1-16.

> The writer is professor of English at Beijing Foreign Language Institute. His interesting reflections are translated into English.

136. Watson, Roderick. *The Literature of Scotland*. London: Macmillan, 1984.

> MacDiarmid is discussed on pp. 349-67, where he is named as the last of the early modern giants of the generation of Eliot, Pound, Yeats and Joyce.

137. Bellany, John, and Alan Bold. *Homage to MacDiarmid*. Balbirnie, Fife: Balbirnie Editions, 1985.

> A portfolio of etchings by Bellany and poems by Bold.

138. Bold, Alan. *Scots Steel Tempered wi' Irish Fire: Hugh MacDiarmid and Ireland*. Edinburgh: Edinburgh College of Art, 1985.

> MacDiarmid frequently celebrated Scotland's cultural affinities with Ireland, and this essay explores the connection.

139. Cribb, T. J. "The Cheka's Horrors and *On a Raised Beach*." *Studies in Scottish Literature* 20 (1985): 88-100.

> An examination of MacDiarmid's intense resolution of the daunting problems posed by a commitment to the meaning that Communism finds in life.

140. Glen, Duncan. "Hugh MacDiarmid and the Small Presses." *Books in Scotland* 19 (1985): 4-6.

> The extract from Glen's autobiography (see 147 below) discusses MacDiarmid's relations with some of Scotland's small publishers.

141. Herbert, W. N. "To Circumjack MacDiarmid." *Verse* 2 (1985): 41-46.

> Focusing on MacDiarmid's method of incorporating other texts--acknowledged and unacknowledged--into his poems, Herbert argues for reading them as "primarily the result of intertextual relationships." He illustrates his point with newly found sources for lines in "On a Raised Beach" and questions readings of the poem based in assumptions of a personal voice as its source rather than what Herbert names "an extended persona."

142. Oxenhorn, Harvey. "Yowdendrift: Gerard Manley Hopkins and Hugh MacDiarmid." *Hopkins among the Poets*. Ed. Richard F. Giles. Hamilton, Ont.: International Hopkins Association, 1985. 42-46.

> Discusses "Cattle Show" and "The Eemis Stane."

143. Stegmaier, E. "Stadt und Land in Hugh MacDiarmids Gedichten der 'Gaelic Idea.' " *Englische und amerikanische*

Naturdichtung im 20 Jahrhundert. Ed. Günter Ahrends & Hans Ulrich Seeber. Tübingen: Narr, 1985. 110-23.

> Questions whether MacDiarmid, in rejecting early 20th-century Scotland's nostalgia for its rural past and inability to deal with modern urban conditions, does not fall into a similar trap himself. Basing his analysis on six middle-length English language poems of the 1930s, Stegmaier argues that MacDiarmid must be read in the context of contemporary economic, political, and literary conditions which affected his ability to carry out the modernization he envisioned. A very valuable discussion of the relations between MacDiarmid's communism as applied to urban representation and the "Gaelic Idea" he derived from a past rural culture. Rather than see these opposing tendencies as failures of vision from one perspective or another, Stegmaier analyzes the extent to which they are interrelated elements of MacDiarmid's larger conception of human development and the liberation of Scotland from English dominance.

144. Watson, Roderick. *MacDiarmid.* Milton Keynes: Open UP, 1985.

> A good introduction to MacDiarmid's poetry.

145. Campbell, Ian. "Gibbon and MacDiarmid at Play: the Evolution of *Scottish Scene.*" *Bibliotheck* 13 (1986): 46-55.

> An analysis of the origins of the book in which "the only Scot alive who can write poetry and the only one who can write fiction" collaborated.

146. Davie, George Elder. *The Crisis of the Democratic Intellect.* Edinburgh: Polygon, 1986.

> The important sequel to the author's earlier book, *The Democratic Intellect* (2nd ed. Edinburgh: Edinburgh UP, 1964), by an Edinburgh philosopher whom MacDiarmid greatly admired (see *The Company I've Kept*, 27 above), discusses the poet's thought and ideas in a novel and profound way.

147. Glen, Duncan. *The Autobiography of a Poet.* Edinburgh: Ramsay Head Press, 1986.

> The reminiscences of the author of the pioneering study, *Hugh MacDiarmid and the Scottish Renaissance* (1964), and editor of MacDiarmid's essays (1969) and the critical study of 1972, frequently touch on the poet's life and work.

148. Hall, J. T. D. "Hugh MacDiarmid, Author and Publisher." *Studies in Scottish Literature* 21 (1986): 53-88.

> Descriptive chronology of MacDiarmid's activities as editor and publisher of anthologies and periodicals in the 1920s. Contains detailed information of MacDiarmid's efforts to create and further a Scottish literary renaissance and suggests the difficulties inherent in establishing outlets for Scottish nationalist work.

149. Milton, C. "Hugh MacDiarmid and North-East Scots." *Scottish Language* 5 (1986): 39-47.

   A discussion of MacDiarmid's attitude to "language" and "dialect" as shown in his articles in *Contemporary Scottish Studies* (5 above) and his share in the considerable correspondence they provoked.

150. Silver, R. S. "Student Culture in the 1930s and Acquaintance with C. M. Grieve." *Edinburgh Review* 74 (1986): 63-75.

   A highly interesting and informative account, less of MacDiarmid than of the writer's own intellectual history. Although Silver takes his account into the early fifties, he focuses on his student days in Glasgow and his acquaintance with MacDiarmid in the 1940s. Contains fascinating detail on curriculum and ideas current in Scottish student culture as well as the impact MacDiarmid had on the writer's developing nationalism.

151. Baglow, John. *Hugh MacDiarmid: the Poetry of Self.* Kingston & Montreal: McGill-Queen's UP, 1987.

   This doctoral thesis, completed in 1973 (but updated), discusses MacDiarmid and the problems of the modern poet, with particular reference to his later poetry.

152. Cox, Kenneth. "The Poetry of Hugh MacDiarmid." *Agenda* 24.4/25.1 (1987): 52-65.

   "Great writers resemble one another much less than small writers do." MacDiarmid's poetry is discussed from the point of view expressed in the writer's opening sentence.

153. Crawford, Robert. "A Drunk Man looks at the Waste Land." *Scottish Literary Journal* 14 (Nov. 1987): 62-78.

   On MacDiarmid and Eliot.

154. Crawford, Robert. "Recent Scottish Poetry and the Scottish Tradition." *Verse* 4 (June 1987): 36-46.

   A "highly selective" essay which takes as axiomatic some knowledge of MacDiarmid's work.

155. Davie, George Elder. "On Hugh MacDiarmid." *Cencrastus* 25 (1987): 15-20.

   The measured judgement of a philosopher and friend who argues that "the poet of the 'Raised Beach' puts forward a naturalist or materialist view that corporeal things explain consciousness, and not vice versa."

156. Dixon, Keith. "Hugh MacDiarmid and the Gaelic Idea." *Pays de Galles, Ecosse, Irlande: Actes du Congrès de Brest,*

mai 1986. Ed. Bernard Sellin. Brest: Centre de Recherche Bretonne et Celtique, 1987. 169-84.

> A commentary on MacDiarmid's political position in two key essays of the 1930s: "English Ascendancy in British Literature" and "The Caledonian Antisyzygy and the Gaelic Idea." Argues that MacDiarmid's underlying idea--present throughout his work--is ultimately a "racist conception of culture and society" at odds with much else in MacDiarmid's work, a contradiction of his progressive positions.

157. Herbert, W. N. "Hugh MacDiarmid: Mature Art." *Verse* 4 (June 1987): 29-35.

> An attempt to find the "proportions and probable form" of the immensely long poem MacDiarmid eventually abandoned.

158. McCarey, Peter. *Hugh MacDiarmid and the Russians*. Edinburgh: Scottish Academic P, 1987.

> A comparative study of MacDiarmid and five Russian writers whose thought concerned him: Dostoevsky, Solovyov, Blok, Mayakovsky, and Shestov.

159. Kerrigan, Catherine. "MacDiarmid's Early Poetry." *The History of Scottish Literature*. Ed. Cairns Craig. Vol. 4. Aberdeen: Aberdeen UP, 1987. 75-85.

> "His poetry begins as challenge and ends in delight."

160. _____. "Underground Men: Dostoevsky in the work of Hugh MacDiarmid." *Journal of Narrative Technique* 17 (1987): 45-50.

> A discussion of the impact of Dostoevsky on MacDiarmid's early experimental forms. Analyzes MacDiarmid's recognition, in Dostoevsky, of an alternative model of "language, literary form, and social order" to that represented by the orthodox Western literary tradition in general and "English ascendancy" in particular. Draws on Bakhtin to suggest how MacDiarmid's multivocalism and use of vernacular language represented a literary experiment "unique in early British modernism." Brief but insightful.

161. Massey, Alan. " 'Creation Shall not be Injured': Notes on the Poetry of Hugh MacDiarmid." *Agenda* 24.4/25.1 (1987): 44-51.

> The poet's tenderness, like his passion, is reserved for ideas. The beauty of his longer, English, poems is in their intelligence.

162. Riach, Alan. "The Later MacDiarmid." *The History of Scottish Literature*. Ed. Cairns Craig. Vol. 4. Aberdeen: Aberdeen UP, 1987. 217-28.

In the later works, themes, ideas, facts, names, languages, cultures, sources and quotations are let loose from any imperial centrality and occur in a free but not directionless movement.

163. _____. " 'The Present is Prologue': Postmodernist Scotland." *Verse* 4 (June 1987): 47-50.

"MacDiarmid comes through, of course."

164. Watson, Roderick. "Seminars in the Glen of Silence." *Cencrastus* 25 (1987): 12-14.

A discussion of Davie's *The Crisis of the Democratic Intellect* (see 146 above) which establishes links between MacDiarmid's modernism-- "that extraordinary conflation of antisyzygytical eclecticisms"--and the Scottish generalist educational tradition.

165. Bold, Alan. *MacDiarmid: Christopher Murray Grieve: a Critical Biography*. London: John Murray, 1988.

An impressively full, fair and very readable account; as the author says, "not a hagiography," but "an attempt to come to terms with the man who created some of the greatest poetry of the twentieth, or any other, century."

166. Buthlay, Kenneth. "The Ablach in the Gold Pavilion." *Scottish Literary Journal* 15 (Nov. 1988): 39-57.

Further hints for source hunters (see 71 above) on some of MacDiarmid's "borrowings."

167. Crotty, Patrick. "From Genesis to Revelation: Patterns and Continuities in Hugh MacDiarmid's Poetry in the Early Thirties." *Scottish Literary Journal* 15 (Nov. 1988): 5-23.

A discussion of MacDiarmid's poetry of the years 1931 to 1933, which to the writer seems to fall fairly readily into two major categories distinguished chiefly by their imagery--the first of water, the second of stones.

168. Herbert, W. N. "MacDiarmid: Mature Art." *Scottish Literary Journal* 15 (Nov. 1988): 24-38.

A version of the essay noted at 157 above.

169. McCleery, Alistair. "MacDiarmid and the Porpoise Press." *Books in Scotland* 28 (1988): 7-8.

The relationship between MacDiarmid and one of Scotland's notable small publishers.

170. Riach, Alan. "T. S. Eliot and Hugh MacDiarmid." *Literary Half-Yearly* 29 (1988): 124-37.

A discussion of the points of contact between the two poets, in their correspondence and in their work.

171. Ross, Raymond. "The Russians Are Coming." *Cencrastus* 30 (1988): 40-46.

> An important essay that is much more than a review of Peter McCarey's *Hugh MacDiarmid and the Russians* (158 above).

BIBLIOGRAPHY

172. Glen, Duncan. "Hugh MacDiarmid: A Chronological Bibliography." *Hugh MacDiarmid and the Scottish Renaissance*. Edinburgh: Chambers, 1964. 245-62.

> A comprehensive bibliography, including a list of anthologies in which MacDiarmid is represented and a select list of his contributions to periodicals. The book contains also a useful bibliography of other writers of the period and of the critical works consulted.

173. Aitken, W. R. "A Hugh MacDiarmid Bibliography." *Hugh MacDiarmid: A Critical Survey*. Ed. Duncan Glen. Edinburgh: Scottish Academic P, 1972. 228-41.

──────────. "Hugh MacDiarmid's Recent Bibliography 1972-76." *Akros* 34/35 (Aug. 1977): 111-14.

──────────. "Hugh MacDiarmid's 'Unpublished' Books: A Bibliographical Exploration." *Of One Accord*. Ed. Frank McAdams. Glasgow: Scottish Library Association, 1977. 57-72.

> MacDiarmid planned and announced a number of books which he either did not proceed with or subsumed in other publications. Some of these mysteries are here unravelled.

174. Glenday, Michael K. "Hugh MacDiarmid: A Bibliography of Criticism, 1924-78." *Bulletin of Bibliography* 36 (1979): 91-98.

> Comprehensive and helpfully annotated.

175. Aitken, W. R. *Scottish Literature in English and Scots: a Guide to Information Sources*. Detroit, Mich.: Gale Research Company, 1982.

> MacDiarmid is included (240-47) in the 160 pages devoted to twentieth-century Scottish literature.

INDEX OF TITLES OF MacDIARMID'S BOOKS

INDEX OF AUTHORS, CRITICS AND EDITORS

INDEX

INDEX OF BOOKS, POEMS, ESSAYS, ETC.
BY HUGH MacDIARMID